I0356885

BOBBY
GRAHAM
PUBLISHERS

THE RIGHT BREAK

Against the odds - a memoir

John Abernethy

All proceeds from the sale of this book will be donated to
The Joel Abernethy Advantage Scholarship
Australian Children's Music Foundation
acmf.com.au/scholarships/

© 2020 John Abernethy

Produced and published by BGPublishers
www.bgpublishers.com.au

All rights reserved

Cover and internal design by David Potter
www.transformer.com.au

Digital edition by SunTecIndia
www.suntecinidia.com

Printed and distributed by Ingram Spark
www.ingramspark.com

First edition 2020

ISBN 978-0-6486686-7-1 (print)

ISBN 978-0-6486686-9-5 (digital)

FRONT COVER IMAGES

Top left: *Saddled up: John off on his first 'Op', Nui Dat, March 1970. Everything is still clean. The red soil would soon change that.*

Top right: *On Media Day, for the Mk1 Seabrake trial off Rottnest Island, 1987.*

Bottom: *Cooling off in the Snowy River after 'brumby running' in the Victorian High Country in the summer of 1989. From left to right, Deb Richardson, Clive Jamison, Pete Richardson – and Budd, Joel's dog. John took the picture.*

For my grandson Joel Abernethy.

Make your own tracks, walk in no one's footsteps.

Everything is possible.

All you need to do is believe.

Contents

Prologue 9

Hollywood comes aboard, 1978 11

The dawn of Seabrake, Bass Strait, 1979 28

A country boy, until 1969 46

National Service, Vietnam, 1969–1971 72

Wendy and Port Fairy life, 1971 99

Seeing the world 118

The long way home 147

The fishing business, Port Fairy, 1976–1978 176

New boat, new son, 1979–1982 182

New beginnings, Ness, 1982 196

Seabrake is born, October 1982 205

America's Cup, Perth, 1986–1987 224

Woodville Lodge, from 1988 233

Farm life to bright lights and back, 1995–2000 256

A home at Millingandi 291

Epilogue 315

Acknowledgements 320

References 320

Prologue

I am an ordinary Aussie bloke from the bush who somehow found himself living an extraordinary life.

As a boy in country Australia, I could never have imagined my life would turn out the way it has. But here I am, older and somehow wiser, looking back at my life – the good, the bad and the almost unbelievable.

I have known considerable wealth and crushing poverty, fame and desolation. My story is one of great success, of trust, betrayal, hope and hopelessness – and struggle in the face of adversity, love and terrible loss. All of it several times over!

I have looked death square in the face and lived to tell the tale. And through it all I have remained optimistic. I have learnt that good triumphs over evil, that innovation, determination and self-reliance are key qualities for survival. I have learnt how to survive.

I was brought up on a farm in the Western District of Victoria, Australia, where life was simple. Farms were handed down to the eldest son; I was the only son, so that was my future – or so I thought. The world's exotic places existed in the movies, along with the beautiful women, the jet-set lifestyle. It wasn't something that could happen to a farm kid like me.

But my world changed when I turned 20 and left the farm for the 'Funny Farm' – Vietnam. I came home a casualty evacuee, a Casevac, never to return to my home, nor to my inheritance.

Through the hand life dealt me I stumbled into a whole new world, a world of dream lifestyles, dream jobs, dream money. I travelled widely, saw amazing places and met amazing people – good and bad – and mingled with millionaires and movie stars. All because, broke and desperate, I made my own lucky star. I created my own 'break', a world-first marine invention that catapulted me into another league.

This is my story. Perhaps you will read this and think, *Really? Did all this happen to one man?* I know I do sometimes.

The story of *The Right Break* is what everybody wishes for. But be careful what you wish for – you may end up getting it, as I did.

Hollywood comes aboard, 1978

Thinking big is the key to success. When running a charter boat operation, putting bums on seats pays off. And like any business, public relations and marketing is the key. In the '70s and '80s, international celebrities in Australia were pretty thin on the ground (and on the water for that matter), but in my business, game fishing, the biggest name in the business – and one of the biggest names in Hollywood, USA – was Lee Marvin.

A Hollywood tough guy of his era, of the war movie and Western tradition, there were few bigger, or better. He was up there with John Wayne, Charles Bronson and Marlon Brando, famous for classic man's man movies like *The Dirty Dozen*. Lee was also a real-life US Marine, wounded during World War II. But in my line of work he was the guru of big game fishing and had made the pilgrimage Down Under in pursuit of our big black marlin when the industry was still in its infancy, operating out of Cairns in Far North Queensland.

Now you could write on the back of a postage stamp what I knew about black marlin and Lee Marvin at the time – but I did know this bloke was the complete package and had been Master of Ceremonies at the 1976 *TV Week* Logie Awards in Melbourne.

If I could get him on my boat, it would put my fledgling game fishing operation – which was based in Port Fairy, in Victoria – on the world map, and into fishing and charter boat circles everywhere. But how?

A little white lie was warranted. It was 1977, and I had a starting point: *TV Week* magazine. Knowing Lee fished Cairns in the Australian spring, I timed my call to *TV Week* accordingly. I said I needed to contact him about the season's fishing and I was having trouble reaching him at home – did they have his agent's phone number in LA handy? It was that simple.

Now comes the hard part, I thought. I can't bullshit this bloke, he seems mean enough to come all the way to Port Fairy just to punch my lights out.

After clearing my throat with a number of hefty scotches, I rang the number in Tucson, Arizona. Lee answered the phone. He had the most distinctive voice ever, like a bear with a heavy flu.

'Hi, my name is John Abernethy – I run a boat out of Port Fairy.'

'WHERE?' Lee bellowed.

'Bass Strait – Australia. I specialise in great white sharks.' I knew I needed to work on his masculine pride, and I needed to do it quickly.

'I'm pulling in 1800lb fish down here … Err – regularly! I guarantee 1000lb fish. That 1560lb marlin world record that has stood since 1953? That's a small, a *very small*, great white shark. I've seen 2000lb fish down here, if you reckon you're up to it!'

'Hang on a minute,' he said.

The phone went silent. I thought he'd hung up on me. A couple of minutes passed, then a lot more. Finally I heard approaching footsteps.

'Lee Marvin. Who am I speaking to?' The very same gruff voice.

'Err – John Abernethy, Mr Marvin.'

'How can I help?' he asked, trying hard to sound different, although it was impossible.

'I was just explaining to your *"friend"* that I specialise in great white sharks – not marlin – down here in the Southern Ocean of Australia. Not far from where Alf Dean caught all his world record great white sharks.'

I'd done my homework, Alf Dean is a legend, and holds the most world records for great white sharks.

Lee Marvin trying out the game chair on **Papeo**: *'When do we fish?'*

'How many have *YOU* caught, personally?' he fired back. Now I was in my element.

'Personally? Just one to test out my game chair – and it went 1009lb. Just a little bloke. But I got a client a fish over here recently that went 1800lb.'

Silence. I knew that would impress him. See, it's all about line-class, catching the heaviest fish on the lightest line-strain. Big marlin and big white pointer sharks are caught primarily on 130lb and 80lb line-class – and the heaviest marlin ever caught went 1560lb on 130lb line.

'Trouble is, I don't get a lot of good anglers down here – yet! That 1800lb fish could have been taken on 80lb line-class, but the angler was a mug.'

He laughed at that.

'I don't mean the guy is a mug,' I added quickly. 'I mean it's the first time the bloke has ever gone game fishing, is what I'm saying.'

Still laughing, Lee replied, 'Well I've never landed an 1800lb fish, so he couldn't be too much of a mug.'

I talked quickly. 'We know what we're doing – before I started catching them on rod and reel I caught a whole bunch on drum-lines. Before I caught the first by rod and reel myself, I had used different hooks, traces, and learnt how to handle them beside the boat. And how, and where, to gaff them. Mr Dean sent me my very first 20-0 hook.'

'How many great whites have you caught in total?' he asked. He was feeding me a bait. Time to be on my toes.

'I'd have to go back over my records to give you a total, but this I can tell you with accuracy, I've only ever taken one *under* 1000lb.' Which was, in fact, true. But as for a total, probably about four at that time.

After some more small talk, he asked for my number and said he would get back to me. He didn't say when.

The following night our phone rang while we were having dinner. Wendy, my wife, answered.

'Lee Marvin – for you,' she said with a smile. I took my time getting to the phone.

'G'day – John Abernethy?'

'Mr Marvin?'

'None of that mister bullshit OK, it's Lee. What's the best time of year to catch one of these BIG great whites?'

'February, if I had to nail it down to a month.'

'Can't do it,' he said bluntly.

'The fish are here all year round Lee, it's just that February is smack in the middle of pupping season. There's blood and young seal pups in the water in abundance for the sharks.'

'How about October?' he asked.

'October sounds fine – just let me see what dates I have available,' I said, flicking pages of the phone directory.

'Oh – I'm sure you'll be able to squeeze me in for a couple of weeks somewhere!' He was right.

Hollywood comes aboard, 1978

And so it came to be, Lee Marvin, Hollywood star and gun game fisherman, was coming to Port Fairy. The interesting thing is that rich people never ask: 'How much?', unlike like the rest of us. The fact was, even I didn't know, I'd never booked two weeks out to anyone before. I quickly did some phoning around.

Now they say it never rains, it pours. I'd just gone from being little old John Abernethy in Port Fairy, who almost nobody knew, to someone everybody knew, when I got another call.

'Hi, I'm John Denver's manager, and I'd like to discuss booking some time while you have Lee Marvin fishing with you.'

'Yeah – right mate, and I'm Santa Claus, and you just blew your Ferrari for Christmas for calling at dinner time, OK!' Then I hung up in his ear. The phone rang several more times that night; I told Wendy to simply ignore it.

This happened again the following night, but before I hung up, the caller gave me the exact date Lee was fishing with me, something only Lee and I knew.

Now to this day I still don't know how this guy got wind of Lee's charter, but he knew, and he was taking me into his confidence by announcing that his client, John Denver, the singer, was going to tour Australia and New Zealand later in the year. They were filming the tour as a documentary, and they wanted footage of catching up with Lee Marvin game fishing Down Under.

I then phoned Lee and told him what had happened. He sounded unconcerned, putting it down to agents talking to each other, but he gave me some good advice. 'You just make sure your pockets are full, OK? Charge them the full charter rate for each day – got that?'

Well I didn't really, but what he was saying was double-book the boat. Whatever I was charging Lee Marvin, charge John Denver the same. And that's just what I did.

Plus, Denver's crew needed extra boats, film boats. They had three 35mm Panavision cameras they wanted placed in different locations around my boat, and on Lady Julia Percy Island – which was part of the trip – and we had to arrange the catering for their crews for the three days of filming. I was truly becoming the number one son of Port Fairy, spreading this financial bonanza all around town.

Now, going from a nobody to a somebody has its drawbacks. Everybody wants a piece of you. Once the media got hold of what was happening, TV, radio and newspapers all wanted a comment.

'About what?' I naively answered. I'm a country kid turned charter boat skipper (through no fault of my own I might add), and suddenly I'm qualified to make *comments*?

'We are going to try and catch a big white pointer,' was about all I could say – and that apparently was enough.

Also keep in mind the 1975 movie, *Jaws*, was still hot property, and everybody was petrified and intrigued by great white sharks.

I was run ragged until Lee arrived, getting my boat, *Papeo*, ready for our VIPs, and arranging everything from hotel rooms to lunches 11 miles out to sea.

Lee and I hit it off immediately. He was genuinely thrilled to know I was a Grunt – infantry, and a Vietnam Vet. Since he was an ex-Marine, we had that military link straight up.

Now, *Papeo* wasn't the style of boat Lee and his wife Pam would have been accustomed to. She was no floating gin palace, she was your basic 38-foot timbered boat with a nice new coat of paint, and was probably as old as Lee and me combined. But she was an honest old sea boat who had proven herself many times over many years. More to the point, she was a Bass Strait-surveyed off-shore vessel – we both knew, Lee and I, it was the bloke behind the wheel, and the crew, that makes any boat work. Lee met my crew, Dip and Foo, sat his arse in the game chair, and gave it his nod of approval.

'When do we fish?' he asked.

This was a totally new experience for both Pam and Lee, fishing in the Southern Ocean. They were used to fishing in Hawaii, Florida, Cairns –

the tropics. Bass Strait before midday, on any day, is bloody cold, and the crew and I spent most of the trip outbound re-dressing Pam and Lee in our own clothes, and cladding ourselves in wet-weather gear until the sun was a little higher, much to their amusement. In fact, Lee wore my roll-neck jumper every day from that morning on, only giving it back the day they left.

Pam Marvin was a very accomplished angler in her own right, holding a Ladies IGFA (International Game Fish Association) World Record for a 607½lb Pacific blue marlin. She had also once gone overboard still attached to a very determined black marlin, as Lee was glad to share with us on our journey out to the island. What many people don't know is that the angler is attached to the rod – not the game chair. A harness, usually made of a flexible but sturdy material, is clipped to the reel. The idea is not to give the angler too unfair an advantage over the fish.

In Pam's case, Lee said that all he remembered was seeing the soles of her deck shoes disappearing over the stern of the boat. Some very quick thinking by the deckhands got her separated from the rod and fish.

We had three days of fishing to ourselves before John Denver's entourage, a cast of dozens, arrived. On the second night, returning to Port Fairy, we had a sudden weather change that came in hard south-westerly. It was nothing to us, but weather like this, for Pam in particular, was bloody terrifying.

My crew went to every effort to make her as comfortable and relaxed as possible until we were safely tied up alongside Port Fairy wharf.

'What a wonderful group of people you have, John,' she said, squeezing the life out of me, teary-eyed from the ordeal. She gave me her ritual kiss on the cheek before slipping into their waiting car. Once she had gone, Lee said he'd never seen her so afraid in his life. Big seas, Bass Strait, it's scared the bejesus out of many people. Pam was so terrified she never joined Lee back out in Bass Strait again. But no holding back the big fella, he was there again with bells on next morning.

The John Denver thing was a three-ring circus from the get-go. I'd never seen so many bosses, or people in charge of anything, in my life. It took two people to tell two more people to get two more people to get one camera out of a vehicle and onto a boat.

'Is it like this when you make movies?' I asked Lee.

'Always, and it'll get worse before it gets better,' he warned.

The scene was planned for John Denver to arrive much later. His father was a retired commercial airline pilot and had flown their entire crew from the USA to Australia and New Zealand in a Jetliner they owned. He would bring John to a boat I'd arranged for them in Port Fairy, which would then meet up with Lee out at sea.

We got away in the early morning, and Lee came up onto the flybridge, leaving the cockpit and saloon to Denver's people.

The sea was calm, we had the flybridge to ourselves, and we got down to game fishing.

The time came. John's boat appeared in the distance, radios reverberated with many voices all talking at once, and Lee was asked to come to his spot down in the cockpit.

I was to remain on the flybridge. I'd begun to look forward to it. I hadn't met John Denver, but I liked a couple of his songs.

Then, completely out of left field, Lee looked up at me and in full voice bellowed, 'Hey, John, who the fuck is this John Denver anyway?'

There was total silence. Complete shock! I laughed. I thought he was joking. He wasn't. Lee knew nothing about John Denver – and I mean nothing, not a thing.

Quickly, very quickly, those people who held clipboards, cameras or microphones, or any position above coffee boy, filled Lee in. I heard him roar with laughter before muttering, '*Rocky Mountain High* – what the fuck is he, a hippie? I don't listen to that shit. No wonder I've never heard of him.'

Lee Marvin was a rough diamond, especially when it came to speaking his mind. But true to the professional he was, when John Denver arrived alongside and they shook hands it was as if they had known each other all their lives. Show business!

Many people have since asked, how come John Denver was a part of a blood sport, being the conservationist he was? In those days, sharks weren't tagged and released as they are today. I really don't know the answer, but I needn't have worried as we never caught a great white that day.

Later, as we headed for home, John came up onto the flybridge with his guitar. Facing into a setting sun, he sang and played for the next 90 minutes, all the way home. I have often marvelled that I was so privileged to have had a private concert from a living legend. He was somebody who became whole with a guitar in his hands.

Back in Port Fairy, we were greeted by a crowd of thousands. The banks each side of the Moyne River were packed with Denver and Marvin fans, all there for a glimpse of their idols. I was puzzled, though, that John Denver wore an additional short-sleeved padded jacket over the top of his wet-weather jacket, even though it was quite a hot day. His bodyguard revealed that John Denver had a phobia of being stabbed – even while on stage performing. It was no normal jacket; it was designed to stop a knife, and when he mingled this close to the public, the body armour remained firmly in place no matter how hot it got.

Pam was always there waiting for us when we arrived back in port. She had fallen in love with Port Fairy and its people.

'This is the only place we have ever been where I can walk barefooted down the street, and simply go shopping, or whatever, without people staring, asking for autographs, or simply being annoying. Everyone is just so nice,' she told me. She and Wendy had also hit it off, and Wendy took her to a local fair one day, which Pam still talked about 20 years later.

To avoid the media, a friend gave me the keys to his beach house on East Beach for Pam, Lee and a few close friends to relax there over a barbecue at the end of the Denver filming.

I was a physical wreck, I hadn't slept for three straight days, and after numerous and various drinks at the beach house, I lapsed into a coma on a couch. When I awoke, many hours later, I was being carried in a fireman's lift by Lee, who insisted on taking me to my truck, as Pam swore she would physically harm anyone who tried to wake me.

At the time Lee would have been in his fifties, and he carried me over loose sand for close to half a mile, refusing to put me down. He was still a very fit man for a heavy drinker and smoker. In fact he was pissed at the time, with a fag hanging out the corner of his mouth, telling me to 'shut the fuck up' before Pam heard us!

Lee and I became lifelong friends during that charter, a friendship that lasted until his death. There are many great memories.

One night during dinner, while Lee was in the men's, Pam told me, with a huge smile, what convinced him to come and fish with me. 'When you said to him on your first call, "If you think you're up to

It's a wrap. The final scene at Port Fairy wharf for the John Denver television special, with John Denver, front left, Lee Marvin, right, and me in the background.

it," he stormed around the house in such a rage, I wondered what had gone wrong.

'He didn't say anything for a while, then he exploded. "Cheeky f...ing Australian – *If I'm up to it!* Who the bloody hell does he think he is? Of course I'm up to it, and I'll show him." That's when you hooked him.'

I remember her laughing, her face so full of joy. Pam Marvin was a beautiful woman, very special to all who met her. It was with great sadness that I learnt of her death, at the age of 88, in April 2018.

In the small township of Koroit, 20 minutes inland from Port Fairy, was the famous Micky Bourke's Hotel, owned by an equally famous hotelier. Mick was quite a character, with a lifelong ban from any horse-racing track in Australia after an indiscretion back in his horse-training days. But he was known far and wide as a great bloke. He had every boxing belt and trophy won by Australian world champion Lionel Rose – and a cockatoo he had taught to play cards.

One day when the weather prevented us from fishing, I took Pam and Lee across to Mick's pub. Built in 1853, it's a museum of sorts, of anything and everything good about Australia, and restored to retain its original Irish character.

Pam and Lee immediately fell in love with it, Mick's cheating bloody cockatoo and, of course, Mick himself. After a full tour of the place, including ducking into an open fireplace with a secret passage hidden behind, and seeing Mick's more precious relics only shown to special VIPs (Lee Marvin was Mick's favourite actor), Mick kept his special treat till last. The Honeymoon Suite, with its original four-poster bed, and beautiful 1853 hand-basin and jug ornaments.

Pam was beside herself. 'I've never seen anything so perfect', I believe were her words.

'How'd you like to stay the night in here?' said Mick.

'We'd love to,' said Lee.

'Only one condition, however,' said Mick. I knew what was coming.

'You only get the room free of charge if you can ring the bell.'

Suspended from the centre frame of the beautiful old bed was the biggest cow bell you can image. I can still hear Lee's raucous laughter carry through the entire second floor. I was never game to ask if they had actually rung the bell.

All too soon the time came for Pam and Lee to leave. I was invited to their hotel on their last night in Warrnambool. Two things remain clear, after all these years.

'You know they offered me the lead role in *Jaws*,' said Lee, sipping his chardonnay.

'I told them it wouldn't work – and turned the role down,' he added, closing his eyes and shaking his head in disbelief.

'I can pick 'em, eh honey?' He smiled at Pam, who stroked his cheek with the back of her hand. For a tough guy he had a very special and unique affection for the woman he loved, and showed it often in public.

Pam wasn't Lee's first love, and for those old enough to remember, Lee Marvin was the front-runner in palimony suits when his ex-partner, Michelle Triola, sued for alimony-without-matrimony, right at the time he was fishing with me.

Although she got nowhere near the amount she asked for, the Marvin v. Marvin palimony suit set the precedent for the out-of-wedlock cases to follow.

In fact, the only bad moment out of that time was as a result of Lee's law suit. I got a call from a well-known Melbourne print-media journalist of the time, who had covered a story on me previously, and who I considered a friend.

He wanted to interview Lee aboard the boat. I was reluctant to even ask Lee, as I felt it might look like I was capitalising on a story for personal gain. It took me days before I mentioned it to him.

'Hell yeah, John … but fuck him, tell him to come early, before we go fishing.' Lee was all for it because he knew it would be good publicity for me. Wrong!

The arsehole got the front page next day, all about Lee's palimony case. The fishing trip barely got a mention.

I rang him first thing next morning from a public phone booth.

'Morning c..t, now I know how low you are – as well as where you drink. Our next interview you're going be on the receiving end. And I'm sure you're smart enough to know how that's going to work out. Never show your face in this area again, as I can guarantee you'll end up on a hook – you have no friends in this town, not one!' Then I hung up.

I was shaking with rage. A voice behind me made jump a foot clear off the ground.

'Well I guess I know who that was.' It was Lee.

'You frightened the shit out of me,' I managed to reply.

'I know what you're saying. I was just taking a pee down there in the dark, and a bloke taps me on the shoulder asking for an autograph – pissed all over myself,' he snarled. We both burst out laughing.

On the walk back down to the boat I tried to apologise, as Lee would have seen the paper, a full front page. 'I thought the prick was a mate of mine – the lying, conniving bastard used me!'

As angry as I was, I was also embarrassed.

'It's OK John, he's only doing his job – I'm not angry with you, or him. Just remember, it doesn't matter what they have to say, just so long as they spell your name right.'

He meant every word of it. He kept his hand on my shoulder on the walk back to the boat.

'But I'd love to be a fly on the wall when you two cross paths again – my money's on you.' He laughed.

Our paths never did cross again; shortly after that, the journalist was posted to the UK. But I have still not forgotten, nor forgiven. Mates don't do that shit.

On their very last night, as we sat in their hotel room, Lee handed me back my roll-neck jumper and, in addition, the very famous, and very recognisable, red spray jacket that he always wore when game fishing.

'I want you to keep this John, it's yours,' he said, laying the jacket across my lap. 'There's only six of these in existence – a unique and special club. Next time we fish you can loan it back to me.' Even Pam looked shocked.

I told him I couldn't possibly accept it.

I honestly thought he was pissed, and next morning he'd be roaring down the phone to bring back his fucking jacket!

But no. He was insistent I keep it. Then he told me the story behind 'Fishing Bums InClorperated' (not 'Incorporated' – as they were all very pissed at the time), and that 'Fishing Bums Inc' logo remains strong to this day, boldly stencilled into the jacket.

Please forgive me if I don't remember all the members, but here goes: Marlin Brando, Richard Boone, Ernest Borgnine, Charles Bronson, Lee Marvin and … Nope, can't remember number six!

I do know, though, that he was great friends with Paul Newman. Another snippet of Hollywood gossip from 40-odd years ago was that Pam and Lee's marriage wasn't popular among the Who's Who of the time, maybe because of the palimony case. So Frank Sinatra loaned them his plane, where they were married over Las Vegas, Nevada, with only close family and friends aboard. Maybe number six is old Blue Eyes himself? Whatever, the six red Fishing Bums Inc jackets belonged to some Hollywood heavyweights, and there will still be people out there today who know all six members. Lee's jacket (which I have never once worn) is still in mint condition and remains one of my great pride and joys, tucked safely away to be hung in a fishing museum perhaps, to honour this wonderful man and the contribution he and Pam made to fishing.

Getting Lee Marvin to Port Fairy and onto my boat was publicity money couldn't buy. To have Lee, Pam, John Denver, and some of the world's leading cinematographers and film-makers in town all at the one time was a major coup. It got me started in international fishing circles.

My phone ran red hot and now I didn't have to bullshit about finding spaces for people, I was booked out for a year at a time. Even my bank manager suddenly liked me.

Shortly after Pam and Lee returned home, I received a call from Lee to say he was making back-to-back movies and to let me know he couldn't visit Australia the next season. Even so, he had been in touch with Jack Erskine, a Cairns rod-maker and legend in the fishing industry.

When Lee had fished with me, he had Jack send down his rods and reels to Port Fairy ahead of him.

'You can't catch big fish on that shit you're using John – I've had Jack make you up a set of 130 and 80, Merry Christmas mate!'

OK, my 130lb rod (my only rod) was nothing flash – but to me it was magnificent. I'd caught a 1009lb white pointer on it … 'piece of shit', was it?

A week later, by special courier, came two items. One contained two custom-built Erskine rods, a 130lb and an 80lb, with my name inscribed through the transparent bindings, and the other, two Penn International reels, a 130 and an 80. Both outfits had bent and straight butts (for those who know the go). The total cost of all this, at the time, was around the price of a new family car!

I rang Lee immediately – I can't remember ever feeling so special, nor so lost for words.

'Now throw that piece of shit you have overboard and go get a serious fish on some serious gear!'

You never got to thank Lee – he wasn't the kind of bloke who took compliments or liked displays of gratitude.

'You need it – now shut up.'

Every fish caught aboard my boats from that day onwards was caught on those two rods, including a Victorian state record of 2257½lb, which can never be broken, as fishing for great whites is banned now.

As much as Lee was part of my lucky break, I know he would appreciate me retelling the story he told me about his.

It was at the end of World War II, and Lee had been shot in the arse (something he'd be really pissed I've made public). And no, he wasn't in retreat, quite the opposite. He and his Marine buddies were pinned down on Saipan during the Pacific campaign, when he took a round that severed his sciatic nerve, paralysing him. 'On your belly advancing up a beach-head, it's better to take a round in the arse than in the head,' I tried to console him, with little success.

When he was back on his feet and discharged, however, things weren't much better.

A Purple Heart you can't eat, medals mean little to combat Veterans, and with soup kitchens on every corner and no work around, Lee was on the bones of his wounded arse.

He found himself standing in a line that ran the full length of a footpath. He thought it was a food line, and it progressed along slowly, for a very long time, until at last he was facing a little old man with thick round glasses sitting behind a table.

'What have you done?' asked the man, without looking up.

'I've caught a 30lb trout,' answered Lee.

'Move along,' said the old guy. Lee stood his ground.

'Where I come from, catching a 30lb trout means something,' said Lee.

The old guy looked up, then further up, until finally he was looking into Lee's eyes – which, with Lee at 6 foot 4, were glaring down upon him.

'OK, go stand with that lot over there,' said the old guy.

The rest, as they say, is well-documented history. Lee's rough gravelly voice, tough appearance, snow-white hair, 6 foot 4 height, and 'take no shit from nobody' attitude took him from an extra (the audition line he wandered into) to being one of Hollywood's great leading men.

He won an Academy Award for his role in *Cat Ballou*, which is kind of ironic as it was a musical comedy, and in Lee's own words, 'I don't even sing under the shower!'

But if my rod was a piece of shit, I couldn't imagine what Lee was thinking about my boat! I had outgrown *Papeo*; I was now in the big league and needed a class of boat worthy of the international clientele who were booking me.

The state government got behind me, as I was promoting Victoria to the world and bringing in international tourists.

I had asked Pam Marvin to christen my new boat, *Friendship*, in 1980, but sadly she was unable to come. She and Lee had commitments that were simply impossible to reschedule.

I still have her letter of thanks, and regret that she couldn't make it.

The dawn of Seabrake, Bass Strait, 1979

Australia's Bass Strait goes from safe to suicidal in hours. A bad weather front was forecast this fateful day, but constant changes in our region meant it could blow itself out well before it reached us, or simply change course and go right around us. We lived with this, but with a careful eye on the barometer ('the Glass'). Should it start falling steadily, get home fast. Or don't leave port in the first place.

It was a typical weekend charter, out Friday evening, back Sunday afternoon. This time it was three VFL footballers from Colac. As a sponsor of Port Fairy Football Club, the big burley Colac ruckman was a familiar sight. For the next 48 hours, as the angler on charter, we would need his brawn to stay with a couple of thousand pounds of angry shark, if we were lucky enough to hook one.

While I was up on the flybridge taking us out to Lady Julia Percy Island, my mate and crewman Phil Wik, or 'Dip', as he was more affectionately known, made our new clients comfortable below. Tricks of the trade to avoid sea-sickness included sorting out their sleeping arrangements, priming them all with alcohol and a deck of cards, and laying out who would be in the game fishing chair should a big fish strike.

It was cold and wet. No one came up onto the bridge until we were inside the lee of the island. The westerly horizon was growing darker and bleaker by the minute when we set anchor for happy hour, a tradition once we were in place for the night.

The dawn of Seabrake, Bass Strait, 1979

Inside the warmth and comfort of the saloon, I made for the Glass and gave it a tap.

The needle dropped like I had never seen a needle drop before. I tapped it again, and my blood ran cold. I just couldn't believe it.

In seven years at sea I had never seen the Glass this low. The wind was picking up, and a storm cloud was bearing down out of the south-west.

I felt sick. This was shaping up to be the worst weather I had ever been out in. Small ships don't survive this weather in Bass Strait.

We had no time to out-run it, and darkness was closing in.

'Don't put a bait in just yet mate,' I said to Dip, who was trying to keep himself occupied between glimpses at the approaching storm.

'Everything OK Skipper?' asked one of the clients.

'Yeah – all's good. Just waiting to see which side of the island we'll shelter, should this rain set in.'

The storm reached us, strong winds along with sheeting rain. I had fished in worse, 30-knot gusts, and 20-foot swells, it wasn't that bad yet!

'That Glass is low mate, lowest I've ever seen it,' I told Dip quietly.

He was never a big talker at the best of times.

'I've noticed.'

'We'll give it till nightfall, and if it hasn't blown itself out by then, we're out of here!' I said, knowing that's often when the wind drops, the rain clears – and we could make a run for home.

Two hours later, the wind was blowing harder than I'd ever known, a demonic high-pitched whistle through the aerials, screaming at us, blocking out any other sound.

Night fell. On my evening radio check with Port Fairy Radio, I said that conditions were too bad to leave the island, but we were OK. I told them I would call again at 7am.

Now we were being tossed from wall to wall in a tiny room. Just sitting and hanging on was a challenge, and Dip and I had to keep checking the anchor was holding and the anchor-line wasn't chafing, which involved a trip out on deck in gale-force winds and blinding rain.

An aerial shot of Lady Julia Percy Island, looking from north to south.

Lady Julia Percy Island lies between Portland and Port Fairy, around 6 miles off the coastline. The island is a mile long by just over half a mile wide; at the southern end it reaches some 120 feet above sea level. It's a volcanic rock rising up from the ocean floor, from 90 feet of water. Apart from the northern end of the island, its sides are sheer rock-face. In Dinghy Cove, the north-western (and sheltered) end, the depth falls away to 30–50 feet, and it's home to some 2000 seals, who haul themselves up the pebbly beach to give birth to their pups during summer and to rest at night.

We always anchored for shelter at Dinghy Cove, where the island blocked the southerly swells, and where the sharks patrolled in search of slow-moving seals. They were not far away even now, on this wild night. It was pupping season.

We were stuck, until daylight at least. The challenge was to keep *Papeo*, a 38-foot timber boat, in as much shelter as we could find. Normally the high cliff faces and the mile-long island offered ample cover. The island serves as a barrier from the constant ground swells originating from Antarctica and rolling northwards year in, year out, to mainland Australia.

The Continental Shelf – with its sheer drop-off into thousands of feet – is closest to the mainland just off the Victorian coast, near where we

The dawn of Seabrake, Bass Strait, 1979

were: it's a natural wave-maker, responsible for the biggest and wildest seas on the planet.

That's why Bass Strait is the most hazardous stretch of water in the world, even more notorious than the North Sea.

There was no shelter that allowed safe anchorage. At any instant, we could 'pull anchor' with the constant reefing the anchor was receiving, tearing it out of the reef below; or we could chafe off the anchor-line, which was dragging over hidden rock and ledges to where the anchor lay on the ocean floor. We would only know when *Papeo* turned beam-on to the weather and began to drift.

The Beaufort wind scale is measured in increments, from 0 (calm), to Force 12 (hurricane). A Force 3 or Force 4 in Bass Strait is enough to keep fishing fleets in port. By midnight it was blowing Force 7–8, gale force. With 25-foot waves on top of a ground swell, the waves were 50 foot. Maybe bigger. It was hell.

The wind screeched like a banshee, the ocean roared its claim against the deadly rocks, and inside the boat crockery was smashed to tiny pieces by a furious hand.

I don't know if I have ever been that afraid. Vietnam included.

I was out of my depth, literally, and without a solution. Lives were depending on me for their survival.

'We have to move.'

I dragged Dip out of the wheelhouse onto the deck, out of earshot of our terrified passengers.

'If we hang back further, to the south-east, we may find a pocket of shelter out there.'

I pointed out a wind-change pattern on the surface of the water close by, as I took to the flybridge ladder.

It meant Dip had to haul the anchor on deck, which was now fully awash and deadly dangerous. I couldn't see him clearly, nor could we communicate. We both knew. These were the worst conditions either of us had ever been in, and we weren't even sure we could pull off.

The bow was rising and falling anywhere up to 30–50 feet on the passing sea.

Dip was blinded by the stinging saltwater as he hung onto the bow-rail with one hand and tried to hold/feel for the weight and direction of the anchor in the dark, against lashing winds and sea.

In total darkness also, I could only 'feel' for our heading through the helm. Keeping my face directly into the wind and 'pointing' – feeling the helm for its least resistance – was the only indication that I was pointed up into the sea and the direction of where the anchor lay. *Papeo* would shudder with every wave that struck her – every square inch of her shook.

I could feel her bulk and dead-weight resist the rise of a wave washing under us, while the anchor remained solidly fixed to the bottom. Then she would swing violently in the direction our anchor-line pointed, hidden to Dip and me in the darkness – but through experience, and the soles of our feet, we knew exactly which way to head.

Slowly, ever so slowly, we edged our way up into the ferocious resistance of wind and waves, Dip gathering in the anchor-line a few feet at a time. At any moment his legs could be swept out from under him by a huge wave, washing him over the side, and we would never find him. In the darkness, in these conditions, it was a certain death sentence. It was the 1970s. 'Real men' didn't wear safety harnesses. You would be laughed out of town.

Please God watch over him, I heard my inner voice whisper.

By the good grace of God – and bloody hard, exhausting, persistent work, not to mention courage – Dip finally boarded our anchor. As I turned our stern towards the island to stream off north-east in search of calmer water, we were laid completely on our side by a wave that hit us a full-on broadside. Had I not been holding onto the wheel, white-knuckled with fear, I would have been catapulted clean off the flybridge.

Dazed and in complete shock, I was simply amazed when she righted herself, cockpit full of water and squirting tons of ocean out through the scuppers – the openings at deck level to let water escape.

The dawn of Seabrake, Bass Strait, 1979

'Fuck – another one like that and we're sunk!'

Then I realised Dip had been somewhere down there on deck. My blood ran absolutely cold.

Like a miracle, he emerged at the foot of the bridge ladder, the water still in the cockpit above his knees!

'Get the fuck inside!' I shouted. 'Lifejackets on all round. And keep that saloon door closed!'

As he disappeared, I fought to bring *Papeo*'s head back up into the wind. The water on deck made her sluggish, and perilously vulnerable to a second blow. A second wave would be fatal, it would bury her.

I had been instrumental in *Papeo*'s refit when converting her from a Motor-Sailor to a Flybridge Cruiser; if anything, I had gone overboard in fitting an abundance of scuppers into her cockpit, to ensure if ever a sea came aboard there were ample ports to let the water run off the deck and overboard quickly. Now it was paying dividends.

A Motor-Sailor, for the uneducated, is a boat that can sail as well as simply motor along. *Papeo* had a round bilge; put simply, at water level her sides were rounded so that when she sailed she could lay over, improving her ability to 'heel over' and have less mass in the water, in order to sail faster. It was that round bilge, and excess of scuppers, that saved our lives. A traditional Flybridge Cruiser wouldn't have survived that first wave.

I have always been a God-fearing man, never religious, but always God-fearing, and more than once in my life, with my back to the wall – like now – I'd have a word to the Big Fella.

I vividly remember having a word to our Lord the moment Dip slammed that saloon door shut. This truly was do-or-die stuff. I'd stared down death a number of times – but never from as close as we were right now.

Miraculously, she drained off the wave without getting hit by a second; as the helm freed up, I kept the dark outline of the island off our bow and used the throttle to maintain our station in the slipstream off the reef. It was a mild improvement on where we had been anchored, and with the engine running it gave some form of false security, for me anyway. For an hour I kept manoeuvring back and forth in the darkness, finding my way by feel and the occasional glimpse through the blanket of sea-spray. Dropping anchor again wasn't an option, even though it would have provided a short reprieve from continually fighting the helm.

I stayed there all night; a long, lonely night with just fear and uncertainty for company.

Fear has an amazing effect on the body. Time becomes irrelevant, food and sleep irrelevant, survival – paramount! As dawn broke it was a reminder of how far from home we were: 11 nautical miles in truth, but it may as well have been the other side of the world. In the grey, weak light, I could see the size of the waves, blocking out the entire coastline for minutes at a time. The wind had abated slightly, or maybe I was accustomed to it by now. I'd seriously doubted I would see daybreak again.

It must have been a great disappointment to our clients to learn we were still at the island when, taking advantage of daylight, I nosed *Papeo* as close in as I dared to the cliffs on the north-east corner, to shelter from the wind at least. The surge coming off the island was short and sharp, but compared to the ground swell we had been in all night, it was relatively calm.

Leaving the helm for a minute, I shot down off the flybridge and was stunned to see all four men, including Dip, bedded down on the saloon floor.

'A brew would be great mate, and relief on the wheel while I radio in – when you're good,' I called to Dip, before charging back up onto the bridge.

Being drawn *into* the cliffs was now as big a risk as being sunk out in the full force of the gale; current and disturbed backwash can quickly pull a vessel towards an obstacle, rather than push it away. But for now we were safe.

As he had done a hundred times before, in all weather, Dip served hot coffee and then he relieved me on the wheel. I knew there would be other boats talking to home, and each other. South Australian fishing boats could be heard on our frequency, and I hoped to pick up one of them. All our weather came from that direction, and what I wanted to hear was a SA boat reporting that the 'blow' had passed through.

But not only were there no SA boats on air, all I picked up was a faint 'Mayday' coming from down the Peterborough direction, from a coastal freighter, talking of running aground.

Apart from being the first time I'd ever heard a Mayday call, it brought home the severity of the storm. Freighters are hundreds of feet long – we were a mere 38 feet, about the size of their lifeboat.

If the army had taught me anything, especially as a section commander in Vietnam, it was keep everyone informed, stay positive and lead from the front. With three sets of eyes glued to me, as my clients huddled on the saloon floor, I began my morning radio Sked (Schedule) calmly.

'VH-3BJ, VH-3BJ, this is *Papeo*, receive please, over.' No reply.

As I waited, I stared at the barometer, which couldn't have dropped any lower – it had effectively bottomed out during the night.

I was contemplating making a 'PAN–PAN' call (vessel in strife but not immediately sinking) on the 2182 emergency frequency, when a voice boomed through the radio loud and clear. Close – very close.

'Vessel calling VH-3BJ come in please, over.'

It wasn't Port Fairy, that I knew. I could hear engines running and knew it was a vessel at sea.

'This is *Papeo*, come in please, over.'

The vessel gave its call-sign and identified itself as an ocean-going tug on its way to the port of Portland – current position abeam 5 miles south of Lady Julia Percy Island – making 1 knot into heavy gale-force seas.

Immediately, myself and our three guests were on our feet, scanning out through the saturated glass of the saloon for this big tug. I told them we were on the other end of the island, 6 miles away, in the lee (for lack of a better word) of it.

There was a long silence.

'What size is your vessel?'

Upon being told it was a 38-foot timber charter boat you could almost hear the Hail Marys.

I think originally they may have contemplated joining us for a break, as they had been in this hammering since leaving Geelong for Portland.

Going by the amount of times he had me repeat our length, his dismay at hearing me right, he didn't want to witness five grown men die. He wished us all the luck he could, with the update that this storm was still 'in the making – worse to come – drive your vessel ashore if you can.'

And then – bye!

It was now becoming clear why that freighter was in trouble further down the coast – survival was less than 50/50, she was going to break her back punching up into the sea. Unlike the tug, which even at 1 knot was designed to cope in such head-on seas, turning to run before seas of this size was certain death.

Our only choices, besides driving her up onto the pebbly beach in Dinghy Cove, were to sit in behind the tug and follow her to Portland, twice as far away as Port Fairy – or to try for home, running the gauntlet (before the sea) and taking our chances by dragging something to slow us down.

I made the decision. I had a sea-anchor on board that should be enough. Old skippers had warned me: if ever you get caught with big seas up your arse, drag whatever you can lay your hands on. Tie a dozen cray-pots to a line and tow that, run out a mile of net and drag that, sink your tinnie (tender-boat) and tow that – anything to keep her from surfing. Surf and you're dead.

Great I thought, I've got no cray-pots, no miles of net, no tinnie, but I do have a fair size sea-anchor. I needed time to batten down all the hatches, pump out our bilges, have stand-by pumps at the ready should we get swamped, drill all onboard to find somewhere to wedge themselves in and stay put, lifejackets on at all times. This was the norm, a simple drill for going home in dirty weather.

The dawn of Seabrake, Bass Strait, 1979

Dip had managed to feed our guests and had taken the wheel while I rigged up the sea-anchor. The concept is to keep a vessel's head up into the weather in depths greater than a ground-anchor can reach. I'd never used one, and they were designed to go over the bow, not the stern.

By mid-morning the wind and seas were increasing, at my best guess Force 9–10. The island, which normally stood out like Ayers Rock, was now almost submerged. Her southernmost end, normally 120 feet above sea level, was awash like a reef; her northern end, with its 90-foot cliffs, was a boiling submerged reef – a terrifying transformation. Only Dip and I realised the enormity of the ocean that had created this.

I nodded to Dip to break anchor and throttled up to drive up the anchor-line. At least this time we could see each other.

With the anchor almost aboard, Dip climbed up onto the bow out of the open hatch.

I saw it happen in slow motion. The hatch cover, which was normally lashed, not hinged, went overboard. We stared at each other, speechless. Without this hatch, the forward section, and in turn the entire vessel, was open to the sea – like a house that has just lost its roof in a cyclone, only worse.

It had never happened in the hundreds – perhaps thousands – of times we had shot and recovered the anchor, and today, in a life-and-death situation, the most important hatch to be battened down, drum tight, was gone. Overboard.

In that instant my mind flashed back. Again, I was paying the price for the life I had taken in Vietnam – first the sight in my left eye, now it was going to be with my own life.

In the wall of sea, mist and foam I saw fins. Oh great, sharks, I thought.

But I made out the raked dorsal of dolphins, a pod of around six or seven. The surface of the water was boiling white, the spray being blown out of the waves was white, the hatch cover was white. Then, flipped up out of the water by the dolphins, came the unmistakable shape of the hatch. Gobsmacked, I pointed in disbelief.

'Grab a gaff!' I screamed at the top of my lungs.

At deck level, Dip was blinded to everything except his handhold on the bow-rail, and the deck below his feet. I shouted again: 'The dolphins – WATCH THE DOLPHINS!'

He gave me a weird look before picking up the gaff while I wheeled around in pursuit. I need not have moved. The pod, in a team effort, pushed and flipped our hatch cover right to where Dip waited with the gaff at midships – and once he had secured it with the gaff, they left.

That moment will remain with me forever. Had those dolphins not salvaged that hatch cover we would never have survived – categorically, we never even had a prayer, as any boater will tell you. Why, and how, they came to be around when they were, or why they chose to push the hatch cover back to us, remains a mystery. But I have four witnesses, and if you want to believe in miracles, this was one, one I shall hold dear for the rest of my life. Those little guys saved our lives.

Did they know that? They are amazing creatures, super smart. I have read about them pushing shipwrecked survivors towards land, but bringing that hatch cover right back to where Dip waited with the gaff, that was a real miracle. It saved our vessel and five lives. I recall reading about survivors during World War II who had to shoot dolphins as they pushed their lifeboat towards a Japanese-occupied island. A real tragedy.

But now, forward hatch back on and lashed down, I edged back out from the lee of the island. The entire island was now awash. Leaving that remote space, or barrier, to face the full brunt of the Southern Ocean, we were exposed to giant swells and the full force of the wind.

Don't ask me why, but I turned on the depth sounder as we headed in the direction of Port Fairy, possibly to ensure we were clear of the natural reef that now had 90 feet of water over it. Approximately 1 mile out of the confused backwash, we got flattened again, laid on our side so badly I almost came off the bridge. Surely this time we were lost – she would never right herself and the sea would swallow us up. But again, miraculously, she came back upright.

The dawn of Seabrake, Bass Strait, 1979

That was it for me, we were dead. If we couldn't keep control before getting out into the open clear water, we had no chance of survival. We were like a matchstick in a washing machine.

We were knocked down again. This time I felt a horrible thud, like the engine had broken free of its mountings. Again, I dragged myself into the helmsman's seat and now, praying out aloud, I hoped for a quick death. This was it. How could we possibly survive, exposed to the full brunt of the Southern Ocean?

How, I shall never know, but I managed to get us back into some form of protection about halfway up the eastern side of the island, which would appear and disappear with the rise and fall of each successive swell.

Dip appeared on deck and screamed out to me: 'We have a guy knocked unconscious down here – fuck it's a mess!'

My first aid was more advanced than his.

It was the 6 foot 6 ruckman, lying in a heap just inside the doorway. He was coming around, shaking his head and groaning. I could see broken skin to one side of his temple and above his ear, but no blood.

'You OK?' He nodded unconvincingly.

'Port Fairy is three points in front, it's almost siren time – now how are you doing?' I asked, forcing a weak smile.

But he was angry and hurt.

'Can we get the fuck out of here, and home?' he snapped.

'I'm working on it cobber, but now you're on the floor – stay there, OK?'

He nodded.

Back on the flybridge, Dip filled me in. This guy was the luckiest guy alive. He'd been sitting behind the dining-room table, wedged in, up until we were flattened. This had launched him across the saloon – all 6 foot 6 inches of him – into the opposite wall, which happened to be a row of plate-glass windows. He hit the frame separating two panes; just 6 inches either side, he'd have gone straight through and out into the sea, unconscious, with no chance of us ever finding him.

Out in the cockpit, the sea-anchor was still there – I threw it over and asked Dip to power forward slowly. Immediately it filled with water; the drag was intense. Good. The tow-line creaked under the load. Great.

'OK mate – slow ahead, and home.'

Standing at the stern, I felt the enormous amount of drag holding us fast.

This is the key, I convinced myself: going in the same direction as wind and waves (which was where we needed to go to get to Port Fairy), stopping the boat surfing, where wave speed is around 35mph. Just when I was beginning to believe the sea-anchor might work, a massive wave rolled towards us. As it arrived at the stern, the sea-anchor groaned loudly, the tow-line hummed like a plucked guitar string and we stopped moving forward. The wave broke into the open cockpit, filling it completely with tons, and tons, of water, which stood *Papeo* on her tail, bow-up.

I was now standing in a cockpit with water up to my groin and feeling *Papeo* going down by the stern – with a second wave about to break, which would sink us instantly. I cut the tow-line with a tomahawk.

The sea-anchor was too severe. It would sink us from the stern. As if on cue, a stainless-steel dairy bucket that we used to hold bait hit me in the shins. Suddenly it became the only option. Up in the forecastle lay just over 300 feet of old hemp rope. If the rope was dry, a man could lift the entire bundle – wet, he'd struggle to lift 3 metres of it, it's such an absorbent fibre.

Both items came into my mind at the same instant. To be doubly sure, I gave the bottom of the bucket, and its sides, half-a-dozen full-blooded whacks with the razor-sharp tomahawk, leaving several slits through the skin. I double-wrapped the hemp rope around the heavy-duty handle, tied it off with a bow-line, turned it around a strong stern mooring-cleat, and tossed the bucket over the stern.

Fear was written all over Dip's face as we crossed on the flybridge ladder.

The dawn of Seabrake, Bass Strait, 1979

'Are we going to get home?' he said.

'Of course we're going to get home, just let that rope run off steady around that cleat until I tell you to stop,' I said, in the most casual tone I could muster.

He believed me, even though I doubted it myself.

But as I stepped in behind the helm, I felt the difference.

Papeo felt twice as heavy and more stable in the water, and half as flighty.

About 100 feet of hemp rope, with the bucket dragging it straight out behind, was holding her back, pulling her up and stopping her from surfing.

With every 20 foot of rope that went out, the better she felt. The effect over the entire vessel was simply amazing, beyond belief.

The look on Dip's face said it all, it was a transformation so incredible it was beyond words. It dawned on me that it was like having a heavy fish under tow. In the past, the trip home always felt better once we had tied off big sharks on a short tow. I'd previously put it down to the celebration/elation – but it was a ton of fish hanging off the stern that had stabilised and slowed the vessel enormously.

The swells were still mountainous and the wind now up around 100 miles an hour – a full-blown Force 12 hurricane. The air was filled with foam, visibility was down to the waves immediately around us, and we still needed to yell in each other's ears to be heard.

'Get down and reassure them, but come straight back up once you have.'

Dip nodded enthusiastically. He could see the calm again in my face. We were going to make it home!

It was blowing harder now than ever, and we were still out in the open ocean, exposed to the full brunt of Bass Strait at her worst. Suddenly it crossed my mind that our tow-line was rubbing back and forth across the stern deck, a deck that I had personally crafted, putting plenty of extra sand into the mix to ensure lasting grip underfoot. It was like sandpaper, and on one occasion towing a shark home had almost chafed through a line. I had practically stopped breathing by the time Dip appeared on the ladder again.

'Get here!' I shouted, passing him before he reached the wheel.

Inside the saloon, I grabbed a section of foam-covered seating and a duvet.

'Neutral!' I screamed out to Dip, who immediately knew my plan. First the duvet onto the deck, then the foam seating doubled over the hemp line, before wrapping the duvet around and around the line over the stern, where the tow-line was tied-off to the cleat. It could never chafe through now.

Fifteen minutes had passed, and we had never looked like being knocked down; we could see far enough astern to pick out the extra-big waves that appeared like they might break into our cockpit. As they reared up to breathtaking heights, I would spin the wheel hard over to full starboard lock, being the same quarter our tow-line was attached to, and *Papeo*'s head would swing across to the right, allowing the wave to pass beneath us, similar to a surfer pulling out of a wave right on the top.

By offering our 'quarter stern' into the wave – not the full flat-faced stern, which was a surface to be 'pushed' – the angled corner, like a bow, allowed the water to separate around our stern. It had worked, time and time again.

Dip actually smiled, briefly.

'Might be better if you go down and reassure them now,' he suggested. I suspect he had had enough of being cramped up inside that saloon, constantly assuring them we were OK.

'Yeah, we get one like this every now and then, just to keep us on our toes,' I said casually, while filling the kettle at the sink.

The lump on the big fella's forehead was now closing his eye.

'You get this all the time?' he asked, with a look of sheer horror.

'Not all the time, maybe a couple of times a year. This one's not so bad – we've had worse.' I couldn't believe I could lie so blatantly, but it worked. They all immediately relaxed.

The dawn of Seabrake, Bass Strait, 1979

'OK – I'll have that beer now,' said one.

'See, I told you – this is Bass Strait, it's normal,' said another.

I put the kettle on and left for the flybridge.

It was still a long way to go, but the boat was as stable as I had ever felt her.

There were two seats on the flybridge, and Dip and I sat there in silence for a long time, taking in the events of the past 16 hours. It had been a living nightmare. Even now, although we were safe and *Papeo* was heading home slowly, we still couldn't see land – nor know exactly where we were.

It was then I remembered I had the sounder running; with a compass heading and knowing our depth, I could get a running fix on roughly where we were.

We both blinked in disbelief at the print-out of the graph for the past couple of hours: 80-foot ground swells constantly across the graph. That is, 160 feet from the top of a swell looking down at the bottom of the trough between sets.

Had that tow-line snapped with us on the top face of a wave, it would have been the same as dropping *Papeo* off a 16-storey building.

Running before a sea is always kinder on a vessel than running into a sea. In seas of this size and ferocity, a vessel wouldn't last long punching up into 80-foot swells, then free-falling 160 feet into the trough. It would break the back of any vessel, and the backs of all aboard.

After an hour we were all very much more accustomed to the environment, and moving about the boat. Dip had prepared a lunch and served it, our guests were now enjoying their beer supply, and one by one they had all come up to the flybridge to get a real feel for this raging sea we were mastering. In fact, I was beginning to enjoy it; the hemp rope was secure, and *Papeo* had never felt as good under the helm as she did now.

The only concern remaining was that we had to round the lighthouse into Port Fairy Bay, and that then meant coming back up into the wind and sea. Slowly, ever-so-slowly, the South-West Passage came into view out of the fog of foam and sea-spray caused by the blinding wind.

'Home,' I said, pointing to the rows of cars flashing their headlights at us, parked in the carpark normally reserved for surfers every weekend.

It was still mid-morning, even though it was dark and bleak enough to be dusk. Once inside the bay, the huge ground swells petered out into short, sharp waves, driven by 100mph winds. *Papeo* stopped in her tracks. We simply weren't moving in the headwind.

'OK guys, time you earned your keep,' I called below. 'That rope and bucket has to come aboard.'

It took all four of them the best part of 30 minutes. With each length retrieved, *Papeo* regained her buoyancy until, when the rope and bucket were fully boarded, she was rolling and crashing as she had during the first early hours at the island the night before.

With the mouth of the Moyne River beckoning less than a mile ahead, I opened the throttles to close the distance as quickly as humanly possible.

The river is stone-walled, and a popular walkway for tourists and locals alike. This day it seemed packed, and as we came into the Gipps Street parking bay area, cars began blowing their horns and people were waving as though we had the Queen aboard.

'You normally this popular?' asked one of our clients.

Dip and I looked at each other for an explanation but found none.

As we tied up, it all became apparent. We had been on the news, reported as missing, and given that it was also the worst storm ever recorded to that date, it had seemed highly unlikely we would ever be seen again.

Also, given that a freighter had been stopped in its tracks and forced into shelter further down the coast, and another commercial fishing boat remained missing (later discovered in another port), it was some sort of a miracle we had made it.

I never made it common knowledge just how we had survived to anyone other than a few close friends.

But from that day onwards, Dip and I had earned a new respect from all along the wharf. Old blokes who may grunt in reply to a cheery 'Good morning' now touched the peak of their caps, blokes who would never say 'G'day' now made the effort, and those who thought, 'who's this young upstart with his flash rods, and bullshit' would leave cray-tails and octopus as bait for our charters on *Papeo*'s deck overnight.

We had earned our stripes, survived where most would have perished. It was the talk along the wharf, and all around the town. And it was all good for business.

That storm to my knowledge has never been surpassed; it took the Shire months to repair the damage caused to the foreshore. Boulders the size of houses had been rolled up off the ocean floor over the South-West Passage and blocked the road for weeks. A few remained there for years, and may even still be there to this day, they were so big.

Dick Cullenward's garden hedge was washed away in that storm. It bordered his home overlooking an inshore beach, some half a kilometre back from the ocean, high up in the sand dunes, 60 feet above sea level. Dick, an ex-fighter pilot for the US Navy, also said that his highly sophisticated wind gauge had recorded winds in excess of 100mph before it disintegrated.

The ruckman nursed a sore head for a week or two, but AFL ruckmen are a very tough breed.

He and his mates even came for another charter. And yes – you couldn't bet on it. It was the flattest Bass Strait gets, like a lake.

'Now this is unique – this just doesn't happen,' I assured them, as we happily sailed off to the island for 48 hours of dead calm.

No shark, but the complete opposite to the first trip, and finally I told them how lucky we really were to live to tell the tale. But then again, we create our own luck.

A country boy, until 1969

I have a vivid memory of standing at the bedside of my dying grandmother; I was four or five, but it's as clear as if it had happened an hour ago. In the middle of the night my three sisters and I had been bundled into a neighbour's car in our pyjamas and driven to Grandma's in Warrnambool, 25 miles away.

We were all standing around her bed. Everyone was crying. I watched in childlike astonishment as a vision of light appeared in a circle around her head on the pillows, before rising up through the ceiling. Someone said, 'She's gone.'

Nobody said anything about the circle of light. It was only years later I figured out it was her spirit leaving her body. I'm positive nobody else saw it; nobody mentioned it then, nor since, not even after I told them what I'd seen. It remains one of life's extraordinary experiences.

Home for us was a sheep stud, which my dad managed for my uncle, Sam Walker, who had lost his leg during World War I and was obviously very restricted in what he could do as a grazier. The property was named Southall, after the hospital where Uncle Sam convalesced in England. Southall was a Corriedale sheep stud of some repute. We sent selected breeding rams all around the world – primarily to South Africa.

And even as a little tacker I would be over at the shed with Dad and Uncle Sam as these very special sheep were loaded up to be shipped to their destinations. Notable, too, were the men in their Sunday clothes, all coming to our shearing shed to look at sheep – and I got to eat Mum's special scones with strawberry jam, served up in the woolshed.

Prior to running Uncle Sam's property, Dad and Mum had lived in Warrnambool, where Dad worked with his father in their trucking business. During World War II, Dad served in New Guinea; after Grandpa died, he returned to take up Uncle Sam's offer.

By the time I stood at my grandma's deathbed, I had three older sisters: Margaret, the eldest; then Elizabeth; followed by Judith, who was two years older than me.

I was the only boy – I was desperate for a brother, which never happened. My younger sister, Ann, I named 'Jack', which has stuck with her for life. Jack bore the brunt of being my little *brother* – including being forced to face my fast-bowling practice.

We were a close family, fortunate to have loving parents who brought us all up to have good manners and good morals.

Being raised on the land meant we all grew up with a strong work ethic and helped one another at all times to ensure that whatever tasks were required were done. We were a happy family, with a large circle of friends, and were well regarded in the community, all involved in community services. It's what country life is about.

I started school while we were at Southall, walking – or riding a pony – the mile or so to Minhamite State School with my sisters.

It was nothing like schools of today. It was just us kids in an old weatherboard building in a paddock. No inter-school activity, no sports days, nothing. All grades were under one roof, one teacher with a total of 25 kids in all. *School of the Air* was the weekly highlight where, weather permitting, we sat outside and listened to a radio program broadcast to rural schools.

For community sport or weekend entertainment, horse riding and bike riding was about your lot – and as horse riding was 90% work-related in any event, the other 10% was merely to get to the neighbours faster than you could riding a bicycle.

Having said that, my earliest claim to fame was riding second in the Minhamite Cup country races, competing against an adult field, aged 11.

Over summer there was a community dam, initially constructed for the Country Fire Authority (CFA) for filling fire trucks. Dad was the CFA Captain for Minhamite and I learnt to swim in that dam, spending hours in there over long hot summers.

Bushfires were and still are a serious risk in Australia, and country life involved preparing for and preventing them. Burning-off season was a community affair. Every family belonged to the CFA, and before summer both sides of all the roads in Dad's zone were burnt. Us kids walked side by side, trailing a kerosene burner – effectively a tube of kerosene with a wick end – to start the fires.

A fleet of privately owned tray-trucks with water tanks and water pumps patrolled to restrict the burn to the roadside only. The aim was to reduce flammable fuel during the summer and create fire-breaks to stop the inevitable fires once they reached a roadway. It also cleaned up the rubbish tossed from cars, which was practically everything back then.

The Minhamite Gymkhana was the big social event in our little rural community. Dad was set on winning the Minhamite Cup. He'd even imported a jockey to ride his chestnut thoroughbred, Chester, a three-year-old gelding he had bred. Chester won alright. Problem was, after he'd won he didn't stop running.

With home in sight of the 7-furlong track in the neighbour's paddock, he left the jockey at the first fence, the saddle at about the third, and was standing at the stables with two short, mangled reins by the time Dad got there. But, he'd won the Minhamite Cup. To be fair, the rest of the field were mainly real station hacks or stockhorses, but there was no telling Dad that.

Dad, being a returned serviceman, had applied for a Soldier Settlement Block, a government-backed initiative through Veterans' Affairs for those choosing to start up their own farms at the end of World War II. I was eight or nine years old, but I remember the excitement when the grant finally came through. To celebrate, Dad took us all on a caravan holiday through Victoria, along the Murray River. It was the first, and only, holiday we ever had as a complete family.

These Soldier Settlement Blocks were allocated out of huge landholdings; as many as a dozen farms could be made up from one larger property.

Our block was part of Affleck's Estate, renamed the Minjah Estate.

We had around 360 acres. There were no fences, no dams, no windmills, no buildings, no plantations, no animal shelters. Nothing, except a boundary fence on the roadside and the survey markers where we had to erect our new boundary fences. Most settlers built their garage first and lived there while their homes were being built. But Dad, Mum and Jack lived in a caravan while our house was built. I was sent away.

This was the loneliest and saddest time of my life.

I was sent to live with an aunt and uncle and their newly-born daughter in Hawkesdale, about halfway between Minhamite and Minjah. I hated

Me and Dad with an export ram for South Africa.

my new school, with hundreds of kids, lots of rooms and lots of classes. I hated the teachers and all the kids. I was alone, and a loner.

I'd go home to an old, cold, weatherboard dump of a house where the new baby never stopped crying, and lie in my bed in the darkness, aching with loneliness. Often I would cry myself to sleep, I missed my parents and sisters and friends so much.

Thank heavens for Lyn Wilson across the road. She was a friend of Judy, my sister. I would go over there and hang out with her. It's where my interest in pigeons began. They had a lost racing pigeon that had made its home in their barn. I could sit and look at that pigeon all day. It was all alone and lost like me.

Time dragged miserably. I could go home and stay in the caravan for school holidays, and occasionally Mum and Dad would visit, but it was really like doing time. I'm sure they knew I was sad and unhappy, but we all had to make sacrifices in order to have a new farm of our very own. My other three sisters were staying in Warrnambool with my aunts, and they were always saying how horrible that was as well. So, I just shut up.

But, as it always does, the good day finally arrived. Moving into 'Woodville', our brand-new three-bedroom house, was complete. Our garage was up, and work was underway on the shearing shed, hay shed, and the dairy. From gloom to glory. I had to share my bedroom with Jack, who was about four years old by then, but hey – after Hawkesdale, I'd have slept in the chook house and shared it with rats.

The school bus ran right past our front gate, to Warrnambool for Elizabeth and Judy, who were at high school, and Woolsthorpe State School for me, just 9 miles down the road. I was in Grade 5 now. It was late in the year when I started at Woolsthorpe, and because of the changes and upheaval, I guess, I was kept back. I had to repeat Grade 5.

But out of the bad comes good. In Grade 5, I made mates who are still best mates to this day. In a new area, all Soldier Settlements, or grazier neighbours, we had the same things in common. Unlike Minhamite, there was lots to do, with small towns close by. And with neighbours nearby, after school and at weekends there were never enough hours in the day to amuse ourselves. Rabbiting and eeling were two of the most popular pastimes, as parents needed little persuasion when it came to putting food on the table.

Or you'd get 7/6' a pair for rabbits – the Rabbit Man would drop by and collect any time you had 'underground mutton' (rabbits) for sale.

Not the same market for eels, however, but my mother loved eels, and only Mum knew how to cook them. Freshly caught from running water – creeks (not muddy dams) – skinned immediately after getting them home, they would then soak overnight in Mum's special solution. After that they were cut into short lengths and rolled in flour before going into the frying pan for breakfast. It was Aussie caviar!

My mate Flynny and I caught heaps of them at night with our home-made spear. This was made out of 6-inch nails attached to a long tree-branch handle; add a spotlight hooked to a 12-volt car battery, and you're in business. We took turns to carry the car battery.

It was 1950s country living – good neighbours, good lifestyle, good life. Neighbours were almost family in those days. Their problem was your problem, and when tragedy struck, the whole community had your back. That great Australian trait, Aussie spirit, arose from such communities. It goes as far back as the First Fleet I guess, when pretty much everybody was in the same boat (albeit a convict ship). There was respect for all those who honoured this spirit.

Woodville combined dairy farming, sheep farming and 'fat cattle' (grown for the beef market). Uncle Sam let Dad take his pick of breeding stock to start his own Corriedale stud – a couple of rams and some selected ewes. As soon as Dad left Southall it was sold.

Dad also had a passion for Murray Grey cattle, an off-shoot of the well-proven Angus, or black poll, beef cattle. Soon we had a Murray Grey stud to complement the sheep stud.

The dairy, however, was our bread and butter – only a small herd of around 50 cows at capacity. I learnt to hate milking cows very early, however, as they have to be milked twice daily. Early morning, then again late afternoon. I had to help Dad with the milking up till school time, then straight off the bus after school it was back to the dairy. Each milking cow has a calf, to begin her milking career, then a calf every year thereafter to keep her place in the herd. My main job was feeding the calves, which are taken off their mothers around three days after birth. The heifers were kept, whereas the bull calves were sold.

The work on farms is endless, it's never done. They say that with sheep you're at one end or the other constantly. First there's drenching, which involves shoving a specially-designed gun into each sheep's mouth and squirting in a formula to kill worms. Then there's the other end. Sheep have a woolly bum, and nobody to wipe their bums. 'Crutching' is shearing the wool from the rear area; if you don't, the sheep will get fly-struck – flies will lay their eggs in this soiled wool, which in turn becomes maggoty, which will kill the sheep. Then once a year the sheep is shorn completely for its fleece.

Merino and Corriedale sheep, for example, are bred mainly for their wool, whereas Polwarth and Southdown lambs are more for meat, the 'fat lamb' market. As an ex-shearer I've been around them all, and – I'd like to add – shearing a bloody Southdown is like shearing a wombat! They are similar in size and shape, and it's like trying to hold onto a greasy log when they wriggle – and they never stop wriggling.

After horses, 'fat cattle', or beef cattle, are by far my favourite farm animal. Drench them once a year, make sure they have plenty of grass and water, and then sell the offspring – simple! More so, it involves horses to work them. This is where most farm kids learn horsemanship from a very young age. It's also where you learn the 'language' to control dogs and livestock and the horse you're astride. Often these are words not used at the dinner table.

It was the first year at Woodville. We didn't have a tractor, and fencing our boundaries involved all three families from each property. Mr James

Affleck, who once owned all three properties, loaned Dad a draught horse and heavy-duty two-wheeled cart. Only Dad had experience with harness horses, from his youth in Ireland.

Unbeknownst to Mr Affleck, we named the horse Jamie. He was a beautiful big Clydesdale, a bay, with a shiny brown coat, black mane and tail, and a broad white blaze down his forehead to match the four white stockings that came up to his knees.

I fell in love with him at first sight; typical of all Clydesdales, he was a gentle giant. As kids we would fight as to who would 'steer' him, hold the reins. Dad never had any problems getting help to take a load of posts or wire down to the fence-line.

To this day I can close my eyes and return to the bench seat from where you steered Jamie, his huge, magnificent rump right there at your feet, and his massive bulk making such easy work of pulling the cart, often loaded with more kids than fencing materials. Such a simple thing, yet as I write, almost 60 years later, it's still a very special memory.

Dad's expertise as a horseman quickly came to the attention of all in the district. His expertise had come at a cost, though; at Southall he had almost paid with his life, and the resulting injuries restricted his time in the saddle thereafter.

It had happened with Chester. Dad was riding out in the fields, far from home, and about to open a farm gate when he saw a snake curled around the gatepost. He was still in the saddle, removing a stirrup iron and leather to use as a weapon, when Chester saw the snake too.

The thoroughbred panicked, and spun round to flee. Dad fell off, his foot slipping through the remaining stirrup iron.

Having Dad helplessly attached to the saddle by one leg and dragging at Chester's side only spooked the horse more; he went into a frenzied gallop. With Dad dragging beneath him, Chester took all before him – fences, plantations, creeks, a mile of hard stony paddock – before the stirrup leather broke. It saved Dad's life but left him badly injured – mainly his back.

But still, anyone in the district with a problem horse would 'send it to Sam'. Dad's back couldn't handle a bucking horse anymore, so he would leg me aboard and control the situation from the ground. Even at 11 years of age, I could sit most horses that bucked, and relished the prospect that they would. 'Just watch the ears,' Dad would say, 'that'll tell you what they're thinking.' Well, actually, that's OK until the head goes out of sight between their front legs; by then you know what they are thinking – buck him off!

My turn for disaster came when we were sent a horse with a reputation for rearing. If she couldn't get her way, she would go up on her hind legs. As a kid's pony, around 14 hands, that's an intolerable and dangerous habit and has to be stopped.

Dad had given me the horse's bridle and asked me to lead her home to start work on her bad manners. But why walk home when you can ride?

I went to fetch her in the paddock, and she let me catch her easily. With the bridle on, I sprang aboard and home we headed. Everything went well until an open gate came into sight, then up she went. All our gates were brand new, and bright red, and she wasn't going through that gateway.

Stubborn as she was, I was twice as stubborn. Instead of getting off and trying to lead her through, I was determined to ride her through it. And so the battle began, me riding hands and heels, and the horse rearing higher with each refusal. Riding bareback gave me confidence – I could just slide off if it all went wrong. Or so I thought! With a handful of mane to help me stay aboard, I forced on. Then it happened. She reared so high she couldn't regain her balance, and she came straight down right on top of me. I remember hitting the ground an instant ahead of her and trying to roll out of her way. Too late.

The horse landed on me with her full weight, as I lay there with my right leg over my left. She quickly found her feet again, but when I tried to get up, I felt the pain. My right leg was twisted in an odd direction, and before my eyes it began swelling to twice its normal size. With blood-chilling certainty, I knew I was in strife. Firstly, Dad was going to be so angry I had ridden her, not led her. And anyway, nobody knew where I was, as I was out of sight of the house, and dairy – I could lie here all night! With that thought in my head, I heard Dad's ute approaching. What a relief that was.

Yes, he was seriously pissed I had not led the horse back, but he never said it – it was just the look. I don't know who got the biggest shock when he gathered me up to lift me onto the ute – my foot pointed behind me! I screamed in agony – then bit my lip. 'Don't cry,' I told myself, 'you're in enough shit, don't show your father you're a sook as well!'

Dad's been gone since 1984, and I never cried to his face, but when he got in to drive, leaving me on the back of the ute, I cried all the way home.

As scared as I was of Dad, Dad was even more scared of Mum if he stuffed up and one of her babies got hurt.

I can still hear her, she never swore, ever, she didn't need to, but she ripped him to shreds.

It was my very first (but not last) ride in an ambulance. I remained in Warrnambool Base Hospital for three months. My femur was snapped clean in half, and the two broken ends were overlapping each other by 3 inches. It all had to be slowly pulled back into position, by traction, till they realigned, then the traction was released slowly so the bone could knit together. Today, you would go into surgery, they would operate, and you'd be home in a week.

It was another lonely, traumatic time. But in the bed beside me was Reg Edwards, a stockman, who had a horse fall beneath him and roll over him while mustering cattle. He had a broken back and was paralysed from the waist down, in a wheelchair for life.

Just down the ward was big Kenny Smith, the Warrnambool life guard who was attacked by a great white shark. Ken had cut his leg in the Surf Club before his morning swim, and Dr Hemingway, a club member, told Ken it needed to be stitched, and to come see him at the

Me with my sister Judy, who always had my back through life. RIP Grub.

hospital as soon as possible. Ken went for a swim first. Fortunately for him, Dr Hemingway was still there when the shark attacked. He dragged Ken onto his surf ski and treated him on the beach; if he hadn't, Ken would have almost certainly bled to death. It was a horrific attack, leaving Ken a changed person.

But I remember him saying, 'I hope that bloody shark chokes on my thumb' – one of his thumbs was severed when he tried to prise open the shark's jaws from around his waist.

People died in that ward in my time there, but I never experienced a glowing light disappearing through the ceiling again. I wondered about that; I'd figured it happened to all people, after I had seen it happen to Grandma. It also scared me, people dying so near – as a little kid it was unsettling. You got to know these people, it was early in life to experience death like that.

My sister Elizabeth was a nurse at Warrnambool Base Hospital at that time, and sometimes would be in my ward.

Her best friend there was Hily Lim, a Malaysian girl who came to Australia to do her nursing certificate. Hily and I became great mates, as she would come out to the farm with Liz at weekends, and she also nursed me during my broken leg time. Later, she was to become my fifth sister.

And as for the horse, there are many ways to teach a horse to stop rearing. Dad knew them all.

On his way home from delivering me to the hospital, he stopped by the Warrnambool Abattoirs to collect some fresh animal blood in a bottle. Weakening the bottle with a file-cut line all around it so it would break neatly and easily, he mounted the filly that had put me in hospital and revisited the gate she had dumped me at. On cue, up she went.

Ready for it, Dad hit her straight between the ears with the bottle of animal blood, enough to shock her into a complete reversal of direction. She never reared again and became a valuable and trustworthy kids' pony. I was also on her back again the same day I was discharged from hospital – I did it for me. Had Mum ever found out, I reckon it would have been Dad going off in the ambulance this time.

Horses have been a huge part of my life, and not long after the broken leg saga, when I was still 11 years old, Dad was gifted an ex-racehorse by the name of Pineleigh, from his racehorse trainer mate.

My sister Judy and I were the two competition riders in the family, attending all the local shows and gymkhanas, both keen on jumpers as well as the dressage ring. Mack, as the former racehorse became known, was an ex-steeplechaser and a big horse, standing at 17 hands. He could jump, that wasn't the problem – detuning him to jump and not race, and turning him into a station hack, was the task ahead of us.

Discovering just how quick he was, I planted the seed in Dad's head. 'Maybe he's quick enough to win the Minhamite Cup, Dad?'

That's all it took. From that night on Mack was on hard feed, grain, and a mix of nutrients combined with chaff, or lucerne, to build him up and put some shine back into his coat.

A dark bay with a white star on his forehead, he was an impressive-looking horse. Each night, instead of helping with the milking, in the lead-up to the Minhamite Cup I would take Mack for his roadwork around our neighbourhood block, a distance of 6–8 miles. Walking, trotting, and at a 'steady canter, no galloping the guts out of him,' Dad cautioned.

Dad was in charge of training. But I got to know Mack and his idiosyncrasies. I had never been on a real racehorse, or a horse with the pure speed of this big fella. He would let me know when he was feeling great and wanted to up the pace. It didn't take long before a stock saddle and a regular bit weren't enough to control Mack when we were pointed towards home, his rug and dinner.

Now I was going out in an exercise saddle with girth and surcingle, and a Pelham bit – with rings to prevent him getting his head up where he was too strong for me to hold back. I was in control again. I knew where the ground was good enough to let him stretch out and gallop. Wow, I can still remember that first night we hit top gear … oh my God, could this big fella run!

Dad is indisputably the best horseman I have ever known, and I've been around more than most. We'd come home just before dark, and Dad would hose Mack down at the dairy, running his hands all over him, like a cabinet maker would over timber he'd been sanding – searching for that perfect feel.

Every day Mack's coat got shinier and he felt stronger. It was becoming a battle to keep him in check, as all he wanted to do was gallop, but I too was getting stronger, and I was still in control.

One night, on our roadwork, Mack was feeling especially strong and simply wouldn't settle back into steady work, constantly on the bit, pulling. 'Alright then fella, you want to pull – let's see how long you can pull *uphill*,' I said to him.

By me talking to him out loud, he seemed to sense my mood, through my tone.

As we approached the uphill stretch he started twitching his ears. He wanted to go tonight. So I hit him with both heels. He charged forward like he'd been shot in the arse. We flew up that hill faster than any time I'd ever been on him. As we hit the top of the hill and I stood up in the stirrups to hold him, I noticed out of the corner of my eye a car right behind, a grey Plymouth. The old man!

I'm fucked, I thought. Sprung! 'Steady canter, don't gallop the guts out of him.' I tried to look like he'd bolted on me. But Dad just stayed well back until the road was wide enough for him to pass without scaring Mack, and gave an interested, casual look. All planned, I later learnt. He'd been following us since we left home.

'If he wants to work uphill, let him. Just keep a tight rein on him.' That was it.

Eventually Minhamite Cup day came. Mack was fit enough to run a Melbourne Cup by then.

The course was effectively an 80-acre paddock, livestock removed for the day, staked out with white markers and mowed. It covered a distance of roughly 7 furlongs, or 1400 metres.

By starting time on race day, Mack had gone from a 50:1 long shot, to odds-on favourite. Dad, of course, never said a word to me. It was simply, 'keep relaxed, keep your horse relaxed.'

And that was pretty much my brief as he legged me aboard. 'Don't pay any attention to what's going on around you. Concentrate on your bloke, keep him off the heels of others – then let them get a good look of YOUR heels all the way to the line.' Simple.

I was a bundle of nerves going to the starting line. There were no starting barriers; when it looked like the field was pretty much evenly lined up, the starter dropped his hand and we were off.

I missed the start, badly. Still, my fear disappeared in an instant, replaced by a huge surge of adrenaline.

There is no greater feeling than a fully fit thoroughbred beneath you, pulling at the bit. Mack had done this over 40 times as a professional on city tracks and won. I was the mug here, but he knew what we needed to do. I took him wide, around the tail-end of the field – the leaders had ten lengths on us, but with Mack's explosive speed, size and brute strength, he was rounding them up like they were standing still. Every vein in his neck was bulging, and his skin was covered with white foam beneath my knuckles.

'Steady mate, steady,' I heard myself saying to him, more to relax me than him. A flick of his ears told me he had heard me, but he only changed his gait, and went up another gear I never knew existed – race-gear! We had now passed two-thirds of the field.

'Look out – here comes the kid.'

'Get that horse over – get him back,' others were shouting.

'You're going too soon, ya mug,' shouted another. Intimidation from all quarters; some were ex-professional jockeys, others amateur jockeys, some just station hands – but all were adults, or certainly much older than an 11-year-old. Mack and I were now neck and neck with the leader. The jockey looked at me in shock as we shot past him – we had hit the front. I kept Mack in a straight line, and drew away. Suddenly it struck me we were going to win – I could see the crowd and the finish line.

'GO – GO BIG FELLA!' I shouted, pushing the reins up Mack's neck, taking all the weight off his mouth. I could see a group of women jumping and hugging each other with joy, and screaming Mack's name: 'COME ON MACK!'

Then I sensed movement – before I saw a horse's nose. We were only feet from the line.

'COME ON BOY,' I shouted in desperation, as the other horse stuck its head in front. But it was all too little, too late, and my fault, not Mack's.

'You'd have won that by the length of the straight mate, had you held him together, balanced,' said the winning jockey, coming alongside to shake my hand. I was disappointed, of course, but second was great. Third, fourth, and the rest of the field were miles behind.

Sam and Myrtle Abernethy, Margaret, Elizabeth, Judith, John and Ann Abernethy.

Dad was grinning from ear to ear, even though I'd rattled Mack out of stride by shoving the reins up his neck in my wild excitement.

'You did great mate, well done Joe.'

Men in those days never hugged, embraced or made a fuss. Just Dad's words made me feel 10 foot tall. And that was my very first horse race, on a racehorse.

Soon it was time for secondary school at Warrnambool Technical College. Start the milking around 6am, catch the school bus around 7.30am, home from school around 4.30pm, into the dairy to milk and feed calves till after dark. Dinner, bed, then do it all again. At weekends I started playing Colts Cricket for Woolsthorpe. I'd thumb a ride in, play, then thumb a ride home. Hitchhiking in the 1960s was safe – in fact almost everything was safe.

The kids who didn't come off farms could go and party – meet girls. Yep, I had discovered them by now, in my early teens. Which gave me the gripes, as I had to milk bloody cows and feed calves before I could go to cricket, then I had to be home again in time to milk at night. There were never, ever, any exceptions.

I was a handy opening bowler. I would never play for Australia – in fact, never play for Woolsthorpe Firsts – but I loved cricket. I still do. My other passion was car racing, Warrnambool Premier Speedway, back when the track was beside the Warrnambool horse racing track in the 1960s.

Daryl Jago and I started the same night. However, Daryl went on to be a Victorian Sprint Car Champion. I went on to less glorious heights – Vietnam – shortly after selling my Sportsman, as they were then called, having my last race in that car at Darlington Speedway the weekend before I enlisted in the army. I built every square inch of her, did all the welding, the assembly of the sub frame, and rebuilt the engine, a straight-six Dodge, bolting a MkII Zephyr gearbox on behind. It went like the clappers.

Girls got very interesting in my teens. Dad figured we had better attend the father-son night at school. A hall filled with fathers and sons listening to a sex education dictation by the principal – how embarrassing. Dad never said a word, until we were about ten minutes from home. Then he cleared his throat and said: 'Just remember, the girls who *let you* let every other bloke just as easy. Steer clear of them, or you'll finish up the father of some other bloke's kid. Or, you'll get a *DISEASE!*' That was the extent of our father-son talk.

What Dad never knew, and thank you Uncle Murray Grant, involved girls and cars. Uncle Murray – not a blood relative – was the sergeant of police in Warrnambool and had served in New Guinea with Dad. I had asked Dad if I could borrow the family car, a Plymouth, instead of my Dodge bush basher, to go eeling with my mate Mick Cameron. Of course Mick and I had arranged to meet two girls from school that night, both with a reputation along the lines Dad mentioned.

Mick and I headed straight for town. We were parked in the main street, necking a bottle of beer, with one arm around a girl; I was sitting behind the wheel and Mick in the back with his girl. Then I got a tap on the shoulder through the open window.

'Got a minute John?' *Holy fuck – it's Uncle Murray, IN UNIFORM!*

'Yes,' I said, in a mouse-like voice, climbing out the door. Sixteen, no licence, drinking beer behind the wheel.

'Dad know you're in town?'

'Err – no Uncle Murray.'

'OK, get rid of that beer, and those two girls – then get home. OK?'

'Yes, Uncle Murray,' in the same mouse-like voice.

As I turned to get back into the car, a size 14 boot caught me right in the arse.

'Take that with you – and no second time, got it?' In spades I got it. They were the good old days. Dad went to his grave never knowing about that night, and Uncle Murray spent days out at our farm with me as if it never happened. Respect – when a foot in the arse did more good than any day in court.

At 16, in 1965, I quit school in Year 9. I was a lousy student in any event, and by Year 8 my only interest was girls. Our farm was too small to support both Dad and me at that point.

I got a job on a large local station, Kuleah, as a tractor driver slashing tussock. I got paid 50 cents an hour and spent the entire day adding up my daily wealth.

Going around, and around, the same 500-acre paddock gets pretty boring after the first week. I also did a stint on the same property as a 'marker' for an aerial super-spreader, spreading super-phosphate, or fertiliser; basically acting as a human marker for the pilot to line up his run – then pacing out 20 strides or so while he was turning, to give him his next alignment. During this time it rained heavily, putting a halt to the aerial spreading. It also allowed the bulk pile of super-phosphate to get wet, creating large lumps, which had to be broken down in order for it to go through the plane's spreader – this was my new job. The guy loading the plane, Nic, would drop the lumpy 'super' onto a mesh grill over the tray of a tipper truck, I would belt it with a sledgehammer, then when the truck was full of powdered 'super' I'd start a new pile he could drop straight into the plane's hopper.

The pilot was paid by the load, not the hour. Hence it was almost military precision to land, load quickly, then be gone again with a ton at a time, every 10–15 minutes. The pilot would take a passenger up with him when he was just a few loads short of stopping to be refuelled. Nic arranged for me to go up – my first flying experience. I was blown away with the ease of flight, how we were off the ground so quickly and looking down on sheep and cattle. I was in awe.

Suddenly, from straight and level flight, only feet above the ground, the horizon disappeared. The skin on my face felt like it was being pulled off around the back of my head, my head felt welded to the seat. Every part of me was like lead. Then it occurred to me we were flying sideways, as the pilot was above me, grinning down at my petrified death throes. He said something – what, I shall never know, but probably 'don't spew on my lunch box.' A horrible nausea overwhelmed me, then I felt a bump that frightened the bejesus out of me. We were back on the ground – taxiing towards Nic. I tried to unbuckle the harness and get the fuck out of there, but before I realised it, we were airborne again! We did four more runs like this; at the end of each run, the pilot, in keeping time to a minimum, banked so hard and fast to get back for his next load we were experiencing a G3, a gravitational force of 3. That's three times one's body weight, so he finally informed me when stopping to refuel.

Charlie Harris had been a station hand at Kuleah most of his life, and would by then have been in his late forties. His house was at the end of the airstrip. On a Saturday morning, while I was at cricket, Charlie, who I knew well, had spent the morning in the Woolsthorpe Hotel loading up on Dutch courage to ask for his turn to take a ride up. Problem was, Charlie, who always wore a hat, approached the plane with his head down to hold his hat on, and he was more than mildly pissed.

He walked straight through a prop close on full power. The pilot thought it was a station dog when his windscreen went red with blood – as had happened before.

There was little left. Charlie was minced into a thousand pieces. The news quickly reached us at cricket, where one of his sons was on my team. It was horrible – horrific!

In 1966, Dad needed back surgery, a long, drawn-out process requiring a lengthy stay in Ballarat Hospital. I was 17 years old and had to step up as the man of the family, taking over Dad's role.

Though I had done three years of agriculture at school, that was books; it was the 17 years living on, and from, the land that taught me what was required. A 12-hour day was the norm – dairy, sheep, beef cattle, fence repairs, machinery repairs, harvesting.

They were long, hard days. My sisters helped me at weekends and after work or school, but I kept the farm running for the best part of that year. Mum did the books, but I did everything else. It was a great way to graduate after three years of theory.

* * * *

The year 1967 saw one of Western Victoria's worst droughts on record; everybody was buying feed to keep their animals alive. Creeks and dams were drying up, there was a severe shortage of water across the region. I was now 18 and had my driver's licence. My old boss from Kuleah asked me if I'd be interested in taking 2000 head of sheep on the road – the great Australian tradition of droving.

On the roadsides there was still ample feed, and with a mob of that size on the constant move we could keep them well fed for months.

I grabbed the offer with both hands. With one of the station's two left-hand drive Willys Army Jeeps and a caravan, two horses, a pack of about eight dogs, and my mate Flynny, we hit the road one Saturday morning with 2000 head of sheep.

We lost about four sheep in the first hour. Hit by a truck.

These animals were starving, they hadn't seen grass for months, and as soon as we let them onto the road they bolted, stopping to graze only briefly before racing further ahead to find even better grazing.

Neither Flynny nor I could get ahead of them without wiping out more than the truck already had. We sent the dogs ahead to slow them, but until they settled we could only follow, and hope they weakened quickly – and that's what happened. However, I had some dead sheep to dress-out and refrigerate for dog food for a week or so. It was a learning curve for both Flynny and me, as it was a first for both of us. And Flynny was only part-time, he was running his own property with a large dairy herd needing him mornings and afternoons.

But he was always there to help me yard at night by the roadside. During the day, Flynny and I would find a place that offered shelter and an L-shaped fence-line – then, using a roll of wire netting, we would erect a 'wing' off the fence-line, to hold the sheep. Where the wire netting ran out, we drove a stake at intervals around the mob and placed a dog at each one. Soon the sheep got the message and bedded down without incident.

It was a great life, out in the sunshine, either on horseback or in the Jeep with the roof off, letting the dogs keep the mob together, moving, safe, and off the road when traffic appeared. I knew every road and laneway for 30 miles in every direction; finding water was the only real problem – and it was essential in the day's planning to reach a creek, river or dam to water down 2000 head of stock. Flynny would come out and join me after his morning milking, freeing me up to go ahead in the Jeep to find the next night's camp, water and the like. It all went without a hitch after that first morning.

It was how I met my first wife – timing, eh! I was out of stores and camped up for the night less than a mile from Flynny's home. After his evening milking he came down to keep watch while I went to Caramut, the closest town.

The Slatterys lived in their store and I knew the family well; the pub was practically next door – everything I needed was there. After the pub I dropped in on Mrs Slattery, the matriarch of Caramut, who had Melbourne relatives visiting: Nancy Slattery and her kids, from the suburb of Mount Waverley. Wendy caught my eye the instant I walked into the store; well, I swaggered in – I was a drover now!

'Hello Mrs Slattery,' said I, smelling of sheep, a week's growth on my dirty face, and a little flushed from four beers at the pub.

'Hello John – this is Wendy,' she said, nodding to where my eyes were riveted. 'Why don't you give me your list and go out to the boys [her sons] while I put all this together? Wendy, take John through."

At 18, I had impeccable taste – I'd seen a lot of Hollywood movies. Wendy was perfect in every way. She had a bright, happy face, shoulder-length blonde hair and green eyes. I stank, and I knew it – but these city folks thought that it was amusing, having never met a real live drover before.

They were playing cards and I was asked to join in; there was a seat right beside Wendy, so I dropped into it. Time passed, conversation flowed, and first our knees touched under the table, then later our hands reaching for cards, for matches – the currency in this game. I started pinching her matches, which, as it turned out, was the clincher.

'Caught you!' she said, grabbing my hand. She didn't let go for the rest of the evening.

At 2am, Mrs Slattery reminded me that Flynny might be getting worried about me. I freaked. Where had the time gone? As I loaded my stores into the Jeep, I asked Wendy if she'd like to go out with me in Warrnabool on Saturday night.

'Yes,' she said.

She was only 16, but the Slattery Clan had it all figured out. They would all go to Warrnambool in two cars, so Nance would know Wendy was chaperoned by adult kids, her relatives. No mention of meeting up with that drover bloke!

'Where the fuck have you been?' Flynny hadn't had a wink of sleep and had to start milking in two hours' time. I told him about my night – till dawn. He agreed to cover for me Saturday night while I dated this hot Melbourne chick.

'I better meet her, Abo,' he warned. I had been known as Abo since pre-school, where the kids couldn't say Abernethy, and it has remained with me throughout my life.

And meet her he did, many times. Our first date that Saturday night was Shandon's Drive-In Movie Theatre, Warrnambool.

As Wendy can attest, on that very first date I asked her to marry me.

She was 16 and I was 18, but she had the most brains.

'Can we wait till I'm a bit older?' It wasn't a no, simply a not yet.

Dating in the 1960s was a vastly different proposition to even the 1970s. Everything took its course. Nice girls, good girls, the type you take home to meet your parents, didn't let you past first base for some time. And it's also worth noting this was the period of panty-girdles, man's worst enemy.

I was besotted, in love for the very first time. That Wendy was a virgin made her extra special. But could we hold out until we were married? I wanted to, but it was a BIG ask! Making matters worse, I had a mother who I loved dearly – but she was a hypocrite.

She had two messages. 'We are all God's children' on the one hand, and on the other, 'all Catholics are evil'.

Now, she had Catholic friends. 'But nobody in *this family* is ever going to marry a Catholic!'

Dad, who would never set foot in a church unless it was for a funeral or wedding, had more real religion in him than Mum ever did.

His philosophy (and he was spot-on) was that the biggest hypocrites in the district only went to church on Sundays to have their cars seen out front. I only went because I was allowed to drive Mum there from the age of 16; the legal age was 18.

It all came to a head one Sunday roast lunch. Mum and I had a huge fight. She even threw a cup of tea in my face because I said something unforgivable – 'sinful!'

From memory, it all started over Wendy not only being a Catholic, but she had worn a black bra!

I packed my bags and left home.

I was now shearing for a living, taking home $100–$150 per week, good money then. I had bought a new Cortina car around the time I met Wendy, which gave me full independence.

I moved in with Judy, my closest sister, both in age and as a friend. She and her husband Ray took me in. To put a little distance between myself and home, I even picked up shearing contracts out of Mildura, which took me into the outback, Broken Hill and beyond, as far as the Queensland border.

The sheep were much harder to shear, the shearers' quarters were a lot rougher, and it was a huge 'growing up' step.

Shearers have a reputation as being fit, tough men, I had seen that from day one. Those outback shearers were another breed altogether.

Most worked under assumed names, either for tax purposes or because they were hiding from the law, but all were men who didn't tolerate fools and who would get as much satisfaction punching you as shaking your hand. Each had their own story, same as jail I guess. But it was the ones who never spoke that you steered clear of.

Don't volunteer for anything, I learnt that quickly. At my first shed, the organiser – the team's Union representative (no 'ticket' with the Australian Workers' Union, no start) – asked: 'Can anyone here kill a sheep?' I put up my hand, as I did all the killing at home.

'Good, go see the cook – he needs a kill tonight.'

It was a 20-man team, you do the maths.

Breakfast always included lamb chops, lunch always included lamb, dinner too. I was killing three sheep every other night, after a day's shearing. But the team at least knew who I was. I had a role.

In order to fit in, when holding the killing knife I developed a different persona – always a fag in the corner of my mouth, and I didn't wash away the blood until I'd been seen by most of the team as they rested with a long-neck of beer in front of the huts. Then I'd sink my first, the whole bottle as I'd been shown, without taking it from my mouth. The message? Don't fuck with this kid, he may not look like anything, but he can handle a knife. Or so I thought, anyway. There were blokes there who could snap me in half with one hand, and I knew it. But nobody did fuck with me, maybe they liked their mutton too much.

Mount Waverley was always my sanctuary, and I would think nothing of driving all night to see Wendy.

She was now in her last year of secondary school and enrolled at Toorak Teachers' College in Melbourne. My group of friends now included all of Wendy's city friends, and a whole new world opened up to me. All my life I had been surrounded by country, and country folk – now I was in the Big Smoke.

One night at a party in Melbourne I met a guy who'd just come back from Vietnam. He was telling his mate how he'd been lying in the dark and an enemy patrol walked by so close he could have touched their legs. It sounded scary, yet exciting. I began to wonder how I would react to something like that – was I up for such bravery? Going off to war? Did I have the balls?

Against this backdrop, Hily Lim's visa had expired, and she had to go home to Kuala Lumpur in Malaysia. She didn't want to leave Australia and all her friends.

Dad made inquiries. When he was manager at Southall, the Frasers from nearby Hamilton were regular customers, and Dad had known 'young Malcolm' from a pup. Malcolm Fraser was now a Minister in the Liberal Party, and would go on to become Prime Minister of Australia.

'Adopt her, Sam,' he said, 'it's the only possible way.' And so he did. Now I had five sisters. All I ever wanted was one brother!

But I loved Hily as a sister and friend, she always made me laugh. She only knew, or used, one cuss-word, 'bloody shit you' – this was for everything from exasperation in traffic to losing something. It just broke me up, especially when her glasses slipped down her nose in her anger.

Hily married an Australian guy, lived in Melbourne, and nursed until her untimely death from cancer at a young age. She had no children.

But at this time we were still young, Hily was very much alive and, for me, New Zealand beckoned, through an opportunity to go there with a shearing contractor. But I was approaching my twentieth birthday, and with National Service on the agenda I was duty bound to tell the contractor I could be enlisted. That did it.

'You're off the list – I can't be replacing men, sorry!'

It would have been my very first time overseas; I had been eagerly looking forward to it.

So I was back at Judy and Ray's, spinning my wheels, going nowhere.

Bugger it, I said, I'll enlist.

Wendy was horrified, she was anti-war. Television had come to Australia in 1956, and every night it brought the Vietnam War into people's sitting rooms. I persuaded Wendy it was my patriotic duty – both her father and mine had served in World War II.

Then I filled out the paperwork.

National Service, Vietnam, 1969–1971

National Service was the raffle everyone was hoping they wouldn't win. Your birth date would go into a draw, like the lottery, and if it came up, you were in. Except I volunteered.

Before I knew it, the Department of Defence and I were exchanging letters, then it was Warrnambool Base Hospital for a medical. The government medical officer was Dr Fisher – wouldn't you know it, another mate of Dad's, who bred Corriedale sheep as a sideline.

He pointed at the eye chart on the far wall. 'As long as you can see the foresight on a rifle they'll take you. You're a good shot so I hear, so we'll skip that. All done – sign here.'

That was it. I was on my way.

After selling all my worldly goods – my Cortina and my Sportsman – I took a free train ride, compliments of the Australian taxpayer, from Warrnambool to Flinders Street Station, Melbourne. There were three of us conscripts in total and, boys being boys, we loaded up with booze for the trip, only to find ourselves in a cubicle full of nuns. We didn't touch a drop until they got off at Geelong – but we drank the lot during the 80-minute journey to Melbourne. And the funny part was, none of us were Catholic. It was just the respect you showed then.

Wendy bade me farewell in Melbourne, a quick, fraught goodbye in a large crowd. Then came the voice of authority: 'Alright, all you lot for Victoria Barracks, start getting on these buses in an ORDERLY manner!'

I was in the army, the 16th Intake of National Service, April 1969.

I knew nobody, but leaning alone against a high stone wall was a bloke just like me, looking equally lost. I found a spot near him. After a while I noticed he smoked the same brand of cigarettes as me, and like me he was practically chain smoking.

'Have one of mine mate,' I offered.

'Thanks.'

'John – or Abo, as most people call me,' I said, offering a hand.

'Frank – Frank Squillacioti,' he answered, accepting my hand in a firm, strong handshake. That was the beginning of a friendship that lasted 31 years until his untimely death in 2006.

We went through the enlistment process side by side, his service number being 3796033 and mine being 3796000. People in the army used to laugh, 'You two are joined at the hip,' we became so inseparable. We left Vic Barracks sitting side by side, and we stood side by side upon arrival at Puckapunyal, 2RTB (2nd Recruit Training Battalion), which is located near Seymour, an hour north of Melbourne. We went into the same hut, with beds in the same cubical; we ate, slept, trained side by side for the 12 weeks of rookie training, and even went on leave together.

He was a motor mechanic from Deer Park, Melbourne, and me, a bushie from the Western District – both off on a great adventure.

At our very first parade at Pukka, one of our RTIs (recruit training instructors), Corporal Dungee, had a huge problem getting his head around Squillacioti: 'Squil ... ak – Squal a – Squill o ... Fuck it – SQUIRREL!'

'Here, Corporal,' replied Frank, and he was Squirrel from that day forth.

Squirrel and I had it all figured out. Stuff staying in Australia painting rocks and saluting people ('If it moves, salute it, if it doesn't, paint it.'). We decided to head to Vietnam – earn extra money and shoot the bad guys, and get a War Service Home at the end of it.

As for the army, like so much in life, the anticipated is never like the real thing.

Recruit training was bloody hard work, and back in the '60s and '70s 'bastardisation' was still allowed. They'd wake the whole platoon in the middle of the night, turning over beds with guys still in them, then make us stand in a deep frost with a sheet wrapped around us for 20 minutes, while they told us what pussies we were. Then we'd get 30 minutes to have the line immaculate again for another inspection, and God help us if it wasn't.

This could happen twice a night; we were belittled constantly, pushed to the limit all day long. Very soon the army knew who's who in the zoo, and so did we. Any guy who continually stuffed up, couldn't march properly, could bring grief on the whole platoon. It was up to his mates to teach him after work – the building of teamwork and mateship.

I hated marching. 'Drill' as it's affectionately known. However, it's a big part of military discipline, and something every Australian commander demands his troops excel at – 'Bang on the Bullshit' as it was known. Nothing looks better than a platoon of 30 men, a company of 100 men, marching in perfect co-ordination. Australian soldiers are good at it.

I couldn't get to the rifle range quick enough; as a shooter since age 11, this was my passion. However, military rifles are a far different proposition to farm guns. My experience was essentially .22 calibre (rabbit rifle) and 12-gauge shotgun (duck gun), and I'd fired a 30/30 calibre rifle on occasion – but a 7.62 semi-automatic 20-round magazine was totally new. All open sights, no telescopic sights like modern assault rifles. The standard issue rifle of the Australian Defence Forces during the 1960s and 1970s was the Belgian-designed SLR (self-loading rifle), which replaced the British .303.

On the first day, I was shooting tight groups, the bullets (the round) hitting the target close to one another – the closer the better. In tech talk 'a 3-inch group' means every round you fired is inside a 3-inch diameter circle. It took getting used to the intimidating recoil. It kicked harder than a 12-gauge shotgun. But once I began to get a feel for the rifle, it was noted, and I was soon given a better rifle.

By month's end I was one of the better shots in Charlie Company – including the RTIs, who were all ex-Vietnam and very handy shots.

Where you spent your time in the army depended greatly upon availability, qualifications, education and luck. The saying was we were given three options – Transport, Artillery, Signals – but really it was Infantry, Infantry, Infantry! My intake, the 16th Intake, was made up largely of professionals completing their apprenticeships and internships. Squirrel had just finished his mechanic's apprenticeship. And the number of doctors and dentists was well above normal; they automatically went into the Medical Corps and didn't complete rookies.

I found out the hard way. One guy was in our hut the first night, then he simply disappeared. A week later I had to go through the dental process, and there was old mate, now a lieutenant.

'Aren't you going to salute me?' he asked.

'No, fuck you, you were a civilian a week ago,' said I. Mistake. He extracted a tooth and the anaesthetic only began to work on the walk back to the lines.

Towards the end of our recruit training, the RTIs became more human, and if they liked you, offered advice. Keeping in mind National Service was for two years only; regular army guys had to sign on for three-, six- or nine-year stints – they could do a trade while they were in. Because Nashos, as we were known, were in and out in two years, infantry is where the majority ended up. Squirrel and I decided to bite the bullet and find out which infantry battalion was the best, and next, to go to Vietnam.

'7 RAR out of Holsworthy Sydney,' Corporal Dungee told us. 'They are rebuilding the battalion right now – I can put you on the list if you want to go straight there instead of Corps Training.' We did.

Again, we huddled shoulder to shoulder after coming off the bus at Holsworthy, the home of 5 RAR and 7 RAR (5th and 7th Battalions, Royal Australian Regiment) – 5 RAR were in Vietnam.

Frank and I got Charlie Company again, 8 Platoon C Company. Our lieutenant was Greg Lindsay, who at one time got a run with the famous

Squirrel and me in Vietnam, joined at the hip.

Rabbitohs, the South Sydney NRL team, before the army got in the way. He was a tough little red-head, built like a Mack truck without the wheels, but he had a great sense of humour. He was also doing his two years National Service. Likewise, our NCOs (non-commissioned officers) weren't like the RTIs – it was a lot more low-key. These guys for the most part had just come back from Vietnam. We were the new guys filling the places.

Now it was starting to feel like the movie version of the army – mateship, real diggers, real training, weapons I had only ever seen in the movies – M79s, M72s, 90mm, M60 machine guns, grenades, Claymore mines, and much more.

It was exciting, being in the company of men who had been there and done it, the real characters who had legendary status like 'Doc' Patterson (our section commander) and his sidekick Nikko, another section commander.

On their last tour of Vietnam, both exceptionally pissed, they decided they'd had enough and were going home. They were dragged out of a US Air Force fighter jet by military police. Doc and Nikko had managed to get some lights flashing and belt themselves in, but couldn't start the jet without ground assistance. Another time, they won an elephant in a card game and were pulling strings trying to get it home to Australia.

It's very hard to put into words how trust, and a sense of belief, comes from simply being around these guys, just normal men like us, yet 10 foot tall and bulletproof when you saw them in dress uniform with citations for bravery. Heroes come in all shapes and sizes, and from my experience the least likely looking guy is normally the greatest.

It would be inexcusable to omit the true story of Dennis 'Bottles' Bathersby, another such legend. Bottles was decorated for bravery on the 1968 7 RAR deployment – awarded an MID (Mention in Despatches).

He was an NCO (corporal) in 9 Platoon when I joined the battalion. Like many, I got to know Bottles and held him in very high regard. I'm not sure how the nickname came about, but he liked a drink, if that's a clue.

His story, as he told me, was that his number two on the gun was badly wounded in a contact. He had picked up both the machine gun and his number two and headed for medical care, but they got separated from the main body of their platoon. Another gun was blazing away nearby and, thinking that was where the command was, Bottles headed towards it. No easy feat dare I say; the gun alone weighed 30lb, God knows what his mate weighed.

But when Bottles reached the machine gun he was confronted by enemy troops, not Aussies.

'What do you do, Abo? I aimed and pulled the trigger.'

What he did was wipe out the enemy gun position.

Bottles refused to wear that citation; I've witnessed him being charged for not 'displaying all his medals' on parade.

As he put it: 'Who in their right mind drags their fucked-up mate into an enemy machine gun position? Had I known who they were I'd have gone in the opposite direction.' He treated the MID as an embarrassment rather than an honour.

Sadly, Bottles left us a couple of years back. He will always remain a true legend of the 'Pig Battalion', 7 RAR.

The name needs some clarification. When the battalion was being formed at Puckapunyal, it had no mascot – until the CO walked into the Mess and said: 'You're nothing but a bunch of pigs.' Someone went 'oink', and so it has remained, to this very day.

Squirrel and I were Pigs, and proud of it. Initially I trained as a machine-gunner, and Squirrel was my number two. A machine-gun group (within the ten-man section) consists of the gunner who carries, aims and operates the gun. The gunner's number two feeds the ammunition into the gun, carries the spare barrel and parts, and in battle ensures the ammo keeps coming. Third in the group is the section 2IC, who oversees the positioning of the gun's site and direction of fire – he's a lance corporal (NCO). I lasted about three months in this role, then was sent off to do a scout's course. Squirrel took over as the gunner.

Being a country boy, I was a natural choice for training as a scout, as it requires a lot of common sense, a sharp eye for detail and a knowledge of the bush.

I probably only had the last thing going for me when I started, but nine years of tracking animals was a hell of a head start.

It stood me in good stead. In Vietnam I noticed the enemy used a whole set of signs to communicate with each other, whereas we had radios to communicate. For example, if a new landmine had been placed on a track, the sapper (enemy engineer) who placed it there could use an obscure sign to warn his mates, something as simple as two strands of grass twisted and tied at the trackside. If you didn't know what to look for, you would never see it.

After the scout course, we were put to the test back in our units – out bush for field exercises. Squirrel now had the gun and I was section scout. We did a number of training exercises out bush, before moving onto the JTC (Jungle Training Centre) at Canungra, in Queensland, just out the back of Surfers Paradise.

One morning our section 2IC hadn't turned up, AWOL – in Surfers Paradise!

'Abernethy – you're acting 2IC.' I remained acting 2IC for the remainder of our 28 days at JTC, effectively Squirrel's boss. A happy family again.

Just before Christmas/pre-embarkation leave of 1969, I was summoned to company headquarters. The major had sent for me. Now when an officer asks you to report, it's normally because you're in the shit, and when it's the company commander that can only mean real serious shit, or that a member of your family has died. I wondered what the hell it was all the way up to HQ.

'Come in Corporal Abernethy,' called Major Skardon's commanding voice.

'Lieutenant Lindsay informs me you have been an acting 2IC. I'm changing that to a full-time 2IC – you're now Lance Corporal Abernethy.'

I was dumbstruck.

'After you come back from leave you'll go up into 7 Platoon,' the major added.

This put a whole new spin on the deal for me, after a year training with 8 Platoon and my best mate Squirrel.

'But sir, Frank ... err, Private Squillacioti and I have been right through recruit training together, we're a team – been in the same gun group all year – we want to stay together sir.' Brave words.

'I don't give a tuppenny stuff what you and Squillacioti want. In fact, you front back here before 1600 hours today, wearing your rank, are we clear on that Corporal Abernethy?'

'Yes, sir!'

I knew Squirrel would be dirty on me, real dirty on me. We had always planned we would do Vietnam shoulder to shoulder together.

I was right, he was pissed – we hardly spoke during the long journey home that night for our four weeks leave. I was as disappointed as he was.

But the good news was Wendy and I decided to get engaged before I left, and she flew to Sydney. I booked a motel and we had one night together.

After our Christmas leave, I relocated up a floor at Holsworthy to join the ranks of 7 Platoon. It was a three-storey building, 7,8,9 Platoons all on a different floor. As a company you get to know all the faces of the 100-plus men, use the same Mess Hall, same boozer, hang out with guys from all three platoons.

So eventually Squirrel got over it, and I had to get on with it – a new lieutenant, new sergeant, new NCOs, new section commander.

As soon as I moved in I hated the place, and I mean really hated the place. I had no mates, and I was promoted over guys who were going back for their second Vietnam stint. I was hated by many, who wondered how I'd gone from a baggy-arsed private to an NCO in six months.

We were pretty much confined to barracks, not knowing what date we sailed for Vietnam, only that it could be any day or night now.

The advance party of officers and NCOs flew out ahead, my section commander among them, leaving me in charge of the section. Now I was subjected to even greater insubordination and outright disrespect.

Our regimental sergeant major and 2IC of the battalion pulled me aside and said: 'Don't bring a man before me on a charge if you can sort it out behind the lines.'

The company bully and I had a run-in, which I won in convincing fashion: he required stitches. It was common knowledge. It only took one; from then on there was no more back-chat or disrespect to my face, but plenty I'm sure behind my back.

The day arrived; the battalion moved to Garden Island Naval Base on buses, and then we were loaded for the journey to Vietnam aboard HMAS *Sydney* (more affectionately known as the 'Vung Tau Ferry').

Wendy and her sister Penny came to see us off. We had just a brief kiss and cuddle as we shuffled along the line towards the gangplank, before disappearing into the maze of steel and heat aboard ship.

'C Deck you lot,' shouted a sailor, directing us below.

'C Deck – we'll be in the fucking sea if we go any lower,' said someone. The further down we went, the closer we got to the engine-room and Messes. It was summer, it was like a furnace below decks.

Wendy. A well-worn image, the original photograph that kept me alive through Vietnam.

All too soon we were underway. Some of the guys on their second tour gave us the drum – once issued your hammock, take it topside at night and sleep on the companionway decks beside the lifeboats. Squirrel and I claimed our spot before Sydney Harbour was out of sight, and there we slept every night.

The only plus for us was the beer ration: 'One can, per man, per day.'

On our last night aboard we were all ordered into the guts of the ship, nobody was allowed on deck. We felt the ship slowing, the noise and vibration died away; hour after hour we edged our way slowly into the night.

Now that we had arrived in Vietnam, I began to ask myself, 'Am I up for this? How will I react when we come under fire? Will I have the courage to fight back – or will I lay low? Will these guys follow my orders?'

'Come on mate, fuck it – I've got to get up on deck,' I told Squirrel.

We managed to get past the navy guard and out into clean fresh air. The night sky was a rainbow of tracer fire, big, small, orange, green. The whole country just ahead in the darkness seemed to be under attack, every square mile of it. 'Fuck,' we said in unison. Our first glimpse of war was a memorable light-show – no sound, just the sight of every battle underway, with the night sky as the backdrop. It's a vision I shall take with me to my grave.

At dawn we were taken to the beach at Vung Tau, where 5 RAR diggers heading home swapped places, and cheek.

'364 and a wakie boys – get some time up,' they called to us as we passed each other across the sand. The wakie is the day you go home – we still had 364 more days to go. For those of us who survived.

1 ATF, the 1st Australian Task Force, was situated at Nui Dat, inland from Vung Tau, about an hour by truck. That would be home base for the next year. Four-man tents at platoon strength had been erected in the rubber plantation; 7 Platoon's lines ran right alongside the airfield, Luscombe Field, with a constant flow of assorted aircraft.

Squirrel and 8 Platoon were situated a short distance away. In all, Charlie Company's three platoons, Mess, boozer and command post (radios and administration buildings) took up barely 5 acres of mature rubber trees.

Now it was 'acclimatisation period', which involved repairing/replacing tents, repairing/replacing sand-bag walls, repairing trenches, working in the heat of day to get our bodies prepared for carrying heavy weight all day in the jungle on patrols.

It was supposed to be 28 days before we were operational. My first night 'outside the wire', in enemy territory, came within the first week.

Night ambushing was a very strong and successful initiative of Australian forces during the Vietnam War. The enemy moved after dark due to the high presence of Allied aircraft – at night they were in their own backyard and could move in large numbers unseen. Ambushing known routes and tracks produced great results for our forces.

Being our first night in enemy territory, which is anywhere outside an FSB (fire support base), or wired-off occupied area, was in itself unnerving. Manning a gun piquet alongside a track that the enemy could appear on at any second, brought home the reality of where we were, and why!

Suddenly there was a huge crash, like someone falling over in the jungle.

'You hear that?' asked a desperate figure at my side.

As 2IC I slept at the piquet site. The gunner was soon behind his gun and the entire patrol stood-to. I looked through the Starlight night vision scope, fearing the worst. Instead of Viet Cong (VC) soldiers, there was a baby monkey licking his wounds after taking a tumble to the jungle floor. 'Stand down!'

A baby monkey scared me that much? What's it going to be like when it really is a whole bunch of enemy soldiers – and they start shooting?

With this on my mind on the walk back to base, we came upon a group of women collecting firewood. Our lieutenant decided to do a security check. Civilians had to carry ID at all times – no ID and you're a VC, or VC sympathiser. I was tasked with guarding a small group while the bulk of the group were being checked. One of the women approached me, panic-stricken, speaking Vietnamese – I had no idea what she was saying, so out of frustration she drew out one of her breasts and began mock crying. By now I was bright red; I'd never had a woman show me her boob before in public, much less in front of all of my section and the other women there.

'She's got a kid, Abo – she has to feed it,' explained the lieutenant, who spoke some Vietnamese. She led me to the infant in a bush not far off. Even she was in on the jibes I got; clearly, she could see this young soldier had a lot more to learn.

Then came the Ops – Operations, out in the jungle for six to eight weeks at a time. Unlike the Americans, we endeavoured to keep our whereabouts quiet. The advantage is being there, but not seen or heard. Once we stepped off those Huey choppers we went 'tactical', hand signals and whispers. If the enemy don't know where you are, but you can see them, that's how it should be.

We were trained to walk on the outside edge of our boots and slowly roll our foot to feel what was underneath, before taking the full weight of our bodies. Snapping a twig or tripping on a root clearly signal that there are men on the ground. And we learnt to spread out. Two men close together make one big target. Keep in sight of the guy ahead – stay behind him, but never on top of him.

Being in virgin jungle, in the middle of nowhere, away from 1 ATF and down to platoon strength of 33 men, keeps you on your toes. Engage the enemy now, and you have to fight your way out. We had seen traces of the enemy, and now all that training was coming together. It made sense, and with each day came a better feel for our surroundings. We were well trained, well armed, and as fit and ready as any diggers before us. Now all that remained to be seen was whether we could fight.

Our platoon had the first casualty of the tour, a 5 RAR guy. With only a couple of months to go, he was shot through the knee while on sentry duty. I was one of the first to reach him; he pointed out seeing the VC aiming at his head only a dozen strides from where we were. But still no exchange with the enemy; 1–0 to them, as it now stood.

Then came more 'hit and run' skirmishes – small forces of VC would detect us and wait until they had us on their own terms and their own turf, then try and kill or wound as many as they could before high-tailing it out of range. This was unnerving as they had the upper hand, and at best we might get one or two of them.

The big one finally came on 30 April 1970, eight weeks into our tour. It came with a vengeance nobody expected, not even the hard-core, battle-hardened boys on their second tour. It was a baptism of fire.

Lieutenant Hughes was tasked with a 24-man night ambush patrol in the rice paddies between the Long Hai Mountains and Dat Do, near the village of Phuoc Loi. That night I was acting section commander, as our section commander was LOB (left on base). That put me in charge of the ten men from our section.

We were taken out on armed personnel carriers (APCs) and then waited until dark before moving in on foot, so the local villagers couldn't tell which way we had gone and give up our position to the enemy. It worked. Too well. Instead of us lying in wait for the enemy to come along, they had also been waiting for the dark – but moved after us. We had been seen.

In setting up an ambush position, Claymore mines, command-detonated mines, are positioned around the perimeter. Sited to strike a standing figure, an electric detonator cord is then run back to the gun position for when the ambush is sprung, to create maximum effect.

Banks of these mines can be connected to one detonation device. My scout and I were out in front of our gun position, setting up Claymore mines, when the nightmare began.

Kneeling beside me in the dark, my scout, Brian Webb, pulled the trigger. A bright orange flash less than a metre to my left, and a loud bang broke the night. I saw a man topple backwards, just a dark figure falling. Then all hell broke loose.

We were a paddy-field length (16 metres) out in front of our gun. The enemy opened up on Webby and me, and we crawled furiously back towards our gun. I had two concerns, the guys with the AK47s on one side, and my machine-gunner at the other thinking, 'Yep, Abo and Webby are history – gotta give these pricks something back!'

We were between both positions; fortunately the enemy aimed high, as if to hit running men. And Peter Riley, my gunner, held out until we rolled over the paddy bun, or he would have killed us both for sure. A paddy bun is a row of dirt raised around 18 inches above ground level to hold the water during rice season.

'FIRE!' I roared, the cue for all along the track to open fire.

A furious exchange ensued; at least seven enemy were seen where Webby and I had engaged them initially. Two lay dead across the paddy bun, and the rest fired directly upon us. Then came the next shock, a pressure wave from an explosion in the pit 4 metres away from me. My guys!

'Medic!'

That horrible word carried above the sound of rifle fire.

I believed it was an incoming RPG (rocket-propelled grenade) that had taken out the entire pit of four guys. Now in a pitch battle, I was pinned down with the gun group, returning fire.

Our patrol fired a flare, a bright white light suspended by a small parachute; it hung above us turning night into day. I glanced behind, fully convinced I would see mass carnage. We were in the setting-up stage of the ambush when the contact started, meaning most of the patrol would have been unprepared. I expected to see bodies everywhere. Instead, I saw just one.

The medic, Ian 'Flappers' Reid, was exposed from his waist up in the pit, attending the wounded 4 metres behind.

'Get DOWN!' I screamed at him, as green enemy tracer bullets filled the night all around him. The flare died, and the enemy maintained a massive attack on our position – the machine gun is the first target both sides want to silence.

At least five enemy were pouring everything they had at us.

The paddy bun – a row of dirt – was all the protection we had. With each burst of AK47 rounds, that low wall was getting lower all the time. I could feel the air above my head ruffle from sustained bursts of incoming rounds, the dirt shot away only inches above my head. The battle raged on, our gun jammed, overheated. Riley was firing long bursts of fire – rapid fire, not short bursts of 10–15 rounds. The spare barrel was quickly fitted, while I put my M16 rifle on full auto to act as section gun until Riley was back in business.

A second flare went up, and again I glanced behind. Flappers, the medic, was still fully exposed from the waist up. I screamed at him to take cover, my voice drowned by fierce gunfire. I could see Flappers had a wounded digger held up against his chest, and I couldn't see any sign of his other three pit mates. Again, our gun overheated; time to change barrels again, and for me to fire on full auto again. A 20-round magazine on full auto out of an M16 is gone in seconds. I was going through ammo at a mad rate.

As we were the closest to the enemy, preventing those behind from firing, my concern was we could be over-run if more enemy were lying in wait. I decided to risk losing a hand, not my head, by putting my rifle-hand above the paddy bun to hold back any potential assault. There was no decline in the enemy intensity. It made me worry they were a larger force.

The firefight had been in progress some 10–15 minutes and showed no signs of slackening off. Riley and the number two continually changed barrels while I covered for them with my M16 rifle. Illumination flares were now coming from our nearby FSB, the 'Horseshoe'. Fired from artillery guns, they were brighter and longer lasting. This simply exposed Flappers – still sitting there – for longer, and in brighter light.

The remainder of my section, to the right of the machine gun, had been involved in the exchange from the outset. A 90mm recoilless rifle (a bazooka-like device) was fired from our position into the enemy force to my immediate front. This had the desired effect. The battle quickly changed direction; now only the occasional burst of AK47 fire rained in on us. Still Flappers remained exposed, shielding his patient with the full width of his back turned to enemy fire.

I was running low on ammunition. Aware that one of the guys in the pit with the medic also had an M16, I crawled towards him. I scrounged up enough from Private Michael 'Chuck' Berry, who had been badly wounded and appeared to be blinded.

Bravely, he remained in position, but was unable to fire as myself and the gun group were in his way; it was the same for Peter Lloyd, who was also wounded but still holding his position. The enemy was now in retreat, but half an hour passed before enemy fire ceased. The flares gave us glimpses of them fleeing; no longer were we pinned down under heavy fire.

It was not until daylight that the full extent of the contact became clear. In the barrage of incoming enemy fire directed at Webby and me, some of that ordnance rained down upon the pit immediately to our rear.

Rounds struck Noel 'Pop' Cooper in the throat and hit a grenade on the end of Chuck's rifle, causing it to explode. Henry Stanczyk died instantly, Chuck was peppered from head to toe by shrapnel and partially blinded, and Peter Lloyd suffered fragment wounds. All were taken out by Medivac chopper as soon as the enemy disengaged. The Big One, the one we feared, had come and gone. The test I needed was over. I was scared, but I did what was expected of me – as did every other man in that patrol.

Flappers had sat with his torso exposed all through the battle to save a man's life. The wound to Pop's throat meant he had to be elevated to stay alive. I nominated Flappers for a bravery award next morning. That award has taken 48 years to eventuate, but his bravery has finally been formally acknowledged. In 2018 he was awarded a Medal for Gallantry.

After the paddy contact, our lieutenant was given the task of training a South Vietnamese (ARVN – Army of the Republic of Vietnam) Company, 100 men, in weapons and contact drills, and he chose me as his 2IC.

With an interpreter, we set about the process. These guys looked like they were 15 years old, and there were most certainly VC sympathisers among them. Upon learning enough, they would simply disappear overnight with their AR15 rifle and anything else of value they could take with them.

The eyes said it all. I could single out four or five who had that 'look', body language that said they were different from the rest. Sure enough, they would be the ones who disappeared during the night.

As problematic as that may sound, without proof we simply did as we were instructed, and that wasn't to cull out men we didn't like the look of.

On the other hand, they were kids just like me, only five years younger, who were as keen as mustard to learn, and wanted to defend their South with their lives.

One of these kids fostered onto me on day one. I would turn to walk in any direction and there he was, grinning. He was like a puppy who never left my side. At the end of the three-week course he handed me his red and green unit scarf (which I still have), telling me the writing on it was a message to Wendy – he loved looking at her picture. He was a lovely kid, who trained hard and really wanted to be a soldier.

Months later, on our way out to a night ambush, sitting by the roadside was a group of ARVN soldiers who started calling out 'Abo'. I then noticed the red and green scarves – but there were only around 20 of them. I stopped our driver and went to them, expecting my little mate to appear beaming with delight. He had cried at the end of the course when we said goodbye.

'Where are the rest?' I asked.

Dead, they said. Eighty men, all dead.

We had been training them up for an assault on the Cambodian border. As they deployed from the choppers, the North Vietnamese Army (NVA) were lying in wait and cut them down in rows – hundreds were slaughtered, including my little mate.

Working with Vietnamese forces wasn't a practice we or the Americans liked – you simply never knew who to trust. However, we were offered Bushman Scouts when we arrived – captured enemy soldiers, NVA, who had undergone a pacification program, had been indoctrinated into the ways of the South. After a two-year re-train under the Americans they went into the ranks of Allied forces as 'on the ground aids'. Many units simply never trusted them – but our lieutenant took two.

Nguyen came into 7 Platoon, and don't ask me why but he also liked Abo – 'Ab-boo' as he pronounced it.

When I was promoted up to section commander, about five months into the tour, I used Nguyen a lot. If my scout saw anything he was uneasy about I would bring up Nguyen, which gave us three trained scouts.

On one occasion he came up the column to tell me we had just passed the entrance to a tunnel.

It was ingenious – someone had surgically cut the centre out of a tussock-type clump of vegetation, big enough to allow a man to squeeze through, and by gathering all the remaining strands and pushing them down through the opening it concealed the entrance completely. Nguyen saw a speck of bright-red soil the enemy had missed.

Bushman Scouts were allowed to carry a rifle, and one 20-round magazine for personal security. They were never to be involved in any contacts, the 20 rounds were to defend themselves only, should our position be over-run. When I took over the section, I brought Nguyen into my pit with my forward scout; that way I had an eye on him at all times.

Nguyen had been with us for months, he was well liked and part of the team.

One afternoon, after we had been stood-down from an evening ambush, my section 2IC allowed the section to drink – we had a beer ration, and some of the guys had iced-down trunks full of canned beer. A no-no, as alcohol was not permitted in the lines. But when we weren't going on patrol for 48 hours, and if it was after 1600 hours, it was OK to drink rationed beer.

However, unbeknownst to me, in my absence the guy in charge thought it would be *funny* to see Nguyen drunk. Nguyen, being a Buddhist, never drank.

Then, at the last minute, late in the day, I was called into HQ to be given a night patrol. When I returned to the lines it was obvious some of the section were pissed.

I was furious. The man I had trusted was pissed. If *anyone* should have been sober, it should have been him, the person in charge in my absence.

'Saddle up,' I ordered. A couple of men were too drunk to go and would remain LOB, meaning fewer men but the same amount of Claymore mines to carry. I told Nguyen he would have to carry one, not even aware he had been drinking – he simply never did.

'NO!' he replied. 'Bushman Scout not have to carry Claymore – Bushman Scout not have to carry anything – only rifle,' he announced, picking up his rifle. Angry that I was short on men – and angry at the 2IC – I lost it.

'You'll fucking carry ONE Claymore,' I insisted, looping the strap of the carry bag over his head. In an instant Nguyen had cocked and levelled his rifle at my chest.

Instinctively, I grabbed the muzzle of his rifle and pulled it away from my body. Furious, I stripped him of the rifle and Claymore, grabbed a handful of his hair, and dragged him off, straight to the RPs (Regimental Police), who locked him up in a storage container that was their base jail.

For two days we could hear Nguyen calling; 'Ab-boo, I sorry!'

But the damage was done. I have often wondered what happened to Nguyen, most likely jailed until the end of the war, then executed by the NVA, his old unit and friends, who wouldn't have liked him being a rat.

But my greatest nightmare from Vietnam, which remained in my dreams for many years, wasn't the rice paddy contact.

It was a much smaller patrol, 15 men, where I was now a fully-fledged section commander (having been promoted again) and the official 2IC of this search and destroy mission.

Acting on good intelligence that an enemy patrol was operating in an area close to one of our bases, we were sent out to investigate. It was to be a three-day patrol – three days rations – and if no enemy were sighted it would be a 'Swan', as they were called, or an easy three days carrying much less weight than usual. A man going on Ops in Vietnam could expect to carry in excess of 100lb on his back: five days' rations, five days' water, his own rifle and ammunition, spare ammunition for the section gun, spare radio battery, Claymore mines, and in many cases a second weapon such as an M69 or M72 – Bunker Busters, or support weapons spread throughout the section.

Our area of Operations was within walking distance of FSB Horsehoe. A day patrolling out, two nights ambushing a known enemy track, and then a day patrolling back to the FSB.

At the end of day two we hadn't seen any enemy, nor much evidence they were still in the area.

Just on dawn of the third morning, as we were packing up from the night ambush, a civilian was seen breaking curfew – curfew being no movement outside Civilian Access Areas from daylight till late afternoon. I caught a glimpse of what appeared to be an old man using a secondary track to our flank; he shuffled along through a deserted paddy, now overgrown by jungle. The hairs on the back of my neck stood up – my gut feelings had never let me down, and there was something that didn't feel right.

'Keep your eyes open this morning, that civvie is early – too early,' I said to my scout.

'Another of your gut feelings?' he answered with a grin. 'There's nothing out here, nothing recent anyway.'

'Just stay switched on, OK!'

He nodded, seeing how serious I was. Then he got to his feet to lead out. As he got a good distance ahead of me, I rose to my feet to cover the arc to my left (his back, as he was covering the right arc) – the overgrown paddy, and the direction the old civvie had gone. Pointing to my eyes with forked fingers (the sign to look), I passed the 'word' to the guy behind me: *Keep your eyes sharp.*

I had taken no more than a few steps when the jungle canopy opened to my left, less than half-a-dozen steps away, and the barrel of an AK47 assault rifle took aim at my scout's back.

In one action I flipped off the safety on my M16 rifle to full auto and emptied the full magazine of 20 rounds.

'CONTACT – LEFT!' I shouted, as a burst of AK47 fire was returned over our heads. The entire patrol was still at our night ambush site.

My scout glared back at me in horror – he had no idea what had just happened, nor that he was the target.

Now that we were in contact with the enemy it was OK to speak. I shouted back to the patrol, 'Enemy seen front left,' for the patrol commander, our sergeant, to put a defensive perimeter into place and have a sweep set up to cover my left flank.

I didn't need to encourage my scout to keep his eyes open, they were the size of dinner plates.

Move forward, I indicated, as I crawled into the jungle where I had seen the AK47 protruding.

The enemy's reaction and the foliage disturbance told me that there was more than one, as well as the direction they had fled. Slowly my scout and I crawled forward, and once inside the wall of vegetation, blood confirmed at least one of the enemy was wounded.

A wounded man, like a wounded animal, is far more dangerous when you're on their trail – and both will seek every opportunity to inflict revenge, or save their lives. Even an animal is smart enough to ambush its pursuer, and this was an armed enemy patrol we were pursuing.

A short distance into the jungle, the overgrown track the old man had used became visible; light filtered down where trees had not yet grown back, and long, thick, green grass flourished beside the unused path.

I took one side, my scout the other, and slowly we crawled forward. Blood was everywhere, that there was more than one wounded became very apparent; if that much blood was coming from one person, we would have discovered a body by now.

I used the barrel of my rifle to gently part the tall strands of grass before moving. My heart was pounding so hard I could feel it raising my chest beneath me, the physical effort and adrenaline had my entire body pulsing.

Anticipating a burst of AK47 fire any second, and at point blank range, was very real, and very unnerving.

Then I saw a movement on the path. I thought it was a snake. The movement of leaves, grass, small twigs first caught my eye – they seemed to be clinging to a long, slimy object.

Suddenly, to my horror, I realised what it was.

All those sheep I had killed during my life had long intestines, very identifiable. I was looking at intestines being drawn across my path. I drew my scout's attention to it before crawling even more slowly forward.

This was real danger – a badly wounded person that close, conscious enough to recover their intestines, *had* to be dangerous. Across the path, on the scout's side, I could make out a foot. I held up my hand to halt his progress, accompanied by the thumbs-down sign: *Enemy!*

I crept forward, holding my breath.

Still very gently parting strands of grass with my rifle barrel, I dragged myself onto the old unused track right alongside the intestines.

Covered in leaves, blood, ants and dirt, the length of gut continued its path between a second foot that now came into view. The body these intestines belonged to lay beneath a small shrub, two rifle-lengths ahead.

I gently raised my elbows beneath me, drawing the stock of my rifle into my shoulder. Only a thin veil of tall grass separated me from the dark figure just a few feet ahead.

It gave a very mild, weak, agonising groan. Inch by inch I raised myself up onto my elbows. Then the head came into view, looking skywards, still unaware of my presence. I took aim, still at rifle-length just ahead. Now I could see the full body, and the trail of intestines being drawn by hands which slowly pushed them back into the gaping hole.

Then, as if suddenly aware of my presence, the head lowered in my direction, a face full of pain and shock, white from lack of blood. Our eyes locked.

We both knew the inevitable.

I pulled the trigger.

My scout stared, struck by the reality of how close he was to his first dead enemy, and then realising how close he had come to being in the same state.

As I moved to kneel over the body, conscious that he may be lying on a live grenade – the last dying act – I was filled with pure horror. It was no he. It was a she.

Her bandana had been blown off, and a full length of jet-black, waist-length hair hung behind the outstretched body. I felt physically sick. Hily, my adopted sister, appeared before my eyes.

My scout saw my shock, he was equally overcome by the sight. But the blood trail led onwards. Our task wasn't over – as the remainder of my section caught up, we moved out to follow on.

For an hour we followed the blood trail. At least two more of the enemy were badly wounded but, through the help of their comrades, they had managed to stay ahead of us until finally we lost them at a river crossing and gave up the pursuit.

It's at this point the shaking begins, when the adrenaline stops.

I was overwhelmed with guilt, shame and a sense of cowardice – this was a woman I had just killed. We were all very aware that the NVA and VC had women soldiers, but confronted by the reality it still made little difference to how I felt.

I carried that guilt for many, many years after Vietnam, even though documents sewn into the seams of her clothes confirmed she was VC, a member of D445, a significant enemy force in our area of operations. She was the same rank as me.

* * * *

Late into our tour I developed a severe cough when I exerted myself, and once I started I couldn't stop.

I could lie around all day just fine – then when we moved out on dark to set up an ambush, and I got hot from walking, I would start coughing. The human cough is unmistakable, and in a night ambush I could give away our position. Just such an occasion occurred one night at full platoon strength. I was coughing blood into my bush-hat when the lieutenant appeared.

'What the fuck, Abernethy!' he hissed. 'How long's this been happening?'

'Weeks now, sir,' my scout piped up.

That was it. The entire patrol was uprooted, and we hauled arse all the way back to the FSB.

I reported next morning to the MO (medical officer), who packed me off to Nui Dat to see a specialist. They took a sample of my blood. I was then placed on a CZE (Combat Zone Exempt) list, not allowed outside the wire again until I was medically cleared.

I scored a great job, however, accompanying the company driver into Dat Do each day to get large blocks of ice for the Mess. Just Private 'Chips' Rafferty the driver, myself riding shotgun, and a guy on the back of the Land Rover manning an M60 machine gun.

A week or so later I was summoned back to Nui Dat to see the specialist, a huge man with a massive black beard, in a pristine white navy uniform.

'Have you been exposed to CS gas recently, Corporal?' he asked.

'What's CS gas, sir?' I asked, having never heard of the stuff. He listed all the weapons and items that contain CS gas, and then he hit upon: 'Also used in tunnel systems – have you been near any tunnel systems of late?' Bingo. Yes, I had, about six weeks earlier – in a tunnel system the enemy had reopened to use in retreat to get wounded soldiers into a secure location.

'Your system is showing traces of CS gas – you're going home, Corporal.'

Yes, I am, I thought. In about four weeks from now we're all going home, our tour is almost over.

A week later I was summoned before 'God Almighty', Lieutenant Colonel R.A. Grey, our commanding officer; I was driven from Nui Dat to FSB Horseshoe to front the 'Old Man'.

'I'm sending you home, Corporal – for Christmas,' he announced. 'A special flight has been arranged for December 24.'

It was 20 December. He went on: 'It's been a real honour having you in the battalion – and if there is ever anything I can do for you back home, you'll know how to find me.'

Shit, really! This is God – he never said nice things? I thanked him, saluted, and as I turned to leave his tent he interrupted: 'By the way, Abo, what's your Christian name?'

'William John – sir.'

'William – I'd never have taken you for a William!'

It's the only time I ever saw him smile.

Ron Grey went on to become the Commissioner of the Australian Federal Police from 1983 to 1988 – and no, I never made that call to him.

I had a few days to raid the PX store in search of gifts for all my family members: five sisters, one brother-in-law, and Mum and Dad. And Wendy.

It was a given I would buy a reel-to-reel stereo, all the go back then, and a Super 8 movie camera.

With all the mod cons cheap and available to us, another opportunity like this was never going to happen in my lifetime, so I bought big time. Squirrel had already gone home a few weeks ahead of me, with a knee injury that needed surgery.

I was scheduled to go into the same hospital, Heidelberg Repatriation Hospital, in Melbourne. It still hadn't sunk in that I was actually going to survive Vietnam, live to tell the tale, and make it home!

The night we flew out, I waited for something to happen every foot the plane climbed above Saigon's Tan Son Nhut Air Base. I actually held my breath looking out that Pan Am 707, awaiting the rocket that would take us out – all the way up to 30,000 feet, and 30 minutes out of Vietnam.

Arriving home was almost like an out-of-body experience.

It's about an 11-hour flight, but it's from one world to another. One minute you are surrounded by green, and war, then you step off the plane into bright lights, colour, and civilisation. Weird! Nobody was armed; in fact neither was I, which felt very strange.

We landed at 2am Christmas morning, so no media to catch this special flight of Medivacs and Casevacs coming home from war.

Just two MPs who thought I should roll my shirt sleeves to regimental height; either above the elbow with a 4-inch fold, or all the way down (mine were at half-mast). I walked straight through them, each bouncing off a shoulder, suggesting they both 'take a flying fuck at a brick wall.' It was left at that, they didn't follow. I had ribbons and they didn't.

Wendy wasn't expecting me, nobody was expecting me – I made it home before any letter would have.

Once on the ground in Sydney, I called my sister Liz in Melbourne to say I was home, alive, and could she meet me in Melbourne when my flight came in.

On my flight I befriended a Melbourne publican and his wife, who insisted Liz and I be their guests for a Christmas drink – it was Christmas Day, after all.

Liz and I fell out of their pub many hours later to take a cab to Liz's flat in Hawthorne. Next day, Boxing Day, I had to report to the hospital administration. I was officially home, on leave, and alive. Any one of the three was difficult to comprehend – but falling asleep in an actual bed was real, there was nothing fake about that after sleeping on the ground for a year.

As for Vietnam, there were many more enemy contacts, more one-on-one showdowns, more killing. War is not a subject I revisit often, nor with any real pride, other than for those I served with.

Ex-servicemen and women are real pacifists; those who glorify war, from my experience, are those who have never come under fire. It's no place to be – but nor can we allow dictators, murderers and evil regimes to take away our freedom.

What our fathers and grandfathers did in World War I and World War II, in my opinion, was worthy of Australia's commitment. Vietnam, Afghanistan and the WMD bullshit in Iraq, again in my opinion, wasn't our war, and we shouldn't have gone there, especially at the whim of the Americans.

Wendy and Port Fairy life, 1971

The year in Vietnam had gone very slowly, and coming home to a hospital only added to my need to be free again. April, and my discharge, couldn't come quick enough. Despite my commanding officer in Vietnam trying to convince me to become a career soldier, and even though I'd been acting platoon sergeant at one point and had completed all three subjects as an NCO to become a sergeant, I'd had enough of the army. More than enough.

My treatment in Heidelberg Repatriation Hospital was nothing short of torture. First they had to determine the lung damage. This entailed inserting a tube down my throat and nose and injecting a milky substance into my lungs, strapping me to a board-like surface and rotating me upside down, sideways, then vertical again, to coat my lungs.

I would then be X-rayed.

It was horrific, dry-retching and trying to breathe upside down with tubes down your nose and throat is like water-boarding. You begin to wonder if you'll survive one more rotation.

This process was repeated weekly. I lived in fear of that trolley coming down the ward for me.

The CS gas had burnt the lining of my lung walls, the left lung being the worst, and as with any burn there is a thickening and thinning of the tissue. Mine was almost transparent in the thin sections. If this was to rupture, even from a simple cough, it could cause pneumothorax, a potentially fatal tear and collapse of the lung.

After weeks of these horrific procedures it was decided they would not remove my left lung. Squirrel and I were discharged on the same day at Watsonia Barracks.

The parting advice from the army medical board was: 'Get near the ocean – salt air is what you need. Your days as a farmer, shearer, drover, tractor driver are over. The dust will kill you.'

Great, I thought, everything I know I can no longer do. The farm I was to inherit also had to go.

But, there were bright parts. Wendy and I set our wedding date for May, her school holidays. We'd even booked our honeymoon to Tasmania for two weeks. And yes, Squirrel was my best man.

Those early weeks of freedom felt different to what you might expect. From war to peace, from the daily routines of the military, to being on your own and not surrounded by a hundred guys, was alienating and lonely. I had lost my common ground with civilian life.

Civilian mates only wanted to know, 'What was it like?' And 'Did you kill anybody?'

Then they'd tell me how *they* had spent the past two years! Nobody cared, nobody knew, and nobody really wanted to know. Vietnam was a dirty word.

Veterans were branded. The My Lai massacre – America's greatest shame of the war – had branded us all 'Baby Killers'. I saw the original photos of My Lai and it sickened me. I could understand the rage back home, but no Australian soldier I ever served with killed babies – rather, we would risk our lives to protect babies – so it soon wore thin if anyone was brave or stupid enough to call me that to my face.

Our wedding was a great day – even Mum enjoyed it, as we weren't married in a Catholic church. Squirrel, however, thought it was harder than Vietnam. Public speaking wasn't his thing.

But Wendy and I had just got married and we were in Launceston, Tasmania, picking up our hire car as Mr and Mrs Abernethy. We were as in love as any two people get.

*Mr and Mrs Abernethy.
Our wedding day, May 1970.*

On honeymoon in Sandy Bay, I noticed a sign in front of our hotel advertising boats for hire, all fishing gear supplied.

Why not? An hour later, Wendy and I were out there fishing. This was Wendy's first time in a boat, ever, and my second. Then it started, beginner's luck.

We began catching fish after fish. Bream, flathead, and then a school of gummy sharks. We could have filled the boat, had we not quit at sunset.

We fed the entire hotel guest list that night; the chef couldn't believe we had caught the lot.

Wendy and I were hooked. We bought our own rods and fishing tackle and learnt from the locals how to catch different species. All in all, we did very well, and our hotel on our last night was again near the ocean, in the inlet right where the *Princess of Tasmania* ferry tied up. We must have landed right on top of the biggest school of bream this time – we were landing them as quickly as we could bait up. Bream topped the billing in the hotel restaurant that night.

Back home again, we moved into a flat in Port Fairy, Wendy's next posting, where she would remain as a permanent teacher.

It is a quaint little fishing village, 18 miles to the west of Warrnambool, with a history going back to early Victorian settlement. Whalers, sealers, fishermen, had all settled in this harbour, even pre-dating Captain Cook.

The mahogany ship – reputedly a Portuguese caravel – that lies in the sand dunes is said to have been there years before Cook's arrival. Some of the old folks in town claim to have played on it before it disappeared beneath the sand, and local Aboriginal people maintain there were white men on their southern coast before British explorers sighted the east coast.

I found an old Clinker inboard ski-boat for sale; it had a blown motor, and was going very cheap. I spent weeks on the hull getting it looking brand new, gave it a coat of bright-red marine paint, then installed a reliable motor – and we were good to go.

Fortunately, I had the good sense to do our maiden voyage up the Hopkins River in Warrnambool, not go straight into the ocean. I blew the motor within 20 minutes; the oil pressure wouldn't hold, which I initially put down to a crook gauge – my engine was good! After I blew a second motor I knew something was up.

Cars and boats are vastly different, for a number of reasons; I was on a learning curve here. On my third rebuilt motor I fitted the original oil pick-up and sump, and this time we hit the water and never looked back – full oil pressure and full throttle. Wendy and I took that boat fishing for a month in the calm of the bay at Port Fairy, then decided to upgrade to a fibreglass 18-foot runabout with 75 HP Johnson outboard. We went further afield, had more success fishing – we were now old hands at this.

Then tragedy struck, as it does when you least expect it.

We were in Melbourne for a family affair.

I was driving, sober, after a dinner, going through a green light, when there was one hell of a bang. Another car had hit us and spun us completely around. Wendy was unconscious, bleeding from her temple. It scared the hell out of me. I knew I was bleeding into my eyes. I wiped them. It made no difference. I could only see faintly out of my right eye.

There was a pair of angels behind us that night, a married couple. He was a Queen's Counsel and his wife a trained nursing sister. The nursing sister assisted Wendy, the husband arranged an ambulance – and the cops, to track down the prick who hit us. He had taken off in a cab.

Amazingly, the cops caught him, through the taxi company, within the hour, where he still blew off-the-scale pissed. He was charged with hit and run, as well as all the other charges, but that got him a year in the nick.

I was taken to nearby Box Hill Hospital, where doctors worked on me for five hours to remove an eye socket packed with windshield and rear-view mirror glass, which had destroyed my left eye.

When I woke, both my eyes were bandaged and my sister Liz was at my bedside. Eyes are sensitive organs, and when one gets badly injured the other one can go out in sympathy, meaning I could be totally blind. The doctors had saved my badly mutilated eye; at first they thought it would have to come out, but they painstakingly removed the glass and repaired the eye as best they could.

Why? Why now, after surviving bloody Vietnam? My messed-up head was telling me that it was pay-back or karma, for killing that VC woman soldier.

Lying there blind for ten days, not knowing if it would be permanent, was an extremely traumatic experience. I would kid myself it was going to be fine – my sight in both eyes would be there when they unbandaged me. I could see the lights come on in the mornings through the bandages, the bright fluorescent lighting that would flicker into life as the night shift was leaving. I asked a dozen questions a day, freaked out that I may be blind for the rest of my life.

When the bandages came off, Liz was there.

I could see – with my right eye anyway, as the left still had gauze and a dressing over it. But I COULD SEE.

However, I got the shock of my life when I saw my face in the mirror. My nose had been stripped of all flesh to the bone.

Over weeks, months and finally years, I adapted to having one seeing eye. Distance is changed enormously; I couldn't pour a glass of water without missing the glass by a foot. Walking down stairs became dangerous – you can never gauge the distance accurately, and I would constantly trip or stumble. But in time I adapted.

Wendy had started teaching by the time I was fully recovered, and we had purchased a house through Defence Homes.

A girl Wendy taught with was married to a commercial fisherman, named Max, whose family owned some three fishing boats, and a boat was short of a deckhand. Was I interested?

Well, that was exactly what the army specialists had recommended – salt air.

I seized the opportunity, and before I knew it I was a deckie on a shark/crayfish boat. There was no formal training back in those days, you simply learnt on the job.

I had an old hand say to me on day one: 'Always remember – one hand for the boat, the other is for you.' In effect, never let go of the ship – always hang on, as it only takes a hair's breadth for you to go over the side, and if you do, you're dead.

Actually, 20 years later, at the Miami Boat Show, a coastguard skipper told me that 80% of all males they recovered dead from the sea had their flies open. Yes, while zipping up or down, using two hands, the boat lurches and over you go!

Max's father was a tough old Norwegian skipper, nicknamed Strangler for the many times he'd had altercations at the pub and would lock onto his opponent's throat. He hardly ever spoke, and when he did it was full of venom and abuse – directed at Max more than anyone.

I learnt to keep a low profile, do exactly what Max told me to, and keep right out of Strangler's way.

Bass Strait fishing is seasonal, always dependent upon weather that is the worst and most erratic on the globe, with crayfishing during the summer months and shark during winter. I did a full 12 months on the

Charles Witton and overcame the sea-sickness early by eating an apple as we left port, and keeping one in reserve for at sea. It worked for me for the best part of 30 years.

But what to do with my life? Each time a fishing boat returned to port it always drew a crowd, locals as well as tourists. The standard question was, 'Can you hire a boat anywhere to go fishing?'

With over a year under my belt as a deckhand on a commercial fishing boat, I qualified to apply for my own skipper's ticket, which I did through the Marine Board of Victoria.

I then got Max to come with me to the Melbourne Boat Show. There I fell in love with a Caribbean Reef Runner – a 21-foot stern-drive offshore runabout, and I sat down with the exhibitors to see if they could build one to Marine Board requirements. They could.

Now all I had to do was convince my bank manager.

I would be the only lemonade stand in the desert, as I put it to him – we get thousands of tourists every year and they are asking for this. Eventually, he agreed.

As I have subsequently learnt, you eat the paint off the walls for your first year in any new business, but if you can survive that and you're still around in year two, you may break even. Year three, you should make money.

It was much tougher than I had expected, long days standing around my signs at a deserted wharf; if I was lucky I might get a 30-minute bay cruise. It was a slow, hard slog. I drove to every hotel in the district asking the publicans if I could put up my posters in the men's toilet – what better place to get a man's attention? Also, every public phone booth in the district (this was before mobile phones), so they had the number to call right in front of them. It worked – slowly. But eventually it caught on.

One day very early into my charter boat career, a single car pulled up and the driver stepped out: a tall, slim, very attractive brunette, a few years older than myself – maybe she was 28 … I was 23. 'Busy?' she asked.

'Not too busy to take a beautiful woman for a spin.'

'The island?'

The island was my big one – four hours round trip, but I needed at least four paying customers to make it viable.

'If you've got four hours to spare, and at a special discount for an exclusive tour, you bet,' I said.

Soon she was in the seat beside me, her hair flowing wildly as we powered out to sea.

It was a perfectly beautiful day, dead-flat sea, not a breath of wind, and the sun was beating down.

Bombora, as I had named my brand-new boat, was skipping across the smooth surface at 22 knots.

I dropped anchor in Dinghy Cove and shut down the motor. The cove was filled with seals, which are all very inquisitive when a boat pulls in. I was still out on the bow, ensuring the anchor had a good hold, when my passenger came up to join me.

I don't know how, or why it happened – or even exactly what did happen, but we soon left the fore deck to come back into the cockpit, and I was going below to drag out every lifejacket on board to make up a mattress of sorts on the deck. We spent three hours on that boat, and not once did I feel guilty that I was married. She knew I was married; she wasn't. I saw her again the next night at her motel. This was the beginning of my infidelity – or should I say, in Australia; it had been Vietnam before that.

After our first three months in Vietnam, where we experienced life and death in an afternoon, repeatedly, we quickly learnt there is no tomorrow. 'Eat, drink and be merry – for tomorrow you may die' had real meaning. It's this mentality that I took away from the army.

There was no de-brief on how we may react back in the real world, or how to deal with it.

Discharge was, 'Rifle here, pack there – now piss off', and no, I'm not joking. Our youth had been stolen from us. I went in a 20-year-old and came out a 40-year-old in a 21-year-old body. I loved Wendy exclusively in my mind, and when I slept with prostitutes in Vietnam I wasn't betraying my love for Wendy – I was satisfying what may well be my last sexual act.

Sadly, regrettably, unforgivably, I kept that attitude from the day the army discharged me till this very day, I guess.

I believe that lady's name was Dawn, and she was the Dawn of my infidelity. Over the next 15 years, running out of Port Fairy, Melbourne, Cairns, Brisbane, it was a continual procession, as any of my crew can attest. It's no badge of honour, nothing I'm proud of. The real irony is I only ever wanted one woman in my life. I have only ever truly loved two women, and I married both of them.

* * * *

Very early into my career as a charter skipper I met Phillip Wik playing pool in the pub. He had just completed university and had majored in pool hustling, as I was to learn the hard way.

Phil was quietly spoken, with a broad, generous smile, and a dead ringer for the famous tennis player of the time, Bjorn Borg.

I had been chartered by the internationally acclaimed wildlife artist Robert Ulmann to go to Lady Julia Percy Island to paint there for five days.

The island being a wildlife reserve, I was granted a permit – but under very strict terms. I had no deckhand and needed help to row Ulmann, his manager and five days' provision ashore.

I asked Phil if he'd be interested and he accepted, having never been on a boat before.

The night before our departure I was visited by an old friend, who introduced me to tequila – not one bottle, but three.

I don't recall a thing from halfway through bottle two, but I've never drunk the stuff since.

Next I knew I was waking up in the cabin of my boat, underway! I freaked, as it became obvious we were at sea.

I staggered out into the wheelhouse to a number of smiling faces – we were on our way home from the island, having landed both men and all their stores safely ashore. I had slept through it all.

Another of my close friends had answered the call from Wendy, and along with Phil, and my mate, they had carried me aboard prior to our departure.

The boys had attributed my 'unavailability' at the helm to a sudden bout of illness.

With a name like Phil Wik, and having saved my life and reputation, I quickly nicknamed him 'Dip', and asked if he was interested in a permanent job. Fortunately he accepted. Besides being my First Mate, he was my best mate, who taught me to play golf off-season, and became my tutor when it came to upgrade my skipper's ticket to Master through the Marine Board of Victoria and Monash University. Without him I would never have obtained my Master's and Engineer's tickets. Not only was he a very bright student, he was a brilliant teacher. I have him to thank for so much in my life. After our time charter fishing, he took over a café in Port Fairy, then a motel with a restaurant in Bendigo, and today he and his wife are relief managers of hotels and motels far and wide. We are still very close friends.

My year as a charter skipper was broken up into seasons, the busiest being from Boxing Day through to the end of May, then public holidays and whatever I could gain at weekends for fishing trips. I had the bug for fishing, big time, and listened and learnt as much as I could. The mecca was marlin fishing, the ultimate for any fisherman, or woman, worth their salt.

Cairns in Far North Queensland was emerging as one of the best locations for big black marlin anywhere in the world; Lee Marvin had even fished there.

Weight and line-class were the real big factors, and Bob Dyer of Australian TV fame had made shark a game fish with a special twist, the added danger.

From my short time in Port Fairy I'd heard the stories of monstrous great white sharks around Lady Julia Percy Island, drawn by all the seals there. How Henri Bource had been attacked out there and lost his leg. The mysterious Big Ben, a shark reputed to be around 36 feet long.

But how do you catch one of these monsters? Tiger sharks were what Bob Dyer had been targeting and, although large and dangerous, they were nothing compared to 'White Death', as the great white shark had become known. Catching it was one thing, but bringing it alongside a boat still alive was another; commercial fishermen who unintentionally caught them in nets shot them, several times apparently, before boarding, or towing them back to port. Shooting them was out of the question if you were taking it on as a sport.

An old hand (and brother to Strangler), Peter 'Runt' Tergersen, had told me of a way of using drums, with a chain and hook baited with meat, with lots of fresh blood. Anchor the drum and keep clear to watch and see what happens.

A shark drowns if it can't swim; the water flowing through its gills provides the oxygen it needs to stay alive – exhaust that and it dies, as they do in nets.

This became my new obsession. I had two 12-gallon fuel drums tied together with wire cable and around 15 feet of chain with a huge hook suspended beneath with a chunk of meat. I took a couple of mates and we gave it a shot.

In theory, everything worked just fine. We anchored in Dinghy Cove, where all the seals slept overnight. Early next morning we saw a huge dorsal fin appear next to the drums, then circle, and keep circling, before it made its charge. Both oil drums disappeared effortlessly; there was a huge swirl of water, then up popped both drums. After some considerable time, long enough to know nothing was connected to it, we edged slowly towards them, 12-gauge shotgun and a .303 as a back-up. Nothing but a straightened hook. Either the hook was too weak, or the drums were too much resistance.

I upgraded both and added an extra pilot drum: a disposable aviation fuel tank. It was around a metre long, made of stainless steel and reinforced with steel rims around the exterior to prevent crushing from pressure, and had a welded ring at each end. Tethering this to the two 12-gallon drums now allowed a shark to pull it under, putting less stress on the hook and allowing the shark to tire with a much-reduced restriction. The two oil drums were still anchored in the calm of Dinghy Cove to stop the shark venturing out into the open sea.

Again, we waited all night, checking the drums with a spotlight every 30 minutes or so. Again, next morning at dawn a dorsal fin appeared. It was a much smaller shark. The pilot drum dipped on its end, went under – and popped up again.

Then we saw the shark again – this time it charged, and pulled the pilot drum down effortlessly. It stayed down. The two 12-gallon oil drums began to move as well, then stopped, but the pilot drum never surfaced.

The fight lasted around 20 minutes. We moved in for a closer look. There it was, still alive but well hooked. I put a shot straight into its brain, and we had our first white pointer capture. We towed it home alongside *Bombora*.

Ironically this was the smallest white pointer shark we ever caught – just on 3 metres. It was also my last by drum-line.

If I was to do this seriously I needed to make a game chair, buy proper rods and reels. That would take some time, but I made some very important contacts, notably Alf Dean, a South Australian, who held the world record for white pointer sharks and knew more about them than any other man who has ever lived – to this day. Mr Dean was amazing in the way he helped and supported me

He was also the first to congratulate me, years later, when I had clearly taken his world record.

I had also taken up scuba diving in a serious way, due to my association with Australian SAS and British Paratroopers who I had met through Colin Holt. Colin came to Port Fairy even before I had purchased

Bombora and started chartering. He was a founding member of the Blue Stars International, a parachute team who put on exhibition jumps all over the world; the entire team eventually ended up living in Australia.

Each was a qualified scuba diver, in addition to all having over 1000 civilian jumps to their credit, but no way were they getting me out of an aeroplane – and they tried many times over many years.

But dive I did. I became hooked, and dived almost every weekend that Colin could get down to Port Fairy. I completed my instructor's rating, bought a dozen sets of scuba-diving equipment, including wet suits, and began a scuba school as a sideline to my charter boat. Diving is a drug; once you experience it you can't give up. Knowing what was beneath the surface was to me as important as knowing what was at the surface. Every canyon, every weed-bed, every reef, where every species of fish preferred to dwell. And being weightless, and free to explore places nobody else has ever been before, has a certain appeal. I loved it.

* * * *

Before daylight one morning, Strangler's third brother, Jumbo, contacted me to say he had something he wanted to show me. Jumbo only worked when he was broke. He was a drunk, and could go on a bender for weeks on end. It was a typical winter's day in Port Fairy – raining and blowing a gale. Jumbo climbed into my truck with a bottle of his favourite Stones Green Ginger Wine, and the sun was still not fully above the horizon.

'East Beach,' he grunted, pointing the way with the neck of the bottle. We stopped the truck, overlooking the ocean, and he drained the wine bottle.

'What de ya see?' he snapped. He was cold, the bottle was empty, and he had no time for small talk at any time.

'I give up, Jumbo – what can't I see?'

'Call yourself a soldier, even a fuckin' seaman, and you can't see your nose in front of your face. TEN O'CLOCK!' he shouted, pointing as he heaved the empty out the window.

Through the wipers I could make out a dark patch behind the break. I knew the coastline well and this wasn't a regular feature.

'School of salmon,' I said.

'That's what I thought – yesterday,' he replied. 'I reckon it's a wreck – scouring out in this blow.'

A 'blow' to Jumbo was anything over 30 knots – it had been blowing 50 knots for three days now, with ground swell as big as I'd ever seen it.

'This blow has moved the sand back – look at the shoreline – and I reckon it's uncovered a wreck. Now it's sucking the guts out of her – that's what all that black shit is.'

'You reckon?'

'No – that's why you're here! You're the fuckin' frogman – go and have a look!'

I marked two reference points to dissect the spot, then went back at last light with a mate, to dive on the spot. The weather had settled dramatically, as it does down there.

By torchlight we worked our way towards the area, checking my wrist compass constantly and guessing how far offshore we should be.

We came across a very heavy old chain.

My mate and I followed it. At times it was partially buried beneath the sand, but it was leading us away from shore – in the right direction.

Then I caught a glimpse of something down by my side: a ship's capstan! Jumbo was right, it was an old wreck.

Together we swam around the black mass of mud-like material being drawn out of the hull with each surge of undercurrent. Night diving can be dangerous, night diving on a wreck can be suicidal. I surfaced first above the wreck to take more reference points back to land for our next dive, then we followed the chain back – discovering the anchor this time.

If it was a wreck, I didn't want to go out to it by boat in broad daylight, in view of the whole town, and drop anchor to dive on it. It had to be kept quiet, and a night dive off the beach was the only solution.

The next day I took *Bombora* and went down alone as my mate circled back out to deeper water. In daylight I could make out the entire shape of the wreck, lying in a dish-shaped gully created by the undercurrent of strong water drawn through and around her rotting timbers.

An open hatch amidships drew me straight to it; through this I would be able to see inside. Treasure was on my mind.

The packing cases I could safely reach were paper thin, soft enough that I pushed my hand through one to find it packed with clay drinking vessels.

Lying exposed through a layer of sand was the top of a very large church-type bell. The wreck was still full of her cargo.

Another legend who lent himself to my cause through good luck and good fortune was Stan McPhee, who had discovered the legendary wreck, the *Loch Ard*, at Loch Ard Gorge along the Victorian coastline. A clipper ship, she had run aground near Mutton Bird Island on 1 June 1878. Of the 54 passengers on board, just two survived.

I had known Stan since my school days. I invited him to dive on the wreck with me.

As we went over the side it became apparent she was covered over: now the ocean floor was once again smooth and even – 30 feet of sand covered her to deck level. Just the very top of the capstan was visible, and Stan and I worked our way to the anchor, also just visible. We tied a marker to it below the surface level and left.

Stan taught me how to lift heavy weights with air. He even accompanied me out to retrieve the anchor. Effectively, all that's required to lift several tonnes is a drum you can fill with water and sink; you then pump air into the drum to push the water out – hey presto, as soon as the buoyancy becomes greater than the weight, up comes the weight.

I couldn't believe the amount of weight I was lifting, nor the effect and efficiency of the drum. As it filled with air, the drum rose off the sand, then the rust around the strong chain we used began breaking away from the stretching links. Still the anchor remained stuck! When I was

The anchor I brought up from the deep.

beginning to think it would never work, the anchor slowly began to part from the sand; the chain was making noises like it would snap.

Before I realised what was happening, both the anchor and I were on our way to the top, me standing inside the flukes!

It was a big anchor, far too big to bring aboard *Bombora*, or any vessel, without a very heavy-duty anchor windlass. We towed it alongside to the wharf at Port Fairy and lifted it onto the wharf with a crane. By now the cat was out of the bag: Abernethy has found a shipwreck and its anchor is down on the wharf – the media had the story.

It became quite a big deal, a flotsam and jetsam stand-off. What, if anything, can be removed from a wrecked ship?

The *Loch Ard*, like many wrecks, had been made a 'sacred site' due to the amount of lives lost. A grave-site if you like.

Our ship was unknown, and on my second dive I removed a couple of objects that could assist in identifying her. One, a very large encrusted old key, remained in my home forever. The other went to Melbourne for identification.

It was later determined to be the wreck of the *Sarah Louise*, a brig that went down on 6 July 1849. An early trading vessel, she was about to set sail for London, fully laden, when a winter storm caught her; she dragged anchor before capsizing with her full complement of cargo. Two lives were lost.

I could never find out officially, but had sufficient knowledge to learn the bell I had seen was one of two aboard.

I was later invited to a lunch with the state premier of the time, who offered to provide dredging support and the necessary equipment to uncover the wreck. I declined to give up its exact location – and his offer.

The facts being the ship and all her contents would immediately come under the control of the state government – including the anchor, which I donated to Flagstaff Hill, the Warrnambool Maritime Museum. It remains there to this very day, while the *Sarah Louise* remains at the bottom of Port Fairy Bay somewhere, covered by metres of sand.

It was also around this time a ghost from the past, or should I say an old army mate, Cubby, found me on his way through to Adelaide with a busload of army recruits. He was a regular army guy from 7 RAR who stayed in after the battalion returned from Vietnam.

Stopping for lunch at a Warrnambool hotel and staring at the wall while taking a leak, there was my name on a poster. He decided there couldn't possibly be two of me, so had the bus driver stop in Port Fairy. He let the bus go on without him.

Not only did he find me but he almost got me shot twice in the next week, more often than in Vietnam.

Kevin Cuthbertson, as all who know him can vouch, is one bundle of fun provided you're on his team. Cubby enjoyed a drink back then, although after 20 you wouldn't think he was anything but stone-cold sober.

We arrived at my favourite hotel, Marty Hearn's pub, and out front was a white Holden ute with a calf tethered in the back – old Danny Madden had been to the Warrnambool calf sales.

Cubby went into the newsagents and bought two books of raffle tickets. We sold both booklets, with the proceeds going to the Royal Children's Hospital. The prize? Oh, a three-week-old calf, announced Cubby. Even old Danny bought tickets.

When it came to the draw, and the announcement of the winner – which oddly enough was old Danny – I came in with his calf in my arms and presented him with it.

'That's mine!' he protested.

Yes it is, we agreed.

Next day, Cubby and I were having a counter-lunch at Marty's when the distinct sound of a double-barrel shotgun snapping closed came from directly behind us. In unison we cleared the bar and bolted out the back door.

Behind us old Danny Madden shouted: 'Sell my calf to me – you pair of rogues, I'll give you a donation alright!'

The gun was unloaded, empty. But try that today – walk into a pub with a side-by-side shotgun and close it up. No matter how good the arresting officer's sense of humour, you'd still be in deep shit.

At the end of my day's charters, it was to the pub with Cubby. Once, we arrived home after closing time to find me locked out of my own home. I knew the window into the lounge-room never fully closed.

'Leg me up,' I said to Cubby.

Pissed, he thought it funny to *really* help me in, with a huge shove.

In the dark, I put out my hand to save myself from falling flat on my face, and Wendy's prize possession – a massive lamp – hit the French-polished hardwood floor with a loud crash.

Suddenly I was looking down the wrong end of a .22 calibre rifle as all the lights came on – my own rifle!

'Out – both of you!' she yelled, seeing Cubby's face at the window. We slept on the boat that night. I doubt she would have shot me, or even that the rifle was loaded, but I told Cubby it was time he hit the road.

Years later, Cubby would save my life.

Actually, as irony has it, Cubby would go on to hold a senior position in the Australian Federal Police, after being recruited by the Australian Army bomb tech to head up the anti-terrorist bomb data centre for the Sydney Olympics in 2000. He was a major figure in the investigation following the Bali bombings in Kuta in 2002, and later he headed up the United Nations bomb disposal unit out of Manila. He received a CSC (Conspicuous Service Cross) for his services.

But, I digress.

Around this time, Wendy and I were made an out-of-court offer, through the other party's solicitors, as compensation for the car crash that had cost me my left eye. Our solicitors encouraged us to take it. So we did.

I had promised Wendy that if she married me I would take her around the world before we settled down to have a family. With the settlement money, now was the time to make good on that offer.

Wendy applied for two years' leave, I found the right people to rent our house, and in May 1975 we boarded a Singapore Airlines 707 for England.

Seeing the world

What a feeling, sitting back in comfort on Singapore Airlines on our great adventure. We had planned to buy a VW 'Pop-Top' Camper – all the rage at the time – direct from the German factory, have it converted to right-hand drive and, after our trip around Europe and the UK, send it home to sell again. Shortly after arriving in England we learnt it was a dumb, bloody expensive idea, as was trying to buy a decent motorhome at Australia House, where every travelling Aussie was trying to sell theirs for the fare home.

This was Wendy's first trip outside Australia; my second, counting Vietnam. I'm delighted to say Australia was giving the Poms an absolute thrashing in the cricket, the 1975 Ashes, with Jeff Thomson at one end and Dennis Lillee at the other.

We found Bertha, an ex-London ambulance converted into a motorhome, in the *Trading Post*. We added a toilet on board, and we were ready. Being diesel, a Bedford, and right-hand drive, it was perfect for me to maintain, and easy enough for Wendy to drive.

We set off north from London, stopping at castles, museums and pubs, such as the 'Trip To Jerusalem', which is built into the cliff that Nottingham Castle sits on. This pub – which is carved out of rock and incorporates some of the cliff's network of caves – was built in 1189 and is said to be the oldest in England. I couldn't believe I was standing at a bar made from a whole split tree, where knights stood hundreds of years before me. Sherwood Forest, Robin Hood – I discovered this history was all true, a bit of exaggeration here and there, but basically these people had really existed.

Scotland had meaning, as 'Abernethy' is Scottish. Our lot were sheep rustlers apparently, who did a runner across to Ireland. Continuing north after Edinburgh, we found a sign-post in Perth and Kinross saying 'Abernethy', and had to investigate. It was only a wee village, with a store, pub and garage. We headed into the pub.

'Are there any Abernethys living in Abernethy?' I asked.

Turned out the owner of the garage was one, but didn't live in town any more.

'We are Abernethys,' I said proudly.

'An Abernethy in Abernethy' became the catch cry; before we knew it the entire town was there – and don't believe the Scots are tight, we couldn't pay for a drink for love nor money. We didn't leave the pub for three days, and I poured Wendy into bed each night. She loved a scotch and I did my best to uphold the family name, but also conceded. We left with enough vegetables to start our own market garden.

After a couple of months touring through England, Scotland and Wales, we arrived at the port of Dover, took the ferry to Calais, and drove off.

Problem. All the traffic was on the wrong side of the road, and a bigger problem, when I got on the correct side of the road I couldn't see what was coming to overtake.

The nightmare began. The passenger seat became the driver's seat, as the driver was blind to oncoming traffic until he was out from behind the vehicle in front. Coming straight down the ramp off the ferry into this was a brutal wake-up!

Paris was different again. Anyone who drives in Paris has to be stark raving mad!

Wendy was into art, big time, we had to visit the Louvre, also the Eiffel Tower – so much to see. But leaving Paris was a godsend, for the driving in any event. Plus Wendy had me convinced she knew French, although nobody could understand a word she said. Only when we left Paris did we find out she could be understood, even if her schoolgirl French was lousy.

A remarkable thing happened shortly after leaving Paris; hopelessly lost, and having no luck communicating with farmers out in the middle of nowhere, I suddenly had enlightenment – don't ask me how, or why, but the road ahead was a place I knew well!

I took off, telling Wendy what was ahead: buildings, bridges, roads, everything was crystal clear to me, and as we progressed everything I predicted was there – exactly as I said. As we came to the main road we were looking for, I noticed Wendy was quite white with shock.

'How did you know all that?' she asked, knowing I had never been to France before in my life (well not in this life anyway). Perhaps there really is something to the past lives theory. It's the only explanation I can think of.

We came to the Mediterranean – everything filmed on my trusty Super 8 movie camera from the army PX in Vietnam – and followed the coast, staying and playing at the Monte Carlo casino, and we even saw Brigitte Bardot naked on the beach at St Tropez.

I met Pierre Abdul there early one morning at a beach bar. A black African in his mid-thirties, Pierre spoke around five languages fluently and offered to translate for me to ensure I wasn't ripped off by the locals, as Bertha was having her brakes checked.

I gladly accepted, although Wendy had a bad feeling about my new friend. He took us, with his doctor friend, to an expensive restaurant/nightclub and paid the entire bill, US$30 a drink – yes, per drink, in 1975! We later found out the same club had been used in Bond movies. By now Wendy was convinced Pierre was a white slave trader. He never let go of his briefcase, was vague about his work, but said he lived in Brussels. He was always immaculately dressed, well mannered, and very kind and friendly towards me. He gave me his address in Brussels.

We had settled into the gypsy life, our home on the road. On the way to Pisa we spotted a roadside trader selling home-made wine – a gallon for like AUD$1. I bought two gallons. Having drunk around half of the first flagon on day one I was so sick I was unable to travel, or even move.

Thirty-six hours later, Wendy had had enough. She got behind the wheel and headed for the Leaning Tower of Pisa. I still couldn't move; as I lay in bed and groaned, I was handed the Super 8 and told to shoot: 'I'm going to climb to the top – film it, OK.'

I swear I'm the only person who has seen the Leaning Tower of Pisa stand perfectly straight – I argued with Wendy that it didn't lean, until I saw the developed film months later. Moral to that story, don't drink home-made wine by the gallon.

Next, Florence. Wendy was in her element – art, history, magnificence all around. The Uffizi Gallery, the Bardini Gardens, the Accademia Gallery, I was getting a history and art degree on the road. A wise man once told me the greatest education you can have is travel, and I couldn't agree more.

When you think you have seen it all, you soon learn you've seen nothing yet. Mum would have been pissed, but I actually went inside the Vatican, dripping with gold and wealth, while just outside beggars lived in squalor. The Colosseum was something else, going down into the bowels, so to speak, where gladiators and wild animals had emerged to do battle to the death for the crowd's entertainment. Makes AFL look pretty tame, I thought.

As for the Sistine Chapel, who would have thought Michelangelo would paint the ceiling? I didn't – and walked all over people lying on their backs on the floor, much to Wendy's disgust! But I shall forever see that image of the touching hands. As for Wendy, to see all this amazing art is something I'm sure she'll treasure for life.

Yugoslavia, no longer a country now, was next, then south into Greece. Arriving in Athens late on a Sunday afternoon, both Wendy and I were amazed at how quiet it was – we drove through the centre of the city with little to no traffic and found a parking space right at Syntagma Square, the city centre.

As we stepped out of Bertha I sensed tear gas, then I heard machine-gun fire.

The streets were deserted except for one old man on his hands and knees on the footpath. He was trying to catch goldfish flipping around on the pavement. His restaurant had been shot to shit – all the front windows were gone, and his fish tank as well. I went to help him, grabbing a bucket and emptying all our catch into it.

'Thank you, thank you – America,' he said, holding both my wrists in sincere appreciation.

'Australia – NOT America,' I said adamantly.

'Thank you, thank you – Australia.'

We were not to know – our Greek was non-existent, and the radio was our only news – but there was major unrest going down that day, possibly a reaction to earlier student uprisings. The old restaurateur insisted Wendy and I take coffee with him.

His English was good enough to warn us to get out of the city – the army had just been through on armed personnel carriers, dispersing students with gunfire and tear gas.

We found our way to the coast, the beach at Glyfada, getting there after dark. Next morning we awoke to the sunshine sparkling off a smooth Mediterranean sea, only sand between us and the water.

We were in luck, we had parked beside a restaurant/grocery store: milk, bread, you name it they had it. By day's end we were on best terms with the owners and, discovering there were no parking restrictions, Bertha stayed in that same spot for two months, our milk delivered to her, the city only a short distance away by bus, so too the Acropolis. The Americans were there in force, air force, to support the Greeks in their dispute with Turkey, who had invaded Cyprus, and unrest continued – but that was all a world away from our little paradise in Glyfada.

We found a packed bar, mostly full of American servicemen, spilled out around the building for a block. Fairy lights covered the trees, with seating beneath – we found a spot and soon had a waitress at our side.

'What will it be?' she asked with an Aussie accent and a gorgeous smile. Sheila Maguire by name, and stunning by nature. Her friend, Ann

Ellis, also worked there – we became instant friends that night. The girls knew their way around, and from then on Wendy and I spent all day on the beach, and the night with the girls.

Sheila was the most naturally beautiful girl we had ever seen, stunning. Everywhere we went, guys appeared out of the woodwork to stare at her.

Then it was off to the Greek islands, to Mykonos – leaving Bertha in Glyfada. Arriving there eventually, we simply followed the crowd and took a death-defying bus ride to the beach.

It took less than a second to recognise that *everyone* was totally naked. That was only half the surprise. Now almost dark, we discovered there was no bus back, and no accommodation. Just a structure of stone and galvanised iron – no bigger than our old shearing shed – which served all meals, and drinks, with Papa the proprietor, and friend to all.

Surrounding Papa's Bar were literally a hundred stone-built shelters, two-person homes, but it took upwards of six months to get one. So, we slept on the beach.

Where Wendy and I decided to crash that night was the first port of call for all newcomers. Next morning, every hour on the hour, small fishing boats arrived with 20 people getting off – fully clothed.

Within minutes they were naked and expanding on our perimeter; Wendy and I did as the saying goes, 'When in Rome ...' I guess we looked safe enough and, being married, both male and female happily joined our expanding family.

Metaxa and coke was the 'in' drink, and the first night Wendy and I consumed our fair share. Next morning, I caught a community donkey and rode him back to town for some vitals. We decided to stay a while.

This was 1975, it was very primitive then, but becoming more and more popular. Other than Papa's Bar/Restaurant, plus a well (which Papa was giving a young couple free meals to dig) and a unisex shower-block, that was it. This paradise of sun and sand, and on any given day over 2000 nude bodies, was it. Any wonder people stayed – some had been there two years.

All Wendy and I had taken with us were the clothes we stood in, our passports and our travellers' cheques. After a week, I purchased a square of tarpaulin to avoid sleeping on the sand at night. It became a popular item, it was nothing to find a dozen bodies on it by morning. In all we stayed there three weeks. We made many friends, but there was no infidelity.

Once we were back in Glyfada, Ann and Sheila were up for a move and decided to come with us in Bertha. Without putting too fine a point to it, there was nothing sacred, nothing! Living in such a confined space it was impossible to even have passive sex with my wife without being given a score next morning.

It was like having two extra sisters, however, and we travelled like this from Greece to Munich over several months, through Turkey, Bulgaria, Romania, Hungary, Austria and Germany. Ann had arranged to meet an English soccer player she'd met in Glyfada at the Munich Oktoberfest.

Istanbul proved to be the best and worst, best bazaars and among the worst people we had encountered so far. The Grand Bazaar is literally a city below the city, endless stalls of everything you could wish for.

Then came the Eastern Bloc, a huge culture shock, like revisiting the sixteenth century. I couldn't believe all the harvesting was still done by hand – those considered reasonably well off might own a horse. People were dirt poor. The basics, milk, bread, etc., were cheap but out of the reach of the vast majority, and cars were almost non-existent – and government-owned in nearly all cases

Romania was a whole new ballgame, a little more advanced than Bulgaria, but a much more fascist regime overall. We couldn't get out quick enough.

At the border between Romania and Hungary, we were faced with a line of parked traffic stretching 3 or 4 miles. We crawled along all day until we got within sight of the border. I watched as a black American guy coming into Romania had his car dismantled – and I mean dismantled. I spoke to him. 'Drugs man, but it's intimidation – they don't want tourists. I've been here two days now!'

Then it was our turn – but going *out* of the country. After a 14-hour wait we finally got to the window to have our passports stamped. 'Sorry – you must go back. Passport no good!'

After a long, hostile debate, we learnt that we were required to have the police in the last town stamp our passports prior to reaching the border. For a fee of course; no stamp, no leaving the country. I was furious, it was simply intimidation and extortion, but they were literally holding the guns. Back we went, slept in front of the police station and were on the road again towards the border around lunchtime next day. Same long queue, at a standstill.

Again, we advanced agonisingly slowly towards the border – only this time they wanted to do the same to Bertha as the American's car, strip her, looking for drugs. I stood my ground. 'It's not going to happen!'

A stand-off began. One boss after another came over with border guards. Bertha was a fibreglass-moulded body on a chassis, not a series of panels to be removed. Eventually we convinced them and, with all four passports stamped, having taken two days to achieve, we were directed towards the final barrier, the boom-gate into no-man's-land. When we approached, the boom-gate was up – then a guard stepped out and lowered it.

That was it, I snapped.

'Take the wheel and don't stop – DO NOT STOP,' I said to Wendy as I swung out of Bertha. I grabbed the barrel of the guard's submachine gun first, then the guard by his throat, shoving him against the wall with one arm and pushing down on the boom-gate with the other. Wendy and the girls rolled on through.

'Now if you want to shoot me you prick – shoot me in Hungary!' I said, stepping over the border.

He was as white as the building he lay against and didn't dare raise his weapon. We were out of Romania at last.

Hungary on the other hand was a lot subtler, more like Bulgaria: poor, full of peasants and no angry standover guards on the borders. We rolled on through without any issues. Arriving in Austria was like coming back from the dead – from one extreme to the other. Wealth, civilisation, normality – it was wonderful. We reached Vienna before dark and found a nice little place in town to park for the night.

I needed space, time on my own for a while to shake the remnant memories of armed and dangerous men from my mind – it had been a bit too much like Vietnam the past day or so. I needed a drink.

I teamed up with a Pommy oil construction bloke in the first bar I came to and proceeded to waste myself very successfully. I returned to Bertha in a horse-drawn taxi, with a beautiful dapple-grey mare between the shafts, and a driver wearing a top hat, much to the girls' amusement.

We visited the Spanish Riding School, those magnificent Lipizzaner horses, something every horse lover should see. That night, as we walked around looking for a place to eat, we could hear Strauss playing – not unusual being in Vienna, but it was coming from an open-air concert in the woods. Drawn on by the sound and the foot traffic, we entered an area under fairy lights where literally hundreds of people sat.

It was the European Dance Championships, being held outdoors. Onlookers were welcome for free. We enjoyed an amazing night of Strauss and dance, and where better than in the Vienna Woods?

Munich was our final destination with the girls. Again we had no idea where to go, but stopped in the Schwabing district, right in front of a busy bar. Again Bertha didn't move for over a month.

I saw something at that bar I have always wanted to bring back to Australia. A scaled train serviced the entire place; the track covered each table with seating for up to six per table, and each carriage was numbered to match table numbers, holding up to six drinks per carriage. You placed your order and money in the carriage and it went to the bar, where three staff furiously filled glasses. Effectively, three people served close to 60 patrons without a soul going near the bar. All very civilised. We had many a night in there. The Hofbrauhaus is a famous beer hall in Munich city, open 365 days a year.

Seeing the world

In the crowd five guys stood out, all in green tracksuits with 'Australia' broad and bold across their backs. One was doing well for himself in arm-wrestling, which is almost a national sport in Germany. Kim quickly homed in on our Sheila.

Soon we had the whole team, the Australian Shooting Team as it was, up for the world championships being held at the same complex as the 1972 Munich Olympics had been. Next day we drove them out to the complex in Bertha. The guys were shooting Running Boar – which is a 25-metre range .22 calibre rifle event, where a target in the shape of a full-size boar (wild pig) is exposed on a track that runs across in front of the shooter for only a few seconds. You aim at the boar's tusk to hit the bullseye a foot or so behind. At the second, faster, speed, the aiming point is closer to the bullseye. The rifles are purpose-built and are fitted with telescopic sights. I took to it like a duck to water.

Over the next week, I went out several times with the team and became their unofficial scorer. On the first day of competition I was asked to be official team scorer, spending the next week of competition taking each score. In fairness, the boys were never in the hunt; the Russian and American teams were made up of full-time military personnel and took out gold and silver. However, it did introduce me to the American captain Charles Davis – who gave me his US address and said when we got there to look him up.

The Oktoberfest was all it was held up to be, huge tents representing various beer manufacturers, with brass bands entertaining a million tourists who drank, sang, and drank more until they dropped – day after day.

But all good things come to an end, and then there are new beginnings. The girls returned to London to work while Wendy and I – and now shooter Kim, too – journeyed on.

Kim wanted to see more of the world; being a young tuna fisherman he was cashed up, and asked if he could go with us as far as Amsterdam – we were happy to have him along.

Amsterdam in the '70s was the place to be for drugs, sex, and rock and roll. Forget about young Kim, I'd never seen anything like it!

From miles out, when we approached the city at night, a sign flashed: 'Real Live Fucking'.

'Is that what I think it reads?'

'Yep,' said Kim. 'That's what it reads.' We found a park, again right in the centre of the action, on top of a canal bridge. Close by was a pub, again with Aussie girls working behind the bar. Kim took a shine to one of the barmaids, and when she knocked off he invited her to join us.

'Do you want to score?' she asked.

'Bloody oath,' Kim blurted out, having no idea what she was offering.

'Hashish – Black Lebanon.'

'Yep – we'll have some,' said Kim.

'How much?' she wanted to know.

Before he could say a couple of pounds, thinking in fishing terms, as it was patently clear he had no idea what he was getting into, I took over negotiations. Kim hadn't even smoked pot, and I'd never smoked hash – and this was premium hash. Wendy was really pissed with me; I was supposed to be looking out for this kid, not encouraging him.

Safely back inside Bertha with our foil of hash, Kim looked on in amazement as I produced a packet of rolling tobacco and papers.

'Do you smoke it?' he asked.

I caught Wendy's glare, and having no idea, figured just roll it about a matchstick thickness, the length of a two-paper joint. It was soft and sticky as plasticine.

'You first,' I offered. 'Suck it in till you feel it hit your toes, hold it, then gently let it out.'

The coughing fit that followed was enough to inform the entire neighbourhood what we were up to.

'Bloody idiots,' said Wendy.

I soon joined Kim coughing my guts out – it was a hell of a lot more potent than the pot I'd smoked.

It didn't take more than about three hits to pull us both up. Soon I was looking at my ejected Chinese dinner on the footpath beside Bertha.

'F A R K – I'm dying,' I heard Kim calling.

By now I was in a state of paralysis and couldn't do a thing for him, much less myself. I fell away from Bertha and joined Kim on the footpath.

I think Wendy would have left us there to die if she could have driven off without driving over us.

The horrible green-out/spun-out period seemed to last all night. At one stage a busload of senior English tourists pulled up and one lady remarked, 'Oh, look at those poor devils in the gutter!' That's another moment I'll take to my grave.

Eventually Kim dragged himself to the bridge wall, which was low enough to look over from a sitting position, and threw up in earnest.

I joined him.

'See if you can hit a duck,' he said.

'What the fuck?'

Kim shrugged his shoulder towards the canal below us. I needed no encouragement; I was throwing up and the ducks below were scampering for every bit.

The worst was over, we could eventually talk, laugh and move – and with a lot of pleading Wendy eventually let us back inside Bertha. But we never saw that hash again.

Amsterdam may have been a fun place, but it was also a very dangerous place at that time. Drugs were available legally through government-approved outlets, and the price of each drug was given over the radio each day. However, street dealing was also big – bigger.

I met street dealers who carried firearms and saw my first 'walking stick rifle' there, a .22 single shot needing only a simple press on a brass plate to release the firing-pin and fire it.

But the real eye-opener for all of us was the red light district. Wendy was equally blown away, women sitting in shop windows advertising their wares – and I mean seeing was believing.

Kim had much to take home, and he took plenty – videos that in those times were not available in Australia, and memories to last a lifetime.

We delivered him to the airport, only to see him taken into custody for having a firearm.

Fuck, never thought about that – we had come from Germany into the Netherlands with a rifle on board. I eventually got the matter cleared up and Kim, his rifle and souvenirs all departed on time for Australia.

Next up was Scandinavia: Denmark, Norway, Sweden. Let me confess from the outset – I hate the cold. And coming into the height of the European winter, heading north was pretty bloody stupid.

The ferries north were all icebreakers – that ought to have been enough insight. It's funny how we build up a vision of what something, or some place, will look like, only to be bitterly disappointed.

I had a vision of what Edvard Eriksen's *The Little Mermaid* would look like, but upon arrival in Copenhagen it was bitterly cold, and Bertha's heater wasn't having any effect. We parked, rugged-up and set off on foot for the famous statue. If X marked the spot, we were standing at X – but no statue?

Cold, annoyed, disappointed we were about to concede we had our directions wrong when Wendy pointed out a little bronze figure placed looking out to sea. 'No way,' I said. It was tiny.

That night was the coldest I have ever been in my life. Discovering that *The Little Mermaid* was very bloody little (it's 1.25 metres tall), the walk there and back to Bertha froze us to the bone. We ran Bertha's engine all night, with the heater going flat-out, to virtually nil effect; we turned on every burner on the stove and, in a final desperate bid to get warm, took it in turns to heat water to submerge our feet and hands in.

'Fuck this,' I announced at sunrise. 'Let's get the hell out of here and get back south.' I had little opposition from Wendy.

We journeyed on to Norway and Sweden – and although different, land of the midnight sun and all, with pleasant enough people, three to four weeks was more than enough.

We left for London, with Christmas fast approaching.

On to Belgium – and I remembered my mate Pierre's offer to look him up. Although still very much anti-Pierre, Wendy reluctantly agreed. The address he had given me was in central Brussels, and at that time a big international trade fair was being hosted there. Eventually we found his street, and we were converged upon by armed Turkish Embassy guards. We realised we were parked right in front of their embassy, and they realised we were no threat.

Wendy sat tight as I hit the footpath in search of Pierre's home. Eventually it brought me to a house with a high set of steps leading to the front door. I rang the bell. The door eased open and I was greeted by a very young, shy African boy. 'Hi – is Pierre home?' I asked. A middle-aged woman wearing European-style clothing appeared.

'I'm looking for Pierre Abdul – he gave me this address, we are friends from St Tropez,' I explained.

The look on her face told me something was up.

'Mr Ambassador wouldn't have given you his home address if you were not a valued friend,' she replied, obviously recognising Pierre's handwriting.

'Say – what, Mr … who?'

'Mr Ambassador is the Ambassador for Upper Volta. He is currently in Paris on business, but will be back this evening, and I'm sure he will be very disappointed if he should miss you. Can you come back after 7pm?'

I was dumbstruck. He was a bloody ambassador!

'Yes – of course I can, I'll bring my wife, who's also his friend.'

She smiled warmly.

'You're a good judge, Wendy, that bloody Pierre is full of it,' I said, climbing back into Bertha, feigning annoyance.

'Told you. I just knew he was no good – was he home?'

'Nope – away on business. White slave trading, or maybe drugs and arms deals. Who knows what ambassadors do,' I said, poker-faced.

'What are you talking about?'

'Your white slave trader, and shifty Pierre, just happens to be the Ambassador of Upper Volta – wherever the fuck that is.'

For the record, it was a landlocked country in West Africa, once part of the French Community. It's now Burkina Faso.

At 7pm sharp, Wendy and I were in our finest, in the diplomatic quarter, and on Mr Ambassador Pierre's doorstep. He himself opened the door, with a smile of pure delight.

Standing directly behind him was a tall, slim, stunning woman in traditional African dress, and two kids, a boy and a girl.

Pierre did the introductions and led us into a room large enough to entertain 100 people.

'I have taken the liberty to have you for dinner, I trust you haven't eaten?' he asked. The table was 40 feet long and set for six.

However, before we sat down, Pierre had a drinks trolley rolled in with every drink imaginable, and with a scotch in hand he led me to his study, leaving Wendy with his wife and children. I had brought along some photos of us at St Tropez, which I had mentioned to Pierre upon arrival.

Once we were inside his study he asked to see the photos, and that's when the penny dropped. St Tropez's famous nude beach and pics of Mr Ambassador (in his shorts) surrounded by naked women is not something for public viewing. Grinning, I showed Pierre a shot of him chatting with a naked lady. His reply was in his native tongue, but I got it and laughed. I took out the non-compromising shots and handed him the packet with negatives. He shook my hand till I thought it would come off.

Pierre's wife, apart from being stunningly beautiful, had the most regal posture of any woman I have even known. She stood tall and proud, perfectly upright – she moved as if she was on a cloud and each movement was almost theatre. I sat in awe of her mystical presence – she barely spoke a word but left me feeling I had truly met a queen or princess.

It was a wonderful evening.

Later, Pierre had his driver bring up the Benz, the embassy limo, and insisted we follow them in Bertha.

'I have somewhere you can stay – please follow.'

We followed them into the countryside beyond Brussels' suburbs.

Wendy and I were blown away; it was a villa for visiting VIPs, he said. With all the luxuries and space you can imagine.

'Make yourselves at home, rest up, enjoy, I will be back the day after tomorrow,' he said.

Submerged in a bath sipping French champagne, Wendy confessed that she couldn't care less if he was a white slave trader – this was pure luxury.

Next morning a box of groceries was delivered by the chauffeur, saying Mr Ambassador insisted – we were his guests and we could not refuse.

Pierre had even gone to the trouble of finding Crown Lager, at that time the only Australian export beer, along with a couple of bottles of scotch to keep us happy.

Pierre was a lovely man, warm and generous. He told us his previous posting had been the USA, but he hadn't enjoyed it due to the deplorable racism over there. He even took us as his guest to the trade fair, driving the embassy limo himself, which turned out to be a nightmare.

He'd not only never had a driver's licence, we were to discover (diplomatic immunity, I guess), but couldn't bloody drive either. I took over the controls for the journey home!

Our time with Pierre in Brussels, like St Tropez, was great.

Back in London after Brussels, we again parked Bertha out front of the hotel where Ann and Sheila worked. The next morning, I listed Bertha for sale in a newsagent's window. Lady Luck was still riding with us; before day's end a gentleman politely knocked on the rear door, dressed to the nines, with briefcase in hand. His wife was into horses and was looking for just such accommodation while eventing around the country.

She sold.

Cashed up, we took the train to Liverpool, then the ferry across to Belfast, across the Irish Sea, to Dad's relatives. It was a rough crossing – Wendy went down with the other 99% of passengers, which left lots of space at the bar.

Aunt Lila, Dad's aunt, had asked James and Renee – who ran the farm – to meet us at the ferry terminal and take us back to Moneyreagh, where Dad's family came from, to the east of Belfast.

The home was a modest two-storey building, with small acreage, and a dairy that housed the herd indoors during winter, which it now was – only days before Christmas. Aunt Lila was in her late eighties and had a disability; she used a leather strap to lift her foot to take a step, a slow process but one that gave her some form of mobility.

She owned the property, but James and his wife Renee and their two sons, Samuel and James, lived in the homestead with her.

Wendy and I were given an upstairs room with a magnificent view across endless green fields and hedged laneways.

In 1975–1976 the Troubles were still raging – the IRA were bombing at will, and the British Army presence was everywhere.

I recall with great clarity waking at night to an enormous explosion, even though Belfast was some miles away.

Next morning it was international news: the Europa Hotel had been bombed with such a large charge it almost bought it down, all 12 floors. As we had to do our Christmas shopping in the city, it wasn't something I was looking forward to – mines and bombs still gave me the jitters.

And it was even worse than I thought it would be. At the entrance to every building there was a body search, or a search of your bags and personal belongings. The queues into each shop ran the length of the footpath, it was a giant pain in the arse – but then again, so is a stick of plastic explosive.

Belfast took me right back into the 'zone'. Wendy had no idea of the paranoia I was going through as she and Renee happily shopped.

It snowed on Christmas Eve, the very first time I had seen falling snow. The kids came up all excited and took Wendy and me outside into this winter wonderland. Hot toddies all round that night.

Aunt Lila gave us her car to do the tour of Ireland, north to south.

I couldn't come to terms with the idea that the car, a Hillman, was three years old with only 500 miles on the clock! It literally was that 'only driven on Sundays by an elderly woman' car, and as town was 6 miles away, that made sense!

However, every morning, before I would let Wendy anywhere near the car, I was under it, over it, under the bonnet, into the boot, even under the spare tyre. With Northern Ireland plates on it, in Dublin, and anywhere down south, it was a target to my mind.

We did all the tourist places, Ring of Kerry, Bunratty Castle, Blarney Castle to kiss the Blarney Stone (the day after Elizabeth Taylor and Richard Burton had), the Giant's Causeway. By the time we had circumnavigated Ireland, I had almost doubled the wee car's three-year mileage.

We left Belfast on 31 December 1975 for Prestwick Airport, Scotland, and took a cab into Glasgow, as it was New Year's Eve (or Hogmanay for the Scots) – and our flight next morning to Halifax, Canada, wasn't until around 8am. Standing in a bus shelter of all places, wondering where to go, we were accosted by a group of party-going locals who drew us into the fold and away we went.

Hogmanay leaves the traditional New Year's I'd known for dead. I think it's even illegal to have your front door locked on Hogmanay, and we simply followed the crowd from house to house. I have no idea how many new friends I made that night, but there were lots.

We partied long and hard, catching a cab back to Prestwick Airport just before daylight. It was now 1 January 1976, and Canada awaited us across the North Atlantic.

When we arrived in Canada, the pilot announced the outside temperature was minus 20 degrees.

'Did he say minus?' I asked. I thought people died when it got to zero degrees! In those days, boarding bridges didn't exist, and our flight stopped well short of the terminal. I will never forget leaving the warmth of that aircraft to walk in minus 20 degrees across to the terminal with my leather-soled boots sticking to the tarmac.

* * * *

Canada was everything I thought it should be. I literally expected a Mountie to ride out from behind every tree.

We took the train from Halifax, Nova Scotia, south towards the US border. The countryside was magnificent, mountainous, endless miles of pine trees, lakes, picture-postcard stunning, but still bloody cold!

Our plan was to buy a VW bug, economical travel, do the round-America circuit and come back to Montreal for the 1976 Olympics. It was also America's Bicentennial year. Fuel prices overnight went from around 20 cents a gallon to 50 cents a gallon.

We travelled by train into the USA, then did the Greyhound bus southwards. For years after, Wendy and I would chant, 'And thanks for going Greyhound!' But it was fast, cheap, warmer than hitch-hiking, and from terminal-to-terminal easy to plan our way down the East Coast.

In Boston we found a good guesthouse and searched the papers every day for a car. I shall never forget seeing Jerry Lewis on TV each morning, live from Miami Beach, then helping the staff shovel many feet of snow away from the door.

Every VW we looked at was miles too expensive, or stuffed. We gave up and headed for the Big Apple, New York City. Big cities have never been my thing, and New York is the biggest. It was no warmer, the people were like their surrounds – cold and hard – and the cars weren't any better than in Boston.

I had my first experience with black ice on the Brooklyn Bridge, taking a test run in a Bug. The owner, in the passenger seat, said, 'Watch out for the ice.' All I saw was a black surface and as I touched the brake the boot passed me! Yes, a complete 360 – twice.

Washington DC was different, very different. We arrived late and found a hotel within sight of the White House. I had noticed a police car parked out front as we entered but took little notice, as they were everywhere.

'A room for two please,' I asked.

'You want it right now?' asked the guy behind reception, looking quite surprised.

'Yes,' I said curtly. Then Wendy nudged me.

Spread out across the stairway was a guy looking very dead – in fact he was very dead, shot at close range, and surrounded by cops.

'There will be a delay getting to your room,' insisted the guy behind reception.

'You reckon? I've been on a bus all day, mate, and my arse is frozen stiff, we just need a key – and a bath,' I said, loud enough for the cops to hear.

'I'm not walking over a body,' whispered Wendy.

'OK – I'll see you when you get up to the room then, because I am!'

She closed her eyes, I took her hand and instructed her step-by-step over the corpse.

'Australian – right?' said the detective as we passed.

'Right,' I replied, without losing a stride.

Wendy and I did the Washington tourist thing to the limit, and being the Bicentennial year, the White House was open to tourists, guided tours throughout. We actually stood inside the Oval Office.

After no luck on the car front, we were back on a Greyhound heading towards Jerry Lewis on Miami Beach – and warmth.

Then one night we rolled into a small town south of Raleigh in North Carolina, got off the bus, having seen a number of car yards, and checked into a motel. Next morning, we met the good ol' Southern boy who owned a large car yard. His sign read: 'All cars $500'.

With the doubling of petrol prices there was a glut of second-hand cars on the market, and the most economical were the most in demand.

A 1964 Cadillac DeVille caught our eye – also a gas guzzler, but wide enough that all my 6 feet could lie across the seat. What we spent in gas we'd save in accommodation.

I got her for US$450. Talk about a Yank Tank – that's how it felt cruising down the highway, in a car as long as my boat back home and wide enough to carry eight adults on her two bench seats. It rode like it was on a cushion of air. No wonder it was Elvis Presley's car of choice.

We did all the tourist spots – Marine World, Cape Canaveral, JFK Space Centre, Miami Beach – and then headed down through the Keys to Key West. Joy of joys, we were now in the tropics.

One afternoon in Naples, Florida, we were sitting in a small pub in the outer suburbs enjoying a beer.

A truck with three black guys pulled into the drive-through bottle shop; they had ladders and work material in the back and were stopping for an end-of-work beer.

A group of white guys playing pool told the barman not to serve them. The barman obeyed. So one of the black guys came inside to ask for a six-pack of Budweiser. He paid for it and, as he was about to pick it up, one of the white pool players came over and placed his hand over the beer.

'Can't you read, nigger – no blacks in here,' he said, pointing to a sign that read exactly that! The black guy saw the sign, and the back-up this guy had, and simply walked out.

My Irish temper kicked in, not my Aussie logic. Wendy went white, she knew me better than anyone.

I got to the bar in three strides and grabbed the six-pack before crashing out through the door to catch the guy who'd paid for them without getting a refund. I handed them to him through the open window of his truck.

'You left these behind, mate,' I said with a wink, then spun on my heels to face the prick who'd shown him the door.

By now he was back around the pool table having a laugh, unaware of what I'd done. I let fly.

'What's your fucking problem mate – they at least are working and have earned a beer. You and your gutless mates are all as weak as piss, bludgers, if it takes the lot of you to intimidate one. Intimidate me – I'm on my own!'

By now I was in this bloke's face – like right in his face.

I was then 27 years old, these guys were all about my age, but not one of them looked like he was a fighter, and I'd been around long enough to pick my mark. The blood ran out of his tanned face.

'And you'll need more than a pool cue, fella, to quieten me.'

He was holding his in both hands. Now I could see he was going to water I looked for the next possible threat. There wasn't one.

The guy put down his cue and backed up.

'You're not American,' he managed to get out.

'So, you're not entirely fucking stupid then?' I fired back. 'No, fortunately I'm not American – I'd be ashamed to be after what I've seen of you lot!'

'It's different down here. Niggers can't just drink anywhere – it's different here,' he tried to explain.

'It was the same in Vietnam as it is down here, gutless whites treating blacks like dogs – did you make it over there, mate?'

By now I was shaking, afraid I was going to step into this bloke and punch the shit out of him.

Wendy came out of nowhere. 'OK boys – cool off time,' she said, taking my arm, having seen this before.

I walked away, as angry as I have ever been. The colour of a man's skin has nothing to do with the man he is, that's how I was brought up.

The guy I had challenged eventually came over with both palms raised in a gesture of peace.

'You were in Vietnam?' he asked carefully. Wendy thumped my thigh beneath the table – be civil.

'Yes, mate, I was, and served with American troops – I do suppose you know a lot of black Americans died over there in the service of this great State in which they can't even buy a drink!' Another thump on the thigh.

He extended his hand. 'My brother fought over there. Real pleasure to meet you, sir,' he said, shaking my hand.

The irony, and I guess typical of most racists, is his racism was inherited. After a number of drinks, he invited us back to his home for dinner.

He explained how his grandfather had instilled in him that blacks were not men, they were less than men, and he had grown up with this every day of his life – as had his father.

He had a lovely wife, and a couple of small kids, too young probably to understand what Dad and this man with the funny accent were talking about – but just a nice normal family. After we left he would still be a racist.

Columbus, Georgia, was up ahead, home of Charlie Davis, captain of the US Army shooting team from Munich. Fort Benning was his home base.

He and his wife Jackie set us up in their spare bedroom and treated us like family.

They were much older than us, in their fifties I guess, but we got along like a house on fire.

Charlie took us everywhere, including onto base at Fort Benning, where I shot some great scores. I went onto the sniper training range, met CIA and FBI recruits going through their basic weapons training, and got access to areas normally off-limits to civilians.

Charlie was very proud of me and showed me off in the officer's club on base – and being an Aussie Vietnam Vet had its pluses. Many of these guys had been over there; the Americans had only withdrawn the year before, just months ago.

On my birthday, 20 January, the Davises' neighbours, Paul and Sue Sutcliff, came over to celebrate with us.

Paul was a captain in the army, a pilot, and had flown in Vietnam; Sue, his wife, was a Kiwi – we instantly hit it off. They invited us to stay with them in their Open Road, which is like a motorhome on steroids. It was huge.

Paul and Sue had four kids – three boys and a girl – who fostered Wendy and me as second parents. Jackie and Charles were just across the lawn, so we were one big happy family.

Both Paul and Sue were into motorbikes. Paul was president of the US Riders, a local motorbike club, so every weekend Wendy and I doubled up behind Paul and Sue respectively and rode all over the state. It was nothing for 50 members to form two files and ride 100 miles for breakfast, another 100 for lunch, and then the ride home of a couple of 100 miles.

The beautiful old Southern homesteads were still there in abundance, so too the cotton – but not the slavery. Riding pillion through these endless fields was almost dreamlike; I filmed as we rode, and lowering the movie camera felt a bit like stepping out of one movie into another, beyond reality.

Also, beyond true, was an experience Wendy and I had one afternoon when both Paul and Sue were at work.

A guy came to the door, telling us he was there to do an evaluation to paint the house. That night, Paul explained the house had just been painted, and all military homes in the area were painted under army contracts.

The place had been cased for a robbery. Paul called the cops, who were straight to the point: 'Have your Aussie mate wait inside. When he breaks in, shoot him. If you blow him outside, drag him back inside, then call us!'

They knew who he was.

'Seriously?'

'Seriously!' they assured me. 'Don't fuck with the bloke, he'll not think twice about shooting you!'

I stayed home alone for three days armed with a .357 Magnum, but the guy was a no-show.

The Fort Benning experience was, for me, one of many great revelations and insights. I'd always had great respect and admiration for Vietnam chopper pilots, both US and Australian. Paul was the real deal, a squadron leader in Vietnam, and now a 2IC of the air wing at Fort Benning.

One night, late, he took me on base and sat me up-front in the captain's seat of a Chinook (a large twin-rotor chopper), and we went through the works and jerks of these amazing birds.

He explained things such as a pressure switch that indicates if a rotor is damaged. They are full of gas for strength – a bullet, or crack, can cause it to fly to pieces. I nearly choked when he showed me the low-fuel light bulb on the controls.

'We'd snap these off when the pressure was on and had no time to refuel – no gas stations out in the jungle. Bloody annoying, and better off not knowing,' he said, with a deadly serious grin.

One of his buddies, Clarke, who was a dead ringer for Australia's Ugly Dave Gray, saw a great opportunity when the US government started selling off its surplus aircraft at the end of the war. Clarke and Paul had flown together in Vietnam. When Clarke heard of a remote development taking place atop some mountain in the middle of nowhere (maybe Alaska) he told the developers he could 'lift' all their pre-fab buildings – from crew's quarters to completed buildings – straight from their factories to their foundations, saving them a fortune in time and cost.

After lowering his first structure, millimetre-perfect, onto the stumps a crew had built, he was in business. It made him an overnight millionaire.

The US Riders had a huge bearing on our future plans. We wanted to go to Africa and then overland home to Australia via Asia; motorbikes would be a great way of doing that.

Wendy loved the open air and freedom of riding, but had never ridden solo. We began putting together a basic plan.

We had established a large group of friends in the USA and I lost count of the amount of farewell parties we had – although we'd never yet left. It was always 'stay a little longer, please'.

But eventually we were back on the road, westbound for California.

It's the equivalent of driving from Melbourne to Perth, and vast stretches of the country look very similar – desert. Las Vegas, the Grand Canyon, Hoover Dam are all in the middle of nowhere.

We enjoyed meeting the Hopi and Apache, and learning the culture of a land occupied, not too unfamiliar to our own. We picked up hitch-hikers, full-blooded native Americans thumbing a ride home from college and university to go and spend holidays and weekends on the reservation with family.

I would love to have bought a real native American blanket – and saw many being woven – but they were worth a fortune, way out of our budget. The trading posts we visited across many states, including Alabama, Mississippi, Texas, New Mexico, Arizona, and eventually California, were a treasure trove of anything and everything you could wish for.

We decided to buy our bikes in Europe and ride on home from there. The XL350 Honda-style bike was what we had been looking at, a mix of road-dirt bike, manageable enough for Wendy to ride, and would serve our purpose; we figured when we hit Africa we would need an off-road capability.

I had my mate sell my boat, *Bombora*, to give us the money for both bikes, and extra cash for the months ahead.

Selling the Cadillac in LA was a joke. If prices were cheap on the East Coast for cars, the West Coast was ridiculous – the best offer I got was US$100! We had bought our tickets to Europe, and the cab fare to LAX airport would have been around US$100. So we drove ourselves to the airport, left the keys in the ignition, gave her a big hug and a kiss and left her in the carpark for anyone who cared to take her.

It was now 10 March 1976, and instead of hanging around for the Montreal Olympics we flew out for Madrid, Spain.

We immediately fell in love with Madrid, and Spain. It remains my favourite country after Australia. Everything is *mañana* and siesta is the greatest thing. If everything happens tomorrow in the big picture, nothing happens today while it's siesta. A wave of the hand with the solitary word, 'siesta', and that's final. You've gotta love it.

In every park around Madrid there were kids with a set of fake horns on a broomstick playing matador, and those without visions of becoming the next greatest matador were kicking a soccer ball around. I tried my hand at both with the kids, much to their amusement, leaving the field of play with a set of horn bruises on my arse on more than one occasion.

Wendy and I checked out every motorbike shop in the city, with no luck; as we were riding back towards Asia, we needed Asian bikes, for parts and service.

We headed back north – hopefully more luck in France.

We did stop in Barcelona and took in a bullfight there. Teaming up with a group of Aussie tourists, we all barracked for the bulls. Talk about a blood sport, and one-sided – the poor bloody bull doesn't stand a chance. By the time the picadors and toreadors have weakened it, it's almost finished before the matador makes an appearance. As a farmer, horseman, hunter and sportsman, I was appalled. I left the arena feeling sickened. I would never recommend anyone witnessing such a cruel 'sport'.

France produced no suitable bikes either, so it was onwards, back to Germany – eventually to the city of Karlsruhe, to the north-west of Munich, on the edge of the Black Forest. From the bus we spotted a large bike shop with 'Honda and Yamaha' boldly displayed. Bingo!

We booked into the biggest and flashiest youth hostel we had ever seen, and next morning we were on the doorstep of the bike shop before it opened. They had no XL350 Hondas, but they had a CB360 Honda, the exact bike Sue owned back in the States. Wendy was immediately in love, she had done her entire biking career on the back of one. The only problem being our German was still non-existent, and the sales staff couldn't speak English!

An American tourist who spoke fluent German came to our aid. The bike shop owner was away at the Berlin motorbike show and, being the world release of the brand-new Yamaha DT400, there were brochures on the counter that caught my eye. Through a call to the boss in Berlin, I was informed I could buy it, but would have to wait ten days – till the show was over – to get it back to Karlsruhe.

I bought it off a brochure; it was the only black one to ever be produced, especially for its launch at the Berlin show. I paid for both bikes there and then.

'We don't have motorbike licences; how do we go about that?' asked Wendy on the walk home.

'Watch and learn, my love,' I replied. I bought an ink stamp pad, then a couple of firm potatoes.

From our vast collection of coins from the various places we'd been, I selected one about the size of the stamp on our international driver's licences. I used the coin and a razor blade to made a 'potato stamp', practising until I had it about 90% right, and then, with a gentle twist/smudge, had it looking as authentic as our car licence stamp. I stamped some paper until most of the potato juice was replaced with blue ink, and then stamped 'Motorcycle' on both our international driver's licences. 'Now you are a licensed motorcycle rider,' I said, handing Wendy back her licence.

Next day we collected the Honda. Wendy was still to ride solo on a motorbike, so I headed for the nearest park. When she had it pretty good, I simply stepped off the back and let her go.

She was still talking to me, asking me when to stop, before she realised I'd gone. 'Slow circle – and back to me,' I shouted from afar.

'F U C K,' I got in reply.

'Don't drop it – it's YOUR NEW BIKE.'

She returned and stopped perfectly. I was then sacked, and every kid in that hostel took turns to chase her around parks and footpaths for the next week – soon she was changing gears like a trooper.

My bike arrived in a wooden crate two weeks later; the shop owner was also back, and his English was better than our German.

'You ride to Australia? Through Africa? You crazy?'

I helped him put my bike together one Saturday morning, then sat back and admired her.

Much bigger, and more powerful than I had envisaged, I too did the park thing for a day before I felt game enough to take on the traffic.

We had crash bars fitted to protect our legs, carry-racks to carry tents, spares, food, fuel, everything we would need for the journey home. With helmets and full wet-weather riding suits, boots, gloves and goggles, we looked the part if nothing else.

One morning the hostel owner said he and his wife were taking holidays.

'I want you to move into our quarters and manage the hostel while we are gone,' he said. 'You stay for free, meals included – yes?'

And so we were official managers of Karlsruhe Hostel for two weeks.

Leaving was sad. We had made many friends – managing the hostel had introduced us to hundreds of kids passing through. Now it was time for the biggest, boldest leg of our two-year travels. Dangerous, yes, but it was my job to get us home safely. Wendy deserves an enormous amount of credit; I know many men who wouldn't, and couldn't, do what she did.

The long way home

We were on our way.

Wendy's Honda road bike could carry more weight than my Yamaha DT400; with the proper carry frames that we had fitted to both bikes, along with high-back Easy Rider chrome rollbars, our backpacks fitted straight on. I bought all the possible spares for both bikes I thought we'd need.

Once more we headed into France, coming back down the eastern border towards Spain. It was April, and we were on the border of the Swiss Alps; it snowed most days.

It's bloody cold on a motorbike! With the constant threat of drama in poor visibility, on icy roads, we moved on, carefully. Spain and sun wasn't that far ahead.

In France we travelled through some of the most beautiful country I'd ever seen. An ancient alpine region tucked away in the most stunning landscape: breathtaking mountains and trees covered in snow, lakes surrounded by the most beautiful woods, and valleys in a green I'd not seen before – as if mixed by an artist to add even more light and beauty.

The rules were, our bikes were our horses. They got fed and watered first, then bedded down safely, before we did anything else. If we didn't hold the key to where they were locked up for the night, we weren't staying! Those bikes were equal to our passports – invaluable.

Only the cold took the edge off the great sense of joy and freedom we both felt. The breakaway point from winter to summer really began at the French/Spanish border, high up in the Pyrenees mountains.

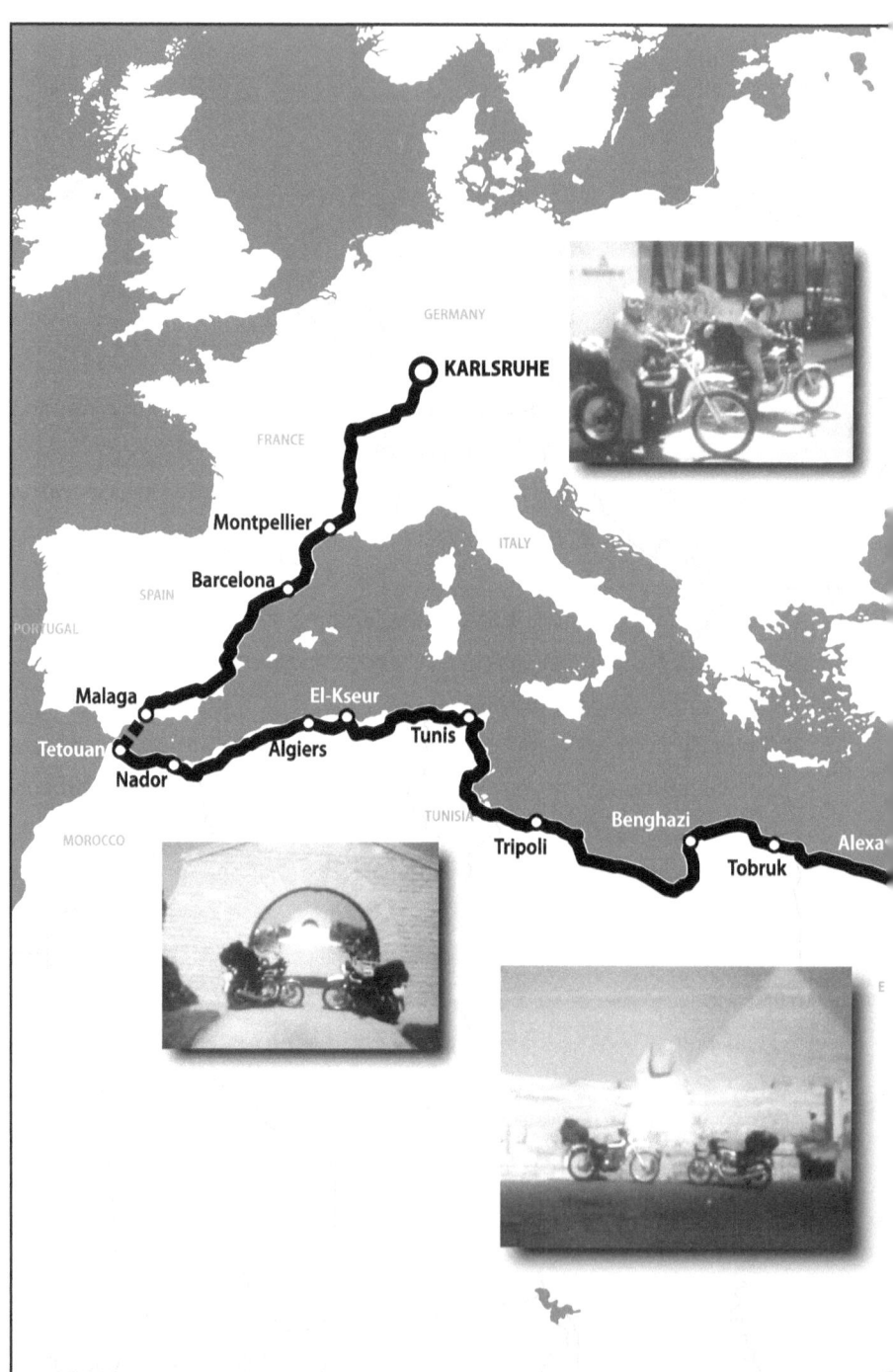

The long way home
Karlsruhe, Germany, to Karachi, Pakistan

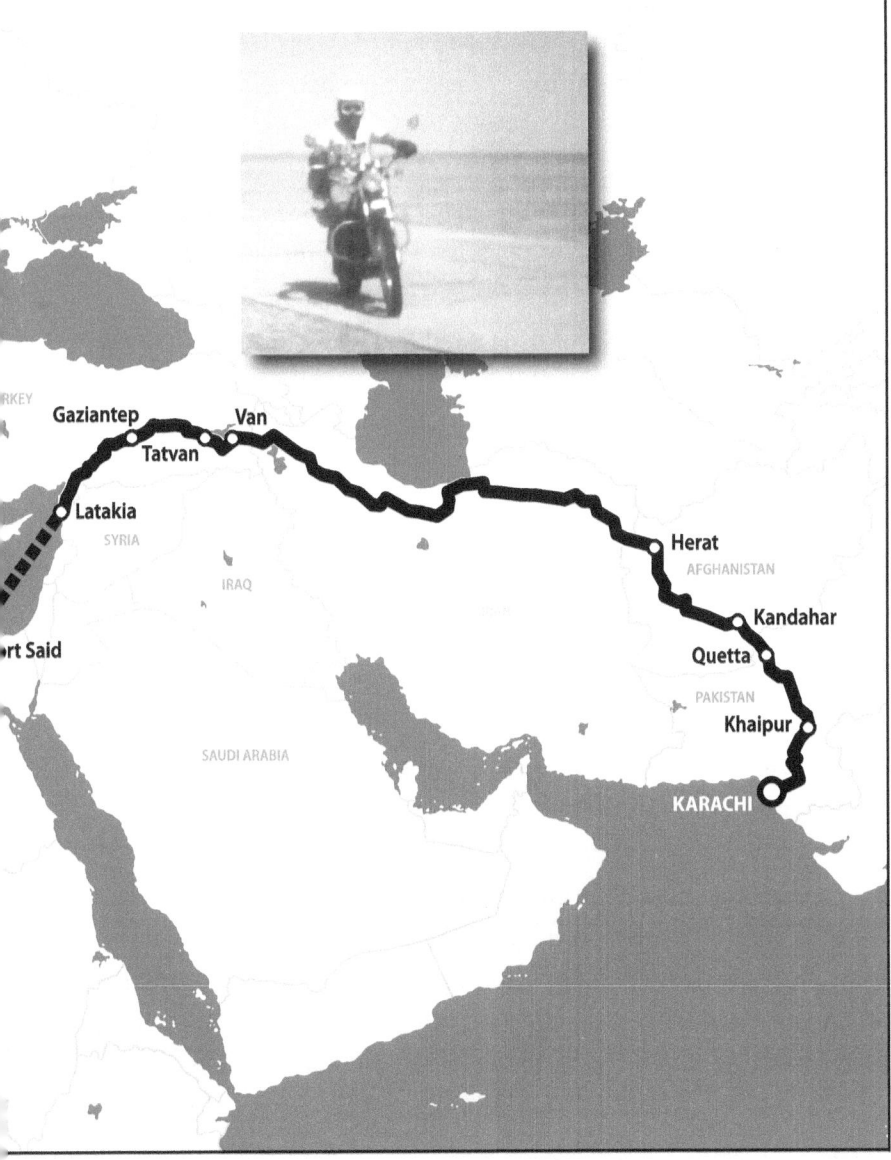

Our passports were stamped under falling snow up in the forest, then we bathed in beautiful blue cloudless skies down in the first Spanish valley at the foot of the mountains an hour later.

Who knew, in the months ahead, that we would witness a possible murder, a few serious incidents in countries on the brink of war, and I would be lucky to escape with my life from a bar in Tehran.

Now it was warm, our journey was a whole new experience. Riding suits gave way to jeans, T-shirts and jackets, the sun felt great on our backs as we headed for Africa.

Wendy and I may have witnessed a murder, or the prelude to a murder, in May 1976, 20km to the east of Malaga, up in the sand dunes overlooking the Mediterranean sea.

We had found a track into the sand dunes off the main highway, stopped early, pitched the tent and started cooking when, in the distance below us, a car pulled in. A young couple proceeded to have sex in and around the car for hours. Then we saw they were also being watched by someone very close to the car, hidden in the bushes – a silent, sinister presence, with a gun. We were miles from anywhere. He stalked them until dark. We never heard a shot, but next morning the car and all three people were gone. If something did go down around that date, I have Super 8 footage of what happened till night fell.

Next morning, the sky was that sparkling Spanish blue that to see is to believe. The ride along that coastline was probably the most memorable of the entire ride home for me.

We were headed for the departure port at Algeciras, as was everybody else, and as we entered the city outskirts it became a four-lane hell. We were the only motorbikes in among thousands of cars. A couple of young blokes in a convertible thought it would be funny to cut Wendy off. It nearly put her down. I rode up alongside her. She was shaken, but OK. I indicated to move over onto the shoulder out of the traffic and wait.

I was furious. In seconds I was at the convertible driver's door, looking him in the eye.

'Yes – me, fucker, now do you want to play?'

He wasn't pulling over. Bikers are mad, dangerous, and this one looked it! Neither of them were laughing now, as I rode up both sides of them and kicked in every panel on that little sports car. I kicked the shit out of it – doors, guards – while the two very embarrassed souls cringed within it. They were of course praying for green lights, and their god answered their call. It was the most expensive outing that car ever had, my number 14s left toe holes everywhere except the grill and floor.

'You bloody idiot, you could have been killed!' Wendy shouted, as she led the way off the freeway to the port.

The ferry was packed next morning as we shoved off from Spain, past the Rock of Gibraltar. Arriving at customs in Morocco, we endured an organised stuff-up of monumental proportions. The bodies of rusted-out cars that hadn't made it through littered each side of the sandy road, going back generations, it appeared.

We got through eventually and found a magnificent place to camp, right on the foreshore of the Mediterranean; sand, palm trees, it was simply perfect. A lone Bedouin approached on a camel, with another two camels in tow. We had a turn on his camel, and when we handed him a pack of cigarettes he was adamant we should not stay there the night. Only weeks before a German couple had their throats cut, murdered by thieves.

We broke camp and moved on before dark. On the road, a mob of 'chamals' appeared right in front of us, settling down on the road for the night, as the concrete held the day's heat and the desert night air is cold. We made for Tetouan and found a camping ground under military guard before re-pitching our tent. Others there had also been warned against desert thieves who will murder without hesitation.

This blew my theory that we would save money camping out in the desert all the way across to Egypt. I had been offered a black-market pistol in Germany but had thought better of it. Instead, I purchased a good tomahawk, and a 6-inch Bowie knife – good for camping needs and enough to keep an unarmed mob at bay.

But I needed a Plan B, there were legs across this vast expanse where we couldn't get accommodation and would have to sleep out.

Night security became my focus, along with keeping two bikes in premium condition when the days were 50 degrees and the nights sub-zero.

Motorbikes have a kill switch, a red switch on the handlebars to kill all power, and this is where I focused, extending the length of lever-switch to make it easier to activate, then connecting a tripwire to that extension. Ironically, the same tripwire flare as in the killing ground of a night ambush.

In the end, it was as simple as two ice-cream sticks, a roll of insulation tape, a roll of fishing line, and extra wire tent pegs.

By taping the ice-cream sticks to the kill switches, it took little effort to flick them on-off. Then I turned on everything – hazard lights, headlights – and taped down the horns, before placing each bike facing in opposite directions with the kill switch off. After that, I ran fishing line around our camp perimeter, 6–8 inches above ground level, and secured it with the extra tent pegs. With the kill switches linked to each other, no matter which direction the threat entered our perimeter, both kill switches would switch on together, instantly.

High-pitched horns blaring, headlights on high beam lighting up the night, and flashing hazard lights, it even scared the shit out of me on my first trial run.

The Atlas Mountains were dark, and eerie rain only added to the gloom. Often we rode through low cloud, which added to the unusual contrast travelling from desert into cold and wet. We stopped every hour for a smoke, to stretch our backs and legs and let the blood flow back into our butts.

On the first stop, a man in a hooded, full-length brown garment appeared from nowhere, simply stepping out of the tree-line.

'*Kief*,' he kept saying, over and over, holding up a leather bag that hung from his belt, and offering me his long-stemmed clay pipe. '*Kief*.'

I had no idea what he was saying, and his dark eyes beneath the hood didn't offer kindness.

'Let's go,' I said. Next hour, next stop, same deal – another guy in a hooded cloak, offering '*kief*'.

It was becoming unnerving.

'He's offering you pot,' said Wendy. I had lost my sense of smell when I got gassed in Vietnam.

'He is?'

I had sworn off hash for life, but pot had never done me any serious harm – so let's not be unsociable.

'OK – yes please.'

I took a hit from his clay pipe. Wendy looked daggers.

'Are you totally insane – riding up here stoned? What are you thinking!'

She rode off. By the time I caught her it was taking effect – mild, not the 'green-out, I'm going to die' effect.

I gave her a smile and a thumbs-up. From then on the journey through the Atlas Mountains became a new, very enjoyable experience. I looked forward to my hourly stops, there was always someone there with '*kief*', which I later learnt was the low-grade leaf, the dregs from the harvest, not the resinous head. But being Morocco it was fresh, and put a smile on my dial every day, much to Wendy's annoyance.

The Western Sahara War was still on. It was sobering to learn the border we had crossed in the morning was attacked later that night, resulting in many deaths, both civilian and military.

We crossed over into Algeria around midday, in pissing-down rain, and pushed on, hoping to find a hotel. We gave up just on dark and headed for an orchard, with me leading the way. Suddenly the headlights picked up a guy in a poncho. He had an AK47 across his chest.

Fuck, I thought, *this guy is a sentry.*

Wheeling around, my headlights picked up a full squadron of tanks backed up into the trees, an entire fucking army!

'Back – back!' I shouted to Wendy, heading back from where we came.

Cold, wet, and back out in the traffic again, Wendy was not happy. We rode another hour in the dark; she took her first spill in that downpour on a greasy dirt road just in sight of the hotel. No harm done, just pride.

Eventually we were warm, dry and comfortable, and over dinner I told her of the army ahead, the reason for the sudden about-face.

'They were probably just army guys on a bivouac – they wouldn't have minded if we camped near them,' she said, still pissed off. Next morning the border attack was all over the TV and newspapers. Our guys weren't out there duck hunting.

We made for Algiers, the capital. On the outskirts of the city, with crowds on the roadside, a motorbike cop on a BMW pulled up alongside me, challenging me to a drag race.

He didn't stand a chance, my Yammie had torque, speed, and was much more manoeuvrable than the slow old Beamer. Then we paced side by side, him smiling like crazy at being beaten.

After kicking his arse right across town, with Wendy bringing up the rear, we pulled over. He was a great guy and conceded defeat graciously. We stood talking, and having a smoke, while the motorbike rally this cop was supposed to be flanking went by. The guy who won it on an old beat-up BMW road bike turned around and came straight back to where we were parked. Yousef, a biker, an Algerian, and known by everybody, including the motorbike cop, introduced himself. He turned out to be our next lucky card. Not only did his family own a guesthouse, his mum worked in an embassy. He invited us to stay.

The ride to his home was like the Dakar Rally, he was still in race mode and knew every street and pothole through the old, crowded city. Wendy and I, fully loaded, struggled to keep up. It was all uphill, but quite spectacular when we reached the summit. The city retained its post-war French influence and the guesthouse was a tall, narrow structure, squeezed between old stone buildings from all sides. It was about four floors high, with a communal kitchen commanded by Yousef's mum, and a mix of many nations on the guest list. Yousef had just finished university in Paris. His mum was single, French and a real sweetheart – she was everyone's mum.

Wendy and I were given a double room and treated like family from the moment we arrived. The other guests were mainly businessmen passing through, or the permanents – students, or construction workers.

Most had a little English, but around the table at mealtimes we could all communicate. It was a fascinating and interesting time.

Through Yousef's mum, we found all the right embassies and over five days had all we needed to make Egypt. I'd also gone right over both bikes. Oil changes, new filters, a steam-clean, tune the motors and spokes, a check for any wear marks. There were tears all round when we announced we had to go. And on the morning we left, a little girl led her baby camel for miles just to show us.

We had learnt a lot: never ride at night; try and ride at first light; stop during the hottest time of day; reach your hotel, or hostel, or stable before dark. We found that riding at 50mph was just right to keep the bikes cool. Any more, or any less, and you could feel the heat radiation against your legs – 50 degrees is hot. Take a piss on the sand, and before you zip up it's gone – that's how hot!

One day's riding on all oils, except Castrol Oil, is all you could get before it turned to milk. I tried every major brand of oil available anywhere in the world (keeping in mind this was oil country), but only Castrol (and this is an unpaid commercial), in both bikes, would go three to four days.

The road had been laid by Rommel during World War II; it was made of sections of huge concrete blocks laid butted up against each other for thousands of miles. Where the concrete had deteriorated, it had been repaired and the surface had been bituminised. In 50-plus degrees all day, the concrete held its heat – hard on tyres by day, and easy on the wildlife at night in sub-zero temps. Hit and kill a camel sleeping on the road at night and it will cost you a motza – even if it's a wild camel, someone will own it. If it's a female you're also dead – that female could have ten offspring, each worth upwards of $2000 a pop. Get the picture?

Making matters worse, the concrete blocks had shifted over time, so it was similar to travelling on a boat. However, it was incredible to be riding along with huge herds of wild camels blending into the heat haze.

We stopped, intrigued by some very young kids with a large camel herd up in the sand dunes. As we approached, it became obvious we were scaring them – they began throwing stones at us. So we took off our helmets and had a smoke. A young boy edged his way closer, fascinated, afraid, uncertain – but still determined to get a good look at us. I told Wendy to ignore him and got the Super 8 out. Being ignored, he decided to catch our attention – pointing to the sky then us.

'He thinks we're Martians,' said Wendy. She's a qualified special needs teacher, she knows kids better than I do. Since the international currency is cigarettes, I placed a pack of French crap I couldn't smoke on a rock. He was onto them like a seagull onto a chip.

Wendy filmed the lot, even him pointing to her helmet then the sky – she was right, we were probably the very first people these kids had ever seen on motorbikes, in full riding suits with helmets, on these strange machines. We probably did look like Martians. Two small girls, perhaps his sisters, took an hour before they were game enough to come close. Through sign language we worked out they were Bedouins from deep south of where we were – their camels followed the feed and new growth.

I thought it never rained in the Sahara, and almost every day since leaving Morocco it had rained every bloody day. We have film of riding in the Sahara with water over our knees on the bikes! That weather had brought these Bedouins north.

I rode one of their camels and they all took turns to sit on our bikes. Then we went back into our respective worlds.

Tunisia, at the time, was biblical. Away from towns or villages it was like travelling through a chapter in the Bible. Men dominated society, to be found drinking short glasses of sweet black tea, large groups sitting in tea-houses all day. Women were covered from head to toe, showing no trace of skin, and the streets teemed with animal life. Donkeys, camels, goats, dogs, these were all a symbol of someone's wealth – and to me it appeared they took all their wealth to town each day to show off. Riding through this traffic was nigh on impossible, it was so thick.

Accommodation in Tunis was rough and ready. I had to lock up the bikes in a stable opposite the hotel, wire-cabled to each other and the building, with the old owner's assurance they would not be touched. Two local cops supervised the exchange of keys. I dropped in unexpectedly every other hour to check, but the owner's two sons were standing guard over the bikes – and *nobody* got near them.

Wendy was in her element. The roadside stores were a treasure-trove, she would sit for ages with the women and girls, capable of communicating perfectly over each item that caught her eye. I had visions of needing a trailer to haul out half of what she fancied. Rolls of handwoven fabric – it was beautiful, even to a rough old bushie like me.

My bike being a two-stroke, with a dual-feed fuel mix – oil and petrol – decided to readjust herself in the heat. Coming out of a sub-zero European winter to 50-plus degrees in the shade, I was tearing my hair out trying to get the right mix. I even had Wendy ride my bike while I followed on hers to see the colour and quantity of the blue smoke. Now we were in the central Sahara we could expect extreme heat; keeping those motors cool, lubricated and happy was life-saving, a blown motor in the middle of nowhere meant serious, life-and-death-type trouble. I messed about with different two-stroke oils, preferring a little more than a little less oil mix, and put her all back together – much to the interest of my audience in the stable. It was like they were witnessing the birth of Christ. Keeping in mind – modern, Japanese motorbikes had never been seen in these parts, a 1942 Norton, or BMW, was a modern bike to them.

One afternoon we stopped at an oasis in the middle of nowhere. A huge animal-skin tent, identical to those of a thousand years ago, sat back away from the oasis. The people from the caravan were all heavily tattooed, the women's faces completely tattooed. They preferred to remain away from the water, and shade, and other people. I took the camera and moved closer to see this amazing piece of history frozen in time. Wendy followed. Suddenly women and children appeared out of thin air, blocking our way.

'Stop filming,' Wendy said, thinking this was the problem. I packed it up and again tried to move closer – same deal, we were blocked. Then a boy took my hand to lead me forward while Wendy was told in sign language, 'not you'!

When I approached the huge tent, a side rolled up facing away from the oasis, and there sat a group of very old men with long white beards. I was asked to sit down, in sign language, and handed hot black tea in a glass – it was sweet as honey. For an hour we discussed them, me, and smoked a hookah water-pipe. I don't know one word of Arabic, nor did any of them speak English – yet we got to know much about each other, which Wendy filmed from a distance. It's a male-dominated society, women don't sit in on such meetings – in fact women don't get spoken to, from my observations, they simply follow on with the animals as a symbol of a man's achievements. Tunisia then was still very untouched by Western influence; even a bottle of coke was almost non-existent.

It was in Tunisia that we slept in the desert for the first time. I set up the tent and bikes with fishing-line tripwire pegged out around our perimeter. We were well off the road, too far to be seen by the naked eye, but a mountain range on the opposite side of the road would have given our camp away to anyone up there. After dinner we tucked up inside our three-man tent, tomahawk and Bowie knife under my groundsheet.

Movement woke me in the quiet night. With my head that close to the ground, and after lots of practice, it was as if someone was ringing the front door bell.

Slowly I took up the tomahawk. Then on cue all hell broke loose.

Both horns were blazing, both headlights on full beam, the whole surrounding area flashed orange from eight hazard lights.

I was through the flap in a second, sweeping both handlebars to scan the night with long high beams. A riderless donkey was bolting back towards the mountains. Neither hide nor hair of the rider. The thief, I suspect, crawled on his belly all the way back to the road. I looked for a long time. Wendy went back to sleep, but I was happier sitting over a fire with my weapons at the ready.

Libya was a sobering ordeal, right from the concrete arrival zone. As different as chalk and cheese – from one time zone to another. Being ex-military, I know a slick outfit when I see one, and those Libyan border guards, all military, were turned out immaculately. Starched jungle greens, ironed to knifepoint creases, highly polished combat boots, and Russian-made assault rifles – brand new, cleaned and oiled. These blokes didn't just look the part, they knew what they were doing. Our bikes were thoroughly searched; everything that was bolted to the frames came off, everything we owned thoroughly scrutinised.

After a two-hour ordeal, and for the first time ever, we were issued new number plates, in Arabic, to cover our German-issued international tourist plates. It wasn't optional.

With our new Libyan tags and stamped visas, we were on our way to Tripoli, on roads like Sydney or Melbourne freeways – big, wide, smooth, beautiful. The country's wealth was on display everywhere, everywhere except in the pockets of the locals. Two-door Mercedes Benz coupes were as common as donkeys, but the guys on the donkeys still had the arse out of their pants.

It was gorgeous riding weather, blue skies, the rain had stopped, and our bikes loved the amazing surface after weeks of uneven concrete blocks. We made for the coast, coming across a massive tourist complex, a 20-storey hotel with a pool and all the trimmings, completely deserted, sand and tumbleweed from the desert taking over everything.

A blue vehicle had followed us from the border, keeping its distance, but definitely following us. We didn't particularly want to go into Tripoli, the capital, so skirted our way around, reaching the township of Misrata on the coast in the late afternoon. We were mobbed coming into town. People ran beside our bikes cheering and applauding, bringing us to a standstill in the town centre.

Out of nowhere, a Sydney Harbour lottery ticket was flashed under my nose.

'Welcome Australia,' said the well-dressed, friendly young bloke waving it at me. 'I have Australian girlfriend,' he added proudly.

Soon the mayor of the town arrived and gave us an official welcome. We were at a loss as to what was going on – but noted the blue car was still parked up the street, watching us. We were taken to the best hotel in town, not surprisingly owned by the mayor!

Our new friend with the Australian lottery ticket hadn't left our side, even pulling up a chair beside us for dinner. Out of earshot he told us what was going on in Libya – in short, Gaddafi had seized all passports, Libyans were not free to travel. The Americans had been kicked out, and the abandoned high-rise development had once housed hundreds of American oil workers. There were billions of dollars from oil money to build new roads and infrastructure – but under a dictatorship. Our mate, who we discovered owned most of the heavy machinery building all the new roads, had lived in Europe with his Aussie (Sydney) girlfriend until he was recalled to Libya. When his passport was seized he was trapped. Well aware we were being followed, we told him about it over dinner. It was common, he assured us.

'All this wealth … cars, machines, trucks, I employ many, many, men. But I have no liberty,' he said in a whisper. 'Tonight, I show you.'

After dark there was a knock on our door, we must be 'clifty', he warned, holding a finger to his lips to indicate no talking.

'I think he means shifty,' I said to Wendy – but from then on he was known to us as Clifty.

We took the back door out into the night, and I couldn't see us, much less anyone else. Clifty led us down back lanes, through people's houses – at one point I fell over a sleeping camel, lying fully across our path.

Wendy and I were in stitches of laughter, with the continual warning that we 'must be Clifty!'

Some way from the last row of streets we came out into the desert; Caterpillar D8 bulldozers, as well as graders, rollers, and row after row of new tip trucks, covered acres of levelled ground.

'Mine,' said Clifty. 'All mine.'

It was literally millions of dollars' worth of equipment, far too much to count. In the centre stood a number of brand-new Mercedes Benz cars, parked around a mud house. American music came softly through the walls as we drew closer. A look-out posted in the cab of a grader waved to Clifty as we passed.

Inside the windowless mud house sat a dozen guys – all of them plant operators at a glance, as they still wore the day's dust and dirt from head to toe.

'Hello Australia – welcome,' came the chorus. I was dumbfounded to be handed a beer. The playing of Western music was enough to get everyone in serious trouble, all alcohol is banned in the country – and by combining the two we could face a firing squad. It only got worse – joints were going around, one after another.

'You had better be the responsible one here Wendy – I'll take a hit just to be social,' I said. *Clifty – you are a legend*, I thought.

We stayed with Clifty and his employees till the early hours. It was odd, to say the very least, to be inside a mud house with a dirt floor with the latest modern electrical appliances from stereos, air conditioners, fridge-freezers, and all the workers driving brand-new BMWs or Benz cars. But the men were miserable.

'No women, no privileges – no liberty,' they all complained. Clifty was a very wealthy young man, from a privileged family no doubt, as he had studied in Europe and must have had influence to get the road-making contracts. He told us his girlfriend, now back in Sydney, sent him a Sydney Harbour lottery ticket every month. He still had plans to marry her and hinted that each day he could cross back into Tunisia through his roadworks. He never said it, but we got the feeling he had plans to simply not come back one day.

Pissed, stoned, and having spent a very political (anti-Gaddafi) night, we stumbled and fell over many more donkeys and camels on our return to our hotel. The blue car was still there, parked down the street.

Next day we hit the road again early, farewelled by Clifty, who shed a tear at our departure. He loved to hear the Aussie accent, he said, but he was grieving his loss of liberty and the girl he loved.

We also learnt from him that Libya was divided into two provinces, Tripoli and Benghazi; a huge archway marked the spot. Legend has it a man from each city ran towards the other, and where they met is where the arch and division of provinces arose.

Along the road we encountered oil refineries, oil pumped up out of the desert from pipelines that extended hundreds of miles south into the Sahara.

These refineries, once American-owned and operated, were now all Gaddafi's; the complexes were wired off, but inside there were still shopping centres for the European staff who had replaced the Americans.

Tobruk had always been a very special place to me. The Rats of Tobruk are famous in Australian history, more so for me as one of Dad's army mates, Garry Martin, was a Rat of Tobruk who had won a Military Medal for his actions there. It was a place I wanted to visit. Twenty kilometres before Tobruk we saw the sign, Knightsbridge Cemetery, the resting place of all Australian, New Zealand and South African soldiers killed during this campaign.

An old Arab, black from the sun, and thin from years of hard labour, greeted us; he was the caretaker.

This ground to him was more than sacred, it was where he looked after all his mates. The place was spotless, immaculate, and he had kids with donkeys carting water continually from a nearby well to water the roses that grew in abundance. I dropped my cigarette butt in the sand and he carefully bent down and transferred it into his pocket.

He had served with these men, they were his mates in life and in death. He took us around this beautiful tribute out in the desert, far from the eyes of the world. To him, it was his world. We shot a lot of film there, and I assured this lovely old gentleman that what he was doing would be taken back to Australia and shared with others who would have served there, who would really appreciate his love and dedication. I can't recall ever seeing a better kept cemetery anywhere. He had turned the desert into a Garden of Eden; he had been at it 21 years, and would die there, 'looking after his mates', as he put it.

On our last night in Libya we stayed in Bardia, in a hotel owned by an Egyptian, in a room with a view clear out onto the ocean just below our window. Over dinner the lights kept going down, then up, then out, then back to normal.

'What's the go?' I finally asked our Egyptian proprietor.

'Censorship,' he said. 'It is Mr Gaddafi stopping Egyptian radio and TV getting to his people. He has the electricity stop when President Sadat speaks.'

It made good sense, as TV and radio signals would travel forever across the flat desert; killing the power was the only way to shut Sadat up. Apparently that night there had been an exchange of pleasantries between the two leaders, calling each other's wives whores! That's when Gaddafi instructed the power station to censor the incoming messages – and disturb everyone's dinner.

So far we had stayed in some rough and ready places, including the desert, and army bases. One night we even stayed in a police station in an outback location, where we locked the two bikes in one cell, and us in another – me holding the keys to both cells. Back then, anywhere at night across the top of Africa was dangerous. People simply disappeared.

We planned our day's ride down to the last kilometre; reaching civilisation before dark was a must for personal safety.

Asking to be locked up for the night took some persuading, both at military and police outposts. But as soon as I had insisted that our embassy had been advised that we would be staying there, under their protection, they would lay it on – we even had breakfast in bed in one jail.

The border crossing between Libya and Egypt proved to be our most memorable. The countries were at the point of war. It had been building up for some time, but now hostilities were at their worst.

'No go!' were the two defining words when we entered the frontier office with our passports and visas.

It was always on, we knew that. The embassy back in Tunisia said as much, and we always had the port to take a ship around to Egypt if worst came to worst. However, I was holding an ace, an ace I hadn't had need for in over a year. If ever there was a time to play it, it was now.

Before I left Australia, Dad handed me an envelope. Inside was a hand-written letter from the Member for Wannon, on official Australian Parliamentary stationery. It said: 'I have known William John Abernethy all his life, and any and all courtesies that can be extended to him while he and his wife Wendy are travelling through your country would be greatly appreciated.' It was signed Malcolm Fraser MP.

When he wrote the letter for Dad he was Minister for Defence; now, in 1976, he was Prime Minister. Knowing the amount of live sheep exports going from Portland (just up the way from Port Fairy) to Libya, I reckoned I might have some pull.

We were at a complete deadlock with the army officers controlling the border. I demanded to speak with an official government representative, unfolded my letter from the Australian Prime Minister and slid it under the boss's nose.

'I would hate to be in your shoes if I have to return to Tripoli to have my Prime Minister's wishes seen to, and God forbid if all that wheat and live sheep were to stop over something as trivial as this.'

An hour later, a big black Mercedes Benz rolled in out of the desert and out stepped four very official-looking types in suits. They asked to see my letter, which I happily produced, retaining it with both hands for them to read. I even helped with a couple of the words.

A very curt nod of the head was followed by an apology, before we were offered tea. The senior officer at the border had been told in Arabic, and I'm sure in no uncertain terms, that we were VIPs and should be given anything we required. We drank tea, I thanked them courteously and added, to Wendy's horror, 'I look forward to our two countries continuing our trade for many years to come.'

The actual frontier was some 10km further down the road, and I was gobsmacked to see what blocked the road when we arrived – 44-gallon drums full of concrete, steel barricades and rolls of barbwire. It took five guys 30 minutes to clear a way for two bikes to pass in single file. Wendy didn't say a word until we were on the bikes again and headed out into no-man's-land, between the Libyan and Egyptian armies.

'I hope our countries continue to trade ...' she yelled, then burst out laughing.

The other side of the border was the complete opposite of the military turn-out displayed in Libya.

Our first sign of human occupation was a tripod of .303 rifles stacked up by a pile of sand – as we drew nearer, a head, then two, and finally a third, rose above the foxhole. We waved and kept rolling forward – keeping in mind this was the frontline of Egypt's defence.

We came across numerous repeats of the three-man foxhole (shell-scrape) with old World War II .303 rifles marking the spot.

No uniforms that I could see, simply Arab garb of pants and flowing shirt. At our first smoke stop, I said to Wendy, 'God help Egypt if Gaddafi decides to come!' His army was a well-oiled machine, with modern, new equipment. Nothing wrong with the good old .303, but it is no match for a modern semi-automatic assault rifle. Moreover, the Egyptian rabble I'd seen so far looked like they'd run if I produced my tomahawk and Bowie knife.

We rolled on towards the coast, hoping to find a hotel before nightfall, as we had heard Egypt was by far the most dangerous Arab country on our route.

An oasis appeared out of the desert haze, shimmering across our vision. It proved to be a huge Tourist Information Centre. A solitary figure headed towards us, pulling on his suit jacket as he ran.

'Welcome – welcome to Egypt.' We were his first visitors in 'some years' from Libya, and given that Libya was their only neighbour, I wondered why he was needed at all. In its heyday, the building could have easily accommodated a thousand people – now there was just Wendy and me, and the tourist officer and his boyfriend. We had tea with them as our passports were stamped, leaving him with the unlikely prospect that he would be seeing anyone else for 'some more years'.

Our first night in Egypt was on the coast at Mersa Matruh, apparently away from the restricted area. If only they knew we had just ridden in from Libya! Town was full of army personnel, and thousands of camels and donkeys.

Next morning, we followed the coast to El-Alamein, another must for me, being a digger. El-Alamein is where the 'Desert Fox', Rommel, got his arse properly kicked by a coalition of Indian, British, South African, Australian and New Zealand forces. It remains a great defeat against, in my opinion, Hitler's smartest, bravest general. Sadly, all that remains (or at least, in 1976), was rusting tanks slowly being claimed by the desert sands. So much blood and hardship, with nothing left to show.

Wendy and I rode on to Alexandria, then south to Cairo. We followed the Nile, rich with agriculture, and bustling with culture old and new – the beautiful old feluccas (sailing boats); herds in their thousands of camels, goats, donkeys, all drinking from this rich source of life flowing through the centre of the country from north to south. Life began and extended out from this river, palms and crops stretching many miles from its banks – but beyond there it was desert, desert and more desert.

We found the central hostel in Cairo and checked ourselves in. It was modern, well-staffed, and central to everything – by foot. The heat was overwhelming. After weeks of riding across the Sahara in 50-plus degree heat, day after day, it wasn't until we were surrounded by concrete buildings that we really discovered its intensity. By midday the bitumen was liquid, a gluey black slime that couldn't be walked on. Come 11am, you found shade and stayed put until sunset. After Morocco and Tunisia, we thought we had seen it all – but we'd seen nothing until we reached Egypt.

With the birth of civilisation coming from this quarter of the world, it was like taking a step backwards in time, to an era before Christ. Modernisation was there, cars, telephones, electricity – but blink and miss any of the three. Sending a telegram from the central post office involved placing your telegram in an empty Johnny Walker box attached by string to the next floor up; watching it get hauled up; waiting 20 minutes for the box to come back down with your confirmation receipt; then praying you hadn't been screwed – which happened by the minute. We were told emphatically *never* to send mail via the post office: stamps are currency, your stamp will be removed, cashed in, and your letter will go straight into the bin.

We learnt all this on day one. But what got me was the paper money may have as many as three values stamped on it, including the original value as printed; because inflation was so erratic, it was cheaper to re-stamp the note than to revalue the currency and print new notes. Some notes were transparent, they were so thin and threadbare – hence $5 worth of stamps was worth $5 in true value. You had to go to the Hilton Hotel and send mail through their daily airmail bag service, the only way you could guarantee your mail leaving the country. We discovered the Hilton had the best restaurant and air conditioning in Cairo. Wendy and I spent at least three hours there every day, watching the local women doing their washing in the Nile just below, while upstream 500 head of camel were washed for market, and further downstream people carted water to sell it.

The main Egyptian Museum in Central Cairo was also a horror show. Your basic bag trolley, as used by potato growers, was the method used to move priceless artefacts around the place where finds from King Tut's tomb and other famous relics are housed. I can still hear Wendy gasp as some dickhead chipped a huge piece out of a water container thousands of years old. It was criminal, clearly there was not enough space to house what they already had – and truckloads more objects were stacking up out on the street. We spent the day in there, amazed at the mummies and the treasures of ancient Egypt. But this was 1976 and it was overflowing then – jam-packed in fact. I can only hope a better facility was found; it was shocking to see how these treasures were being treated.

Market day was Tuesday. Thousands of camels were herded through the city centre, to the saleyards, as has probably happened since Christ was an apprentice carpenter. Do you know how much camel shit that is to wade through afterwards? For all its history, Egypt was a dump, and we couldn't wait to get the hell out of there. We hung in and suffered in order to get our visas from the Australian Embassy.

One night, a couple came around the hostel asking if anyone was interested in being extras in a movie – at five quid Egyptian per night, Wendy and I said why not. They had a bus outside and pretty soon filled it with European kids. We were driven within sight of the Pyramids, then unloaded at a studio, for lack of a better word, where we waited, and waited and waited – almost all night. In short, the movie entitled *Where Have They Hidden the Sun?* was an Egyptian production, and our bit was supposed to be a European nightclub scene – debauchery: drinking, smoking, dancing etc. It was a week's work.

On the last day of shooting, we rode our bikes out to the set in the morning and toured around the Pyramids, the Sphinx, and mixed with the desert traders. Just when I thought I had been rocked to my socks by the ways of our Egyptian kinfolk there was a final shock. Why has much of the smooth rock surface on the Pyramids gone? For roads, of course. Ingenious Egyptian road-makers dismantled the outer layer to create a smooth road surface. On your drive out to the Pyramids, you are actually driving on the Pyramids! Were it not for the Wimpy Bar and the Hilton Hotel, I don't think I could have survived Cairo.

Finally, cashed up and with the visas we needed, we hit the road back north to Alexandria.

Visiting Israel was a no-go; with all the Arabic, especially Egyptian, visas stamped in our passports, Syria was our only way forward. We bought tickets for a Russian cruise ship out of Alexandria to Latakia in Syria. It was US$65 for a cabin, and the two bikes were US$15 to go as deck cargo, but I have never been as thankful in my life to leave a place as I was to leave Egypt. On board ship, Wendy and I made friends with a couple of English guys who had been working on oil rigs.

We hadn't expected a war to break out while we were approaching Syria. Well, an ongoing border skirmish was perhaps the correct term, as Turkey and Syria had been 'at war' for centuries.

As we entered the port of Latakia, the captain announced he would be stopping only long enough to disembark passengers; after that the ship would be returning immediately to sea.

Then, when we reached port, the captain and crew said, 'No unload bikes – no time.'

A huge argument broke out.

There was a crane on the foredeck. 'Can you drive that?' I asked one of the Englishmen. He could.

I sent Wendy ashore with our packs, then slung each bike, one at a time, for the guy in the crane to lower over the side and down to Wendy. The captain was going berserk, the wharfies too, but we, and the bikes, were ashore.

By the time we cleared customs, the ship was gone. Panic spread as locals and tourists alike were told that the Turks were invading across the border.

We made for the Turkish border, riding into the night for Yayladagi, on the Turkish side.

We reached the frontier to chaos: guards were fleeing, people were loading their belongings into vehicles and leaving en masse. In the border crossing complex I spotted a guy boxing up stuff frantically.

'Stamp passport?' I asked politely.

He looked at me in utter disbelief. I spotted the pad and stamp.

'Yes?' I asked, holding them up. He nodded and continued stuffing files into boxes. I stamped our passports and we mounted up and rode north.

An hour after we crossed the border into Turkey I found a great place to camp, high up in the mountains among pine trees, where the lights of Syrian towns could be seen. We bedded down.

Heavy machinery woke us just before daylight.

'Tanks,' I told Wendy.

We quickly hit the road, which we had to ourselves – the tanks were advancing in the cover of the forest. I waved at the first tank that came into view, they waved back – then we saw dozens of them.

'Wave,' I told Wendy, and they all waved back and kept advancing on Syria. We rode on all day without incident.

The roads soon deteriorated into the worst surface we had encountered. That night we quickly discovered just how uncivilised southern Turkey was. Blonde women seemed to be a source of great pleasure to these Turkish men – groups of a dozen or more sat and stared at Wendy for hours at a time. On our first night I had to rearrange the bed so it blocked the door – only to wake in the night to find a guy had removed louvres from a window and was halfway inside. Southern Turkey in 1976 was probably the most dangerous place I have ever been to.

Finally, we arrived at Tatvan on the shore of Lake Van, which is more like an inland sea. We checked into a grotty hotel and soon after met the ferry boat skipper, Raymond, in his pristine white uniform, who took it upon himself to show Wendy and me around. We were then introduced to his tourist officer mate, who would look after us – it was better to take the ferry across to get to Iran than ride all the way around Lake Van.

The tourist officer owned a British Land Rover and offered to take us for an advance inspection of the ferry. It was getting towards dark, but we piled in with three guys and headed off, away from the lake.

I had that gut feeling again. The plan was: get us pissed on vodka, which they were drinking like water, overwhelm me and rape Wendy – or worse! The further we went, the more ominous it became.

With my foot, I found a large shifting spanner under our seat; I grabbed a handful of the front passenger's hair and hauled him backwards over the seat to immobilise him. Then I aimed the shifter at the driver's head.

'Turn this car back to town – NOW, or I kill the driver first,' I yelled. Even Wendy jumped.

The Land Rover quickly headed back towards civilisation, and I didn't let go of either advantage until we pulled up in front of our hotel.

'And you, motherfucker, had better keep your gob shut – or I'll shove this spanner up your arse for my night's entertainment,' I said, throwing the shifter at the tourist officer as we bailed out.

We often wondered how many other innocent tourists had been subjected to this little scam – the skipper, the head of tourism and the local cop (from what we made of it) were all in on it.

Wendy and I hit the road early next morning to ride around Lake Van – a two-day ride as opposed to a comfortable ferry ride, but at what cost!

We were on our way to catch up with Ann Ellis, an airline hostess with Iran Airlines in Tehran. But not before a farewell gift from the Turks.

As we rode past a work crew at 80km/h, a guy on the back of the truck threw a shovel full of gravel into my face. It was like being blasted with a shotgun. I knew the border to Iran was close, very close, and the look Wendy gave me said, *Don't even go there – suck it up*. And so I did.

The crossing into Iran was a godsend. Everyone was friendly, it was clean, rich, the roads and country were a delight, mountainous when we first crossed over the lakes and forest, quite the opposite to where we had been.

We made our way towards the capital, Tehran, and I have never seen so many Hillman Hunter cars in my life; 80% of all cars on the road were Hillman Hunters – 50,000 in all, we later found out, being a trade settlement with Britain.

Ann stayed in a plush suburb shared by the Shah of Iran – you could see his house from the Iran Air compound where Ann shared a house with around six other girls, American, English, and Aussie Ann.

The place was a palace, with 10-foot stone walls, a full-size swimming pool, full-time gardener and full-time maid. The girls were transported to and from the airport by private shuttle-vans. It was Hollywood, and it only got better for me, being the only guy in residence – the girls all sun-baked nude. After Turkey I truly thought I was in heaven.

I set about pulling down both bikes until they were fully restored to brand new and gleaming. Then I couldn't but notice the pool was filthy, and that a duck by the name of Jakob had free rein of the place, including the pool. Jakob had come home alive and stayed that way after the girls discovered poultry was sold live in the markets.

The pool had no pump nor any filtration system – that's why it was black. Once a month the gardener would drain it and refill it with clean water.

I found an abandoned washing machine under the house; the electric motor and pump still worked. I dismantled it until I had a motor and pump, which I bolted to an old door as a base, then I hooked up two hoses: one suction, the other out into the garden. I plugged in my apparatus, held my breath, and hey presto it worked – water pumped at 50 times the rate. However, Iran had no earth to its electrical system; putting a finger in the pool gave enough of a shock to make you keep away.

In an afternoon I had drained the pool, which normally took three days. I was a legend.

Then one night I decided to drain the pool while we were out at dinner. When we arrived home it was down to the dregs – with a black thing out in the middle. Poor old Jakob was taking a late-night dip and got his arse zapped big time! I went from hero to zero in one night.

Back in the 70s, under the Shah, the Americans were everywhere: military bases, American radio, McDonald's, Kentucky Fried Chicken. One of the girls was dating an American radio DJ, which got us invited to all the top spots in town, including a huge party given by Americans in downtown Tehran. Wendy and I stayed the night, crashed on the floor.

They say it's a small world, but coincidence only makes it smaller. After dragging our hangovers out into the street next morning, I realised I'd left my sunglasses behind. Leaving Wendy in a cafe, I literally collided with Ronnie, a former lover from Australia. She was with her partner, and I took them in to Wendy, then went back for my sunnies.

I returned to chaos, a massive brawl was spilling out onto the footpath. Inside I saw Rob, Ronnie's 6 foot 7 partner, fighting people all around him. He was being gang-tackled by the mob. I'd never met him before, but he was Ronnie's partner and he was getting killed. I jumped in.

Always drop the biggest first is my motto. I lined up the guy putting the boot into Rob, catching him flush on the chin with a big right hand. He went down like I'd used a sledge hammer. The guy beside him got a right hook into his left eye and he went down.

I was now convinced we were going to die.

'Get the fuck out of here and keep going,' I yelled to Wendy and Ronnie. To my astonishment, the 30 guys who had been in a blood-lust frenzy were now all backing away. Rob found his feet and bolted down the street, never to be seen again.

Then I saw all these guys were carrying curved knives in their belts – obviously to carve up stupid Australians. The big guy I had dropped was receiving a lot of attention. Now was a good time to go.

Wendy and Ronnie were on the footpath. 'Let's go.'

Just when I thought we were safe, the mob caught up.

They had a cop in tow, and they were carrying the first bloke I'd punched, who was still groggy. They wanted me locked up. The cop had his hands on me and was going for handcuffs. I tried to explain, there were 30 of them and one of me, I never started it.

Then Wendy and Ronnie stepped in to explain the situation to the cop, who fortunately had fluent English. The handcuffs were put away as he feasted upon Ronnie's cleavage.

'You are very lucky man – you fight with your hands,' he explained.

In Tehran, in those days, men who fought with their fists were to be feared. Knocking out the big bloke was a smart move, it probably saved my life.

The drama was over Ronnie – she had just never got it, even after many previous encounters. Being blue-eyed, with long blonde hair, and bra-less under a T-shirt, it wasn't just dumb, ignorant and disrespectful – it was fucking stupid, and I told Ronnie so in no uncertain terms! We never saw Rob again, but Ronnie came over to the girls' house one night, properly dressed I was glad to see.

It was time to get back on the road. We decided to take the northern route – up near the Caspian Sea, the country had a little of everything: national parks, lakes, desert, and good and bad roads. The heat was stifling, 120 degrees some days. There is nowhere to hide from such heat.

Along the way we met people coming in from Australia who had ridden up from Asia. All were telling us tales of massive payments at the Indian border, a 'pass' to be paid to the value of the bikes then reimbursed upon leaving at the other side! The further we went into Afghanistan, the more we heard of it.

The alternative was give the Khyber Pass the arse and travel south down through Pakistan.

Upon reaching Kandahar, in Afghanistan, we had made our decision – go to the embassy and get our visas for Pakistan, then head south. We struck gold; there was an Australian Embassy there, where we were given the VIP treatment by staff upon hearing of our journey thus far.

We were warned, however, that a survey team had been fired upon only days beforehand in the Bolan Pass, the road we had to take to Pakistan. Tribesmen in these parts can take offence at strangers passing through, and as it wasn't a tourist route, we were fair game.

We decided to take our chances. After Ireland, the Spanish Sahara, Libya, Egypt, Syria, Turkey – what were the odds of being nailed with a muzzle-loader this far down the track?

It was primitive, outback of the outback, and bloody hot and dry. But Wendy, God bless her, stuck to the plan. One night, in pouring rain, the road was blocked by 2000 head of camels. Wendy was exhausted, in tears, and over it. Then her bike quit. I walked her with her bike through a raging river, up to our waists and getting higher by the minute, which is why the camels had stopped. Then I went back for my bike. I was washed off my feet getting to it, then bike and I were both washed off. Soaked through, and with my bike not starting when we did emerge, I punched the fuel tank in a rage, leaving a dent still there the day I sold her. But she started very next kick.

We had endured sandstorms, thunderstorms, heat, threats and calm – now the finishing line was in sight, nothing was going to stop us. Pakistan was a tropical paradise once we emerged from its deep endless deserts, and nobody took a shot at us. Riding into Karachi was the end of the road.

'We box the bikes up here baby, put them on a ship to Melbourne, and we fly on home sipping wine.'

Wendy was all for it. And so it was. I spent a week stripping down both bikes, boxing them myself, and seeing them loaded for Australia.

During that week we took a lovely hotel overlooking the main street; we had two house-boys who I paid 50 cents a day to help me clean and pack the bikes. Back then, that was about as much as the receptionist earned a day! At night I would invite the kids in to watch TV, which was a huge treat for them, but not so for me, as Pakistan were kicking our arse in the cricket – not that either kid dared mention it – and the name Imran Khan was forbidden to be spoken, much to their delightful smiles! They cried when we left.

The fishing business, Port Fairy, 1976-1978

Returning to Port Fairy after 20 months on the road, a lot had happened, and a lot had changed. We still had four months until we could get back into our house, for one, and Marty Hearn had sold his pub!

The pub had been my office, and coming home it was a must to inspect – meet the new owner, catch up with old friends.

But it simply wasn't the same; Marty had made the pub. The new owner was the complete opposite to Marty.

However, in time, he asked what I intended to do now I was back, given I'd sold *Bombora*. He offered me the hotel security job – which I accepted. The settlement money was gone, and Wendy and I were now broke after being unemployed and travelling for almost two years.

One night, shortly after our bikes had arrived safely in Melbourne, the new publican made me an offer: 'I'm buying a boat – would you skipper it?"

After finding out which boat, and knowing its previous owner, I agreed. However, the boat – a 38-foot Huon pine timber Motor-Sailor – badly needed a refit.

The publican's father-in-law was a shipwright, retired, and keen to rebuild to *my* design requirements. The plan being, once the boat was in survey, I could skipper it for exclusive hotel guests. I worked from daylight till dark on that boat, *Papeo*, removing her short mast, constructing a flybridge, installing a new engine, and turning her from a Motor-Cruiser into a Flybridge Cruiser, working with the shipwright.

One morning I rang the hotel and it rang out. After many futile attempts, I rode down to the pub – it wasn't until I was removing my helmet and goggles that it struck me the pub was gone! Burnt to the ground. The fire brigade were still there, pushing in the remaining brick walls, but everything else was gone, simply rubble.

It was suss – big-time suspicious! After a lengthy investigation, nobody went to jail, but the dude left town after selling me *Papeo*.

I had no money, but Wendy's mum, Nance Smyrk, God love her, staked me. We were back in the charter boat business.

There was a saying that certain boats would 'roll' on a dead-flat lake. *Papeo* would 'roll' on a wet lawn! She was a sailboat, round bilge, and adding height in the flybridge only made matters worse – she rolled constantly. But ballast and stabilisers fixed 70% of her movement; I filled her below decks with concrete house stumps and lengths of railway track until she sat like a duck on water. Now we had a good sea boat, and one the Marine Board of Victoria surveyed and passed with flying colours. From *Bombora* with ten passengers, to *Papeo* with 35 passengers, we also had improved revenue, and now I had a boat with a cockpit large enough to fit a game chair. Game fishing was now feasible.

Mr Alf Dean, of South Australia, just over the border, held pretty much every record for white pointer sharks worldwide. Out of Streaky Bay and Ceduna, he had been catching these monsters on rod and reel for years, holding the record for the heaviest fish ever caught, at 2664lb. The world record for marlin, on the other hand (although they are big and hard fighters), was 1560lb, which had stood since 1953.

I called Mr Dean and told him who I was, where I was, and that I'd like to start catching white pointers on rod and reel. He was fantastic, encouraging, helpful, he even sent me my very first proper shark hooks, and guided me through each step of the journey in catching one as per the IGFA (International Game Fish Association) Rules.

He also told me how to get my hands on whale oil, a 44-gallon drum of it from the Albany Whaling Station in Western Australia. I was in business.

All set up with an affordable 130lb 'off the rack' rod, basic International 130lb reel, compliant wire trace (under 30 feet) and again a compliant 'double' (line under 30 feet). With an Alf Dean hook swaged into the wire trace, and on a home-made game chair, we headed off in pursuit of our first fish. With my trusty mate Phil 'Dip' Wik, and a crew of locals – five of us in total – we set off for a 48-hour trial run.

We dropped anchor in Dinghy Cove in perfect conditions: glassy smooth seas, not a breath of wind, and in prime seal pupping season. From here on it was a case of winging it.

Fishing by IGFA rules, we had to use fish bait, not horse meat or the like; likewise, we burlied with whale oil, a steady drip going into the water to create a slick and scent for our quarry to hone in on. Using a 20lb southern bluefin tuna as bait, we sewed chunks of foam soaked in whale oil into the fish's body, our thinking being: sharks are dumb, it was the same bait as the scent, they'd just eat it.

Rumour has it that sharks are night feeders, hence we sat up all night just waiting for a strike. Keeping the bait off the bottom is also important, hence a couple of party balloons tied to the eyelet/swivel on the wire trace kept the bait under 30 feet from the surface – about mid-water, as we were in 60 feet of water. Nothing happened; all night we took it in turns to keep watch.

Mid-morning next day, however, produced activity. A flock of seagulls hovering above the surface of our whale-oil slick and coming towards the bait caught all our attention. I'd seen seagulls do this straight after a shark had made a kill; small bits float to the surface for easy pickings. Then we saw it, first the tip of a dorsal fin, then the full dorsal fin and tail fin. Alf Dean's record was safe should we get lucky, as it wasn't a big white pointer. All day and all night that shark patrolled around the bait, up and down the whale-oil slick, but no action.

I got some of the greatest footage of this shark in crystal-clear water as it swam under the boat; Dip even touched its back with a deck broom it came so close, but it wouldn't touch that bait.

On deck I had a heavy-duty stainless-steel dairy bucket, as it was longer than the average bucket and we could stand a couple of tuna in it, tail up, to hold the blood as they thawed out. Putting on our last fresh tuna bait, Dip pitched the blood out of the bucket and over the side with his bait.

WHAM! Pop, pop, two balloons went off as they went under, and the reel started to click faster and faster while we all watched in disbelief. Knowing only that nobody other than the angler could touch the rod, I grabbed it out of the rod-holder and figured I'd work it all out as things unfolded.

Mr Dean had warned me not to strike too soon; often they are just mouthing the food – don't pull it out of their mouths.

I let heaps out, like 200 metres, while Dip got rid of the anchor and had *Papeo* running with the shark off our quarter.

I pushed up the strike, applying 80lb of pressure before reefing back in the chair to set the hook – hopefully in the gut! Suddenly my butt was off the chair, and there I was with locked knees and spread straight legs on the footrest – this fish had pulled me to my feet.

'SHUTE!' – or words to that effect, as I backed off the drag a little. I didn't fancy a swim with a pissed-off great white. And so I was 'hooked-up', as they say in fishing. Through that rod and line, I could feel every movement that fish made. After setting the hook, it exploded, peeling off 600 metres of line in no time. All I could do was hold on with both hands and watch the line go out.

It was a first for all of us, on-the-job-learning. Too much drag on a green fish, fresh and full of fight, isn't what you do. You give just enough to prevent being spooled, all the line taken off the reel; then, as the drag starts to slow the fish down, you up the drag – to the 80lb strike limit if you can hold it – and keep your bum on the chair. The trick to retrieving line is bend your knees, dip the rod tip, and wind like a mad man – then pull long and hard until the rod tip is high again. If the fish isn't pulling away, repeat the same: dip, wind, pull.

On the first run, when it felt the hook, it took 500 metres of line with my arse off the chair. It did that twice more over the next two-and-a-half hours.

The guy on the ship's wheel is far more important than the guy on the fishing reel – he has to keep three steps ahead of the fish, or it's all over in less than a heartbeat. This was Dip's first fish as skipper – we were both learning as we went, and as it happened we made a great team; he kept the fish off our stern quarter so if it rolled he was ahead of it, and if it wanted to change direction he was again ahead of it and could adjust accordingly.

It was becoming apparent the fish was stuffed; if it drowned, died, we may never lift it with only 130lb line, so we had to bring it to gaff and get a tail rope on it sooner rather than later.

'Flying gaffs' are gaffs where the hooked end detaches from the handle. Once the gaff is firmly into the shark's flesh, you quickly secure a tail rope to the shark and the boat; towing the shark backwards rapidly ends its life.

All went according to plan, but shooting the fish would immediately disqualify me, and the capture. It wasn't required – by the time we towed it back to the island to collect our anchor and float-line, the shark was dead. It weighed in at 1009lb. I was a member of the thousand-pound club with my very first fish.

It was great grounding for Dip and me, we both had a first-hand, hands-on background and now – with the prospect of having anglers aboard, paying us to take them shark fishing – we had actually caught one. From here we had something to build on.

Ian Fritsch was our next big achievement. Ian and his mates from up in the Wimmera/Mallee area came down to Port Fairy for a 48-hour shark fishing charter. All big, strong, young country boys, on an end-of-year footy trip from memory.

Ian set a hook into a 1792lb white pointer that took four hours to bring to gaff. Dip and I rotated from cockpit to helm, and Ian's fish was taken in the dead of night, adding to the task of keeping away from Lady Julia

Percy Island as well as in front of the fish, which constantly rolled like a crocodile to rid itself of whatever was controlling its head and direction.

A fish on the gantry always brings a crowd, a big great white shark brings the media; we were getting headlines, and Victorians, as well as interstaters, all wanted a slice of the action. To serious game fishermen, our bringing in these weights was temptation beyond belief – anything over 1000lb was momentous.

We were now established, catching fish over 1000lb caught everyone's attention, and combined with the hype of the movie *Jaws*, everyone wanted to see a great white shark, if not catch one.

I had Australian celebrities and international celebrities calling me! My bank manager was delighted, and seeing the commercial value even more than I did, insisted I get a 16mm motion-picture camera to have on board at all times.

I couldn't afford the camera but had a 'permanent loan' of one through a friend. Demand and supply are the ruling factors of commerce. Being the only lemonade stand in the desert, I had the monopoly and could up my pricing, which became essential if I was to entertain to a higher standard.

My bread and butter was family cruising around Port Fairy Bay, fishing parties, and four-hour cruises to the island. If the weather was too rough I could run a scuba school in the South-West Passage.

But fishing for great white sharks was the bonus, the big bonus, and it was catching on.

New boat, new son, 1979–1982

My chartering business was taking off, and Wendy was pregnant. It felt like the greatest achievement in my life, that I would be a father. After years of trying, we had almost given up when the wonderful news came.

I had been to Queensland, skippering a marlin boat and seeing how the other half lived … in warmth, with calm, flat seas offering marlin, sailfish and much more.

I also had a custom-built boat under construction, much bigger than *Papeo* – a whisker under 50 feet. I remember physically pinching myself to ensure it was all true, everything was just falling into place.

Friendship was to be the name of my new vessel, designed from a slightly larger version of *Sea Strike*, the boat I had been skippering in Queensland for Bill Smith. He had contacted me soon after Lee Marvin had fished with me; he wanted to bring *Sea Strike* to Port Fairy to go for the great whites, which resulted in me skippering the boat.

'Dollar Bill', as Bill was called by his rivals, had tried in vain to get Lee Marvin on his boat up in Cairns – he figured having me as his skipper might change Lee's mind. I knew it wouldn't work. Bill wasn't liked in Cairns; although, in fairness, he hadn't had an easy start in life, left in an orphanage by his mother.

However, being new to it all, I had agreed to fly to Queensland at Bill's expense. I had skippered *Sea Strike* at the Tangalooma Sailfish Competition off Moreton Island, with the legendary Paul 'Wheels' Whelan on deck as my number two. Wheels came from down our way, Terang, before he made it into the big time as one of, if not the best, game-fishing skippers in the country. Pretty much everything I learnt about game fishing, from rigging baits, to boat handling, to boat design, all came from Paul Whelan.

Wheels and I had some great times – none better than when he went down into the engine-room and opened the screws on our new V12 Baudouin engines to show the Yank Peter Wright a clean pair of heels.

Peter Wright was captaining the very first Black Watch game boat into Australia. We beat her back to Tangalooma by a country mile, and Wright drowned every electrical item on the flybridge just trying to keep us in sight. Some victories are sweet, but there was none sweeter than that for Wheels and me. It was an America's Cup to us.

It took a full year to construct *Friendship*; Wheels built her fuel tanks and game chair as she went through construction in Port Fairy.

Friendship was the very first interstate vessel built under the new USL (Uniform Shipping Legislation) code, allowing her to ply commercially up to 200 miles off the Australian coastline. Prior to this, boats built to each state's regulations meant they could only be surveyed one state at a time, and every state had different rules. It was a nightmare! Each state I crossed into meant a different survey ruling.

But no longer, and *Friendship* could accommodate 11, including a crew of three. She had the best of both worlds – she was double diagonal planked with (Tasmanian) King William pine, and Dynel fabric was applied over the timber, giving a 2½ inch, solid, strong hull with a fibreglass-style finish.

As *Friendship* was growing, so too was my child, all through 1979.

We were busy, charters kept coming in, more and more from the USA and Europe.

Then came the big question from our doctor: 'Which year do you want your child born, 1979 or 1980?'

Wendy, like her mum, couldn't have a natural childbirth, it had to be caesarean, and soon. We decided on 31 December 1979, and that was the happiest day of my young life. When my son Joel was born, all my

The Friendship *team: Dip, Linda, me.*

dreams came true. He was a gorgeous little man. I held him first, and it was a moment I shall treasure always.

He became my whole world.

However, there is something in male genetics (or certainly mine) that means when things are going perfectly, something, or someone, throws a spanner in the works. I had the world at my feet, everything – *everything* to lose. If I could just keep faithful to my wife I was set for life.

I loved my wife, adored my son, and I was practically the toast of Victorian Tourism, certainly in Port Fairy, since game-fishing successes had helped put it on the map.

But I had created a rod for my own back, with a number of lovers, and one in particular who lived in town. I had been cheating on Wendy for years, and had never come close to being caught. I was naive enough to convince myself that what Wendy didn't know could never hurt her.

I also made sure I was extremely discreet; Dip was the only friend I truly trusted with my extramarital affairs, and even though he was disappointed, even upset, that I was cheating on Wendy – who was his friend also – he never voiced his disapproval nor interfered.

With the launching of *Friendship*, performed by the Victorian State Premier's wife, April Hamer, my life took a sudden turn for the worse.

For starters, the boat was badly out of trim from the moment she went into the water. With only the engine and the fuel and water tanks installed, she was 'head down' – too much weight forward. When the superstructure went on and the construction was finished, the head-down aspect remained. During the initial sea-trials it became glaringly apparent there was a trim issue: the boat simply wouldn't plane, that is, lift her head clear and skim across the water. Instead, she 'pushed' water, never reaching her designed hull speed of 20–24 knots. The project was a disaster – her top speed was 11–12 knots.

While I could sit for hours just watching Joel sleep, the nightmare around *Friendship* never went away. I tried half-a-dozen different propellers as the boat-builder insisted that was the problem – at $1000 a shot, it was an expensive trial-and-error process, which did nothing to improve the boat's speed or trim.

I was booked out solid on the new boat. And crucial to the investment was the requirement that the boat would perform at 20 knots, getting us to and from Lady Julia Percy Island twice as fast as *Papeo* had.

In simple logic, the fuel tanks and 300-gallon freshwater tank needed to be moved further back in the hull, something that the builder refused to do.

Litigation became inevitable. The Victorian Tourism authority and a state-backed bank collectively put up two-thirds of the money, and I put up a third. I, however, was responsible for the entire amount eventually.

My legal advice was to sue the builder if he wouldn't do the fix, and that's what finally happened. Nobody likes court, and the Victorian Supreme Court in Melbourne is no place to cut your teeth.

In the meantime, Dip and I had to battle on with a boat that was *almost* magnificent – if only it would go over 12 knots.

I wasn't having much luck with shark fishing either, with some charters experiencing disappointing catches.

Then in March 1980, Terry Morton and his two friends chartered us.

We headed out to Lady Julia Percy Island. I was exhausted – it had been a long week – and told Dip I would crash early and relieve him at midnight. Our clients had already drawn cards to sort out the fishing order, highest to lowest, aces high. Highest first in the chair for the first hour, then change hourly by next-best cards. I fell asleep quickly.

'FISH – wake-up!'

Dip charged into my cabin at 8.30pm.

As I arrived in the cockpit I felt the whole 48 feet of *Friendship* lurch. There was not a breath of wind, nor any waves.

'What the fuck was that?' I asked Dip, who was scrambling up the flybridge ladder.

He flicked on the two huge floodlights.

'The bait's gone,' he yelled. 'It's feeding on the burley bag!'

I edged my way to the stern, gathering up the 130lb bait rod, and I found myself staring into the gaping jaws of a huge great white, which had just torn the bottom out of a bag full of fish guts and burley that we had suspended over the stern.

'Don't start her!' I yelled to Dip, frantically winding in the 130lb tuna bait.

The bait came over the stern and the huge, gaping mouth followed it. Instinctively, I aimed the tuna to the back of the great white's open mouth. I even saw it get swallowed.

I spooled off all the wire trace, 30 feet of double and then some.

'Who's in the chair?' I called.

'Me,' came a faint response.

They had all seen the monster shark in the floodlights; and it was by far the biggest I'd ever encountered.

Terry Morton is around 60 kilograms wringing wet; his two mates however, were about 160 kilograms bone dry.

'You're kidding?' was all I could muster, as I jammed the rod butt into the gimbal. He took over the rod. He now owned it, till the end. No assistance from anyone.

Dip had slipped the anchor onto a float-line and fired-up *Friendship* while I instructed Terry when to strike.

Dip needed to be pointing away from the island, with the fish off one corner of the stern, and be travelling in the same direction as the fish.

'Lock up the strike, pull like all hell – and keep your legs locked and straight!'

Terry's eyes were like hub caps.

'NOW!' I yelled at him, as everything came together at once.

Someone had to steer the game chair – the back folds down (allowing the angler to lie straight back when pulling) and makes a good 'rudder' for steering.

I was steering the chair when the shark felt the hook deep in its gut.

Terry adopted the standing position in the same instant. The hook was well set, and he simply couldn't hold 80lb of drag peeling off in a cloud of smoke

'Back it off – SLOWLY,' I said calmly, feeling him lower back onto the chair as he got the idea. 'It can pull you over the back,' I reminded him. 'Simply hold – do nothing more than hold at this point.'

This was a massive shark, hurting from a hook in its gut – the boat was getting on its nerves as well. I was in two minds; I knew sharks would attack boats, and this one was big enough to do serious damage. We needed to end this quickly.

I swapped places with Dip at the helm.

'I'm going to try and keep it in shallow water – keep him busy, put as much pressure on the shark as you can without losing him over the stern.'

And so it began.

The island showed up nice and dark without needing the spotlight too often. Keeping the shark shallow meant it had to swim harder to keep away from the threat of the boat, which required more energy from both fish and angler. Dip kept the strike up as much as he could without losing Terry. Good old Palmolive green dishwashing detergent squirted under Terry's bum and all over the game chair seat helped the angler slide back and forth when recovering line: dip, bend, wind, PULL and slide – then repeat.

When the reel is smoking, warm water applied through a rag or sponge can save friction snap; line dragging over itself on the spool can get seriously hot, and hot line is weak line.

Into the third hour, Dip came up onto the flybridge.

'I don't think he's going to last – he's rooted now, and that shark is far from rooted! But he won't hear of handing over the rod to anyone else.'

I handed over the helm and went down. Terry was shaking from head to foot, exhausted, close-to-tears exhausted. His mates were looking at me for the word to replace him; skipper's word is law.

I stood behind him and steered the chair, he had worked out how to gather line, how to rest, how to stick it to the fish when needed. What he lacked was power – he was a small guy. But it was his fish; hand over the rod and nobody can claim it, it was automatic disqualification under the IGFA rules.

He was making odd, painful noises.

'It's only a fish Terry – what seems to be the problem?' I asked calmly. The line screamed and he bent forward, watching all the line he had only just retrieved going back out as the shark made another run.

'Seriously Terry – the hostess could have landed this by now. Stop fucking around and catch it, OK?'

Linda our hostess stood watching on; he cast a look at her, then back at me.

'You've got 30 minutes – then it's her time.'

Two cans of rum and coke and an hour later he brought the fish to the boat. He was incoherent, shaking like an autumn leaf in a southerly gale, but his determination was steadfast. Nobody was catching that fish but him, and he did – all by the rules.

It was an even bigger fish than I had anticipated. It wasn't until it was alongside the boat that we saw how big she was, 18 feet 6 inches, or 5.6388 metres, to be exact.

This is danger time, and it's not the jaws that do the damage, it's the tail.

With one full-blooded swing of its tail into the hull, a fish that size could easily snap timber. Getting a gaff into its head was crucial, but getting a tail rope on was paramount.

After four-and-a-half hours, the fish was under tow by the tail, homeward to Port Fairy. Terry was a gibbering wreck on the cockpit deck, exhausted but ecstatic.

It was the world record fish, I knew it, 3000lb-plus.

Sadly, it had been caught at night and my borrowed 16mm camera didn't have lights for night filming, but as the sun rose I took lots of 16mm film all the way to the gantry.

We had another problem. As we entered Port Fairy Bay and shortened up our tow, I watched in horror as our catch threw up her entire intestines; her liver alone would have weighed several hundred pounds.

But I was still confident we had a world record fish – even completely self-gutted.

Next problem, there wasn't a set of scales in town that weighed over 2000lb.

We had to revert to the weighbridge, which meant loading the fish onto a truck and weighing the truck empty, then weighing it again with the fish on the tray to get the actual measurement – all the time in the sun with dehydration stealing more weight. She weighed in at 2257½lb, 406½lb under the world record.

The official weigh-master was present, and the sergeant of police, as well as my bank manager – three independent witnesses – all by the rules, but it was a world record fish that no longer counted.

Terry Morton and me after his epic battle with the huge great white. It's still the heaviest fish caught on rod and reel in Victoria.

By arrangement with the Victorian Game Fishing Club (VGFC), I signed up anglers as members prior to charters. That way, should a fish be a record, it could be claimed under IGFA rules. Terry and his two mates had all paid their nominal fees. Even though the fish was caught strictly by IGFA rules, on legal equipment, which was sent to the IGFA, the VGFC refused to accept the capture, saying they had revised their policy on temporary memberships. They simply disallowed the capture.

That ended the long association I'd had with the Victorian Game Fishing Club.

I figured the sudden change to a longstanding policy was due to the fact Terry would have cleaned up on a number of pending annual prizes – one being the heaviest shark caught for the year, and another, the heaviest fish. Terry's 2257½lb shark beat a smaller shark (well under 1000lb) and remains the heaviest fish caught by IGFA rules in the state of

Victoria. The record will remain unbroken since the banning of fishing/killing great white sharks came into effect shortly thereafter.

* * * *

With a court case looming with the boat-builder, and a new boat that wouldn't plane, instead of it being a time to really capitalise on the international game-fishing location we had established, it was a struggle. Fuel costs were almost double, as we were running flat-out to achieve half-speed, repaying the loans put enormous pressure on me. We sometimes fished in conditions that were not good, just to pay the bills.

Bill Smith offered me work on *Sea Strike* out of Brisbane, which helped; Dip ran *Friendship* while I was up north.

And then I blew it completely. One lunchtime in Brisbane, Bill introduced me to a well-known female TV presenter, who I won't name. We spent the afternoon in her bed.

A week later, I flew back to Port Fairy to be greeted by Wendy, distraught, in tears, holding a letter. She thrust it at me and stormed out.

The Brisbane TV presenter had taken the time to write to Wendy, in detail, about everything that had taken place between us that one afternoon in her bed. Joel was coming up to one year old.

My life was in total ruins.

Don't ask me why, but I thought a clean slate would help. I loved Wendy, only Wendy, and the extramarital sex meant nothing. I thought if I came completely clean, we could get our lives back together – there was too, too much to lose. So I told her of the others.

That afternoon and night we tried to work our way through the mess. I'd been relegated to Joel's room and never slept. The harder and longer I thought, the more obvious it became; we hadn't just grown up, we'd grown apart.

Our interests had become totally different, her teaching and my fishing had driven us further apart, we were ships passing in the night.

At one stage, before *Friendship*, Wendy had asked me to give up the charter business; she could see where it was taking me, but I was blind to what was right under my nose. Now it was too late.

* * * *

I employed a manager to do the bookings, left Dip as skipper, and returned to Brisbane where I was met at the airport by Bill's wife Lizzy. Bill was in the USA.

In a year my whole world had been turned upside down, I was trying to put on a brave front, but I was gutted.

Back at Bill's, a stunningly beautiful blonde girl was sitting at their bar; behind the bar was a guy snorting cocaine and arguing with the blonde. I'd never seen cocaine before, nor Lizzy lose her temper, but all hell broke loose. I quickly made myself scarce beside their giant pool. The blonde followed, as Lizzy aimed her unwanted coke-head out the front door and into a taxi.

'Hi, I'm Julie,' the girl said, as I swam to cool off in the tropical night. Without being chauvinistic, or trying to sound like a playboy, I had met some beautiful women in my 31 years. Julie, a model, was by far the most stunning.

We started a conversation that simply flowed, we drank champagne, then Julie stripped to her underwear and joined me in the pool. It was well after midnight before we realised Lizzy had gone to bed, and another two hours later Julie and I were also in bed – together.

As much as it should have been the furthest thing from my mind to do, it was the easiest and most natural relationship I'd ever started. We became a couple from that night onwards.

* * * *

Sea Strike needed larger horsepower; when I came on as skipper she was into her second set of engines and going through gearboxes like tissues – and she wasn't even a year old.

New V12 Baudouin engines went in, and I was still familiarising myself with this state-of-the-art ship, the most modern and magnificent game boat afloat outside of the USA at the time – and at 56 feet she took some familiarisation.

Julie came to the boat with me on the days that she had free, and at night I would go down to the Gold Coast with her, for her modelling assignments.

When I left Wendy, I had made myself the promise I would keep in constant contact with Joel; I never wanted to lose him, nor lose contact with him. It was a straight 21-hour drive from Kenmore, Queensland, to Port Fairy, Victoria, stopping only for fuel.

At the end of every month I left on a Friday afternoon, arriving Saturday morning, spent Saturday and Sunday with Joel, then hit the road home, arriving early Monday morning.

I did this every month for a year. At only one year old, Joel was too little to really know what was happening, but he always knew who Dad was when I arrived. It made the entire trip worthwhile, just for that moment alone.

Julie had a son of around three who spent equal time with his father. She was also going through a separation with a child, which gave us something else in common.

From a disaster that had uprooted me from my family and home, I now found myself living in a palatial, Hollywood-style estate with a gorgeous model, and driving the best game boat in the land. I was even cruising around in the latest-model Mercedes Benz convertible, Bill's car, which he never drove as he was pissed 99% of the time. Happy you'd think, even ecstatic? But I wasn't.

Dollar Bill was an arsehole to everyone except me, I missed my family, Joel especially, I missed Port Fairy – and believe it or not, I missed the weather!

Every bloody day in Queensland was perfect – why didn't it rain, blow and get cold just one day a week?

Skippering in Queensland was a whole new thing. Every day was a good day to fish. Even right inside Moreton Bay I managed to catch my first black marlin, as well as my first sailfish. Shark fishing had taught me to be patient, and what it feels like for the angler being in the chair; this experience, new species, and fishing much lighter gear, broadened my knowledge. I never caught any big 1000lb-plus black marlin, but if the smaller ones are any indication, they are one hell of a fighting fish.

I was also fortunate to have great deckhands, wire men (manhandling the trace) and gaff men, who got it right the first time, every time. Game fishing is a team sport, anyone who brags they caught a big fish has their head up their arse – they may have been sweating in the chair at the time, but three other guys made it happen. That is what I took away from big game fishing.

Port Fairy was a much different pace: there I was getting four seasons in one day. My trips home only emphasised this.

But more importantly at this time, what I needed was a six-foot mirror – to watch myself go broke.

The business, *Friendship*, was going down the tubes. People charter skippers, not boats, when it gets down to the nitty gritty of game fishing. Dip was every bit as good a skipper as I was, but my name was associated with all the publicity and hype surrounding the boat, the business and our success. Plus, I was the spokesman – Dip rarely spoke!

Bookings were falling away and I still owed around $130,000 on *Friendship*. Something had to give.

Julie and I did a run down to Nimbin, and on the trip back I broke the news to her – I was returning to Port Fairy.

Bill wasn't happy, but whenever was he? I packed up everything and headed south.

* * * *

I rented a place with spectacular views of the Southern Ocean, and was able to see Joel regularly now; he loved being by the beach.

Wendy and I even gave it another shot, which we both knew wasn't going to happen, but we established a friendly relationship that has only strengthened through the years.

The business was screwed.

I tried re-establishing old contacts, and stuck out the summer, but it was inevitable that *Friendship* had to be sold. The bid in the Supreme Court to have the builder fix the problem had failed. It was my headache now – and mine alone.

New beginnings, Ness, 1982

Then one morning there was a knock on my door from an actor friend of my landlords. They were away in Queensland, so their friend stayed with me.

That fluke meeting led to many great friendships, which I established through that guy – who I also won't name – when I moved the boat to Melbourne, to try and find work there.

I was living in and around Toorak, and partying hard with my new friends. One in particular was a very wealthy entrepreneur who owned shopping centres, simply collecting the rent for a living.

His friend, Gabriel, a Frenchman, had a place in South Melbourne, where it was party night, every night. And this was how I met my second wife.

My entrepreneur friend woke me early one morning, still in bed with a girl after a party.

'I need you to come with me,' he whispered. I left without waking the sleeping beauty at my side.

He drove a white Rolls Royce Corniche, the first I'd ever seen, much less been in.

'I met these two girls last night – English girls, you have to meet them,' he explained. 'One is a movie star.'

'A real one?' I asked naively.

'Should be if she's not,' he said.

We were met with a full brilliant smile at 8am on a Saturday morning.

'Hi, I'm Mandy.'

She introduced herself with a firm handshake. Mandy was tall, blonde, a typically beautiful English lady, who invited us in for coffee. My mate was shaking his head to indicate she was not the movie star.

By now the night's activities were beginning to take their toll, I was feeling very second-hand, when a flash of bright red entered the room.

'Morning everyone,' beamed the other English tourist. 'I'm Vanessa.'

She extended her hand.

'John,' I replied, without taking too much notice. She fetched me a mug of coffee.

'You're quiet,' she said.

'I had a huge night last night, I'm paying for it right now,' I replied, suddenly seeing her for the first time.

She was beautiful, she did look like a movie star. Slim, brunette, deeply tanned and wearing a bright-red Japanese kimono.

'My God – you have had a big night, just look at your eye!' she said

When I had a big night or was tired, my blind eye became very bloodshot. I immediately went off her, thinking that she was making fun of me.

Soon my friend suggested I take the girls to Port Fairy, as they hadn't left Melbourne since arriving in Australia. I had taken the boat back to Port Fairy, doing fishing charters at weekends to keep some money coming in, as Melbourne hadn't worked out. I had a charter on the Sunday – with a bunch of bird watchers.

The girls liked the idea. I took them along the famed Great Ocean Road, it was a perfect sunny day. Mandy sat up front with me, and Vanessa climbed into the back. I decided she was way out of my league.

We reached Port Fairy after dark, having had a great day on the road. I deliberately pulled up beside the smallest, dirtiest boat in the fleet, the deck littered with cray-pots.

'That's it – that's where we're sleeping tonight?' asked Mandy, in a strained voice.

'Yep – welcome aboard,' I said, trying to look proud. The girls shared a look of sheer horror.

'That is unless you'd prefer to sleep aboard *her*,' I added, pointing down to *Friendship*.

Dip knew I was coming with female company, he'd gone the whole nine yards – every navigation light was lit up, the saloon lights were turned down low, music was playing, and the fridge was stocked.

Shrieks of delight from the girls. 'That's YOURS?' they said in unison.

With too many banks and family to name, I took the credit.

I needed to deliver something to my mate Dick Cullenwood, and took the girls up with me once they had settled into *Friendship*'s comfort. Dick, as always, was in his hot tub when we arrived.

As an abalone diver in Bass Strait, a hot tub was a must, simply to thaw out at day's end. Soon we were all in it with drinks in our hands.

We stayed late; eventually it was only Vanessa and me left in the hot tub – at opposite sides. My eye had settled, I was loaded on bourbon, and I'd had a joint or two. I felt her foot under the water, and it had to be deliberate, unless I was stoned beyond all reasonable assessment. We moved closer, until we were sitting side by side.

I don't know how, or even when, but I know we eventually kissed. She was hot, Jacqueline Bisset hot … that's who she looked like.

When we arrived back at the boat, Mandy took a cabin of her own and Vanessa moved in with me. That's how it remained; except for one night, we didn't sleep apart for the next six months.

We took the ornithologists out next day over the Continental Shelf, saw thousands of dolphins migrating, stopped at Lady Julia Percy Island, and the girls were delighted. We stayed a week in Port Fairy, and Joel met Vanessa – or Ness as I now called her.

I was head over heels. As crazy as it may sound, I have got to know many women in my life, yet only Wendy and Vanessa had that WOW factor, the love factor, and it's a feeling so unique it can't be confused with anything as simplistic as good sex.

New beginnings, Ness, 1982

I was in love again.

But I was in for a shock.

At 21 years old, Ness came from a very privileged background. The shock came from how she reacted to alcohol. From a happy, sociable drinker, she became a completely different person in an instant. It wasn't predictable. It would go on to shape our relationship, and her life, in many tragic ways. But then we were both too young to understand that she suffered from a very real – and rare – illness, an extremely high intolerance to very small amounts of alcohol.

We talked about it at length, how drinking changed her and how it would never work with us if that's how she was.

'It will never happen again,' she promised. Many times.

We all moved into a flat in South Yarra: myself, Ness, Mandy and Ina, a friend of Mandy's.

Bill kept calling me from Brisbane to come back and skipper his boat. 'I have my own problems Bill – my boat!'

'Bring it to Queensland,' he said. 'Sell it,' he said.

I didn't have the $3000 for fuel to Queensland, just for starters.

'I'll cover it until you sell her and earn money driving for me in the meantime.'

What's that saying – desperate people do desperate things in desperate times? I qualified.

Mandy drove my car from Melbourne to Brisbane. Ness and I – and some photographer guy she had met modelling who wanted to bum a ride off us – were going to take the boat. *Friendship* was really a three-man ship, bow, stern and bridge – especially going in and out of strange ports, the extra set of hands would be very useful.

I vividly remember calling my parents and speaking to Mum the night we left Queenscliff, south of Melbourne, standing under Norfolk pines in a roaring gale, ringing from a phone booth.

Something kept telling me it would be the last time I would get to speak to them, and Dad hadn't spoken a word to me since I left Wendy.

Deep down I believe I was afraid; the weather was horrific, I'd never done a trip this far, I was taking two crew I hadn't taken to sea before – and one of them I loved.

Getting off the phone in the dark and almost being blown off my feet in the walk back to the boat, I saw the *Princess of Tasmania* ferry making her way up the bay from Port Melbourne, lit up like a Christmas tree.

'OK guys – we're off, get those lines ready to let go,' I said, heading for the bridge to start engines.

'NOW?' came both responses.

It was around 9pm, and I planned on sitting right in behind the *Princess* as she flattened down the southerly buster, turning The Rip into a fury of confused seas – nothing anyone would try in anything smaller than an ocean liner.

I caught her at the entrance of The Rip and stayed so close to her I could name the brand of cigarettes people were smoking on the stern.

Ness was at my side all the way, up on the flybridge, and when I peeled off her stern to head east, we were exposed to the full brunt of the gale. All night we moved through the darkness and huge waves. *Friendship* and I had been in worse, but not Ness or her photographer mate, who we hadn't seen since leaving Queenscliff.

Next morning, we were heading into the islands that lie off Wilsons Promontory, the weather had improved and the sun was out; we made hay while the sun shines as they say – full power ahead.

Every hour I like to visually go over the engine-room, not rely totally on instruments. I asked Ness to grab the wheel while I went below; after all, she said she had done a lot of sailing with her brother, and she liked to steer. When I disappeared down into the engine-room, Australia was on our left; as I came up to check something, Australia was at our stern – next time I came up, Australia was on our right side. We were going west, not east.

'Everything OK up here skipper?' I asked, amused at Ness standing over the compass, not behind the compass. It's commonly called chasing the compass; so long as you keep turning that wheel, the compass is going to follow.

All that experience she had talked about eventually shrank into rowing a 14-foot timber dinghy on her dad's dam. And I still hadn't seen her photographer mate since he threw off our stern-line in Melbourne.

As it turned out, Ness was worth three blokes. She was doing a watch on the helm day and night, cooking meals, and playing nursemaid to her mate – who had locked himself in a cabin, wearing a lifejacket, and drinking scotch around the clock, after disclosing he had a fear of water and had come on the trip to overcome it.

In Sydney, we collected Mandy and Bill en route to Brisbane. Mandy freaked me out with news she had met a nice old man who gave her a suitcase to deliver when she got to Brisbane! 'Drugs, Mandy – what were you thinking?'

No drugs, as it happened, but this man was, ironically, to play a bigger role later in my life. Life is full of surprises.

Upon arrival in Brisbane, Bill rang home to speak with Lizzy, only to get the housekeeper. Lizzy had left Bill.

If ever I needed a joint it was that day – we sat around *Friendship*'s dining-room table smoking, even the photographer emerged for the occasion. Later, Bill returned to help move the girls and me up to his home – what was left of it. He was really pissed off. Lizzy had outsmarted him, and was truly gone.

In the end, the pre-made plans never even got started, with the exception that Bill had booked *Friendship* in to have the water and fuel tanks relocated further astern.

The work on *Sea Strike* was non-existent, all bullshit, it was mid-winter, and nothing was happening – nothing except Bill was working around the clock to financially ruin Lizzy and get full custody of their son. After a week or so of this, and Bill making a prick of himself making moves on Mandy in the privacy of her bedroom at all hours, he finally gave me the excuse I needed to leave.

He stuck an affidavit under my nose denigrating Lizzy as an immoral lesbian, druggie, you name it, he included it, and wanted me to sign it. I asked the girls to pack and we were gone within the hour.

Lizzy was my friend as much as Bill was, more so. And Ness and Lizzy liked each other. Lizzy invited us to crash at her place until we found a place to rent.

I expected shit from Bill and wasn't let down – we had the place raided by ten Drug Squad coppers. This was in notorious Queensland Premier Joh Bjelke-Petersen's reign. You got jail for one joint.

A hired private investigator kept watch over Lizzy 24/7, and Bill had asked me to keep his pot in the boot of my car after we brought the boat up, as he was paranoid about Lizzy springing him with dope to use against him in their custody war. Guess where the cops went straight to? They found nothing – but I can assure you the frogs in the Brisbane River were on a high for a week on Bill's pot.

Mandy, or Tinks (Tinkler being her surname), got a good job as a legal secretary, Ness did some modelling, and I went on the dole for the first time in my life.

It was 1982 and the Commonwealth Games were on in Brisbane. The day of the marathon, Ness and I were having a matinee. She went to the loo, returning at a run.

'There is someone in Tinks' room,' she whispered frantically. Mandy was at work.

I had a Franchi shotgun in the wardrobe, but no ammunition. Stark naked, I snuck down the passageway. There were people in Tinks' room.

As I stepped into the room one guy burst out through the flyscreen wire, leapt off her balcony, and was gone. The other followed, and winded himself on landing. He lay there on the back lawn looking up at me – stark naked, pointing a shotgun at his head.

'Mate – I'll blow your head clean off your fucking shoulders if you as much as move, LAY PERFECTLY STILL,' I said, loud enough that even the neighbours could hear.

New beginnings, Ness, 1982

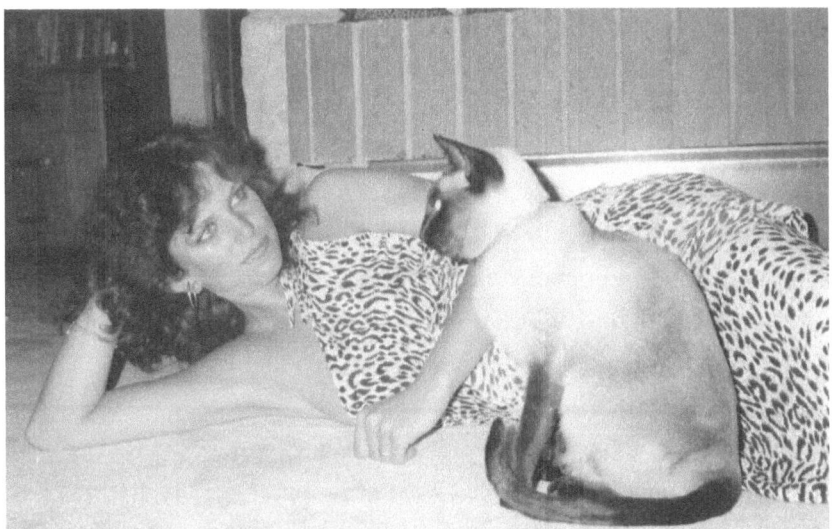

Ness in Kenmore, Queensland, when we first started dating in 1982.

'At this range – with a 12-gauge, you're fucked – I can't miss. GOT IT?'
He nodded.

'Call the coppers,' I whispered to Ness.

I continued to bluff my way into scaring the bejesus out of this guy, who was slowly regaining his breath.

'You're going to have to shoot me – I'm not going back to jail,' he said.

I changed my angle and tucked the gun tighter into my armpit.

'Your call … but you're getting both barrels in the leg if you move – then you can go back to jail with a limp.'

He actually thought about that, I could see the fear in his eyes. .

Ten minutes must have elapsed, it certainly felt longer – no cops, no sirens, no warning shot. He simply got up and jumped the back fence as both barrels went click – click.

'The police are coming,' said Ness, as I checked nothing had been stolen.

Then I noticed that she was wearing make-up. We had no phone, but the guy upstairs did, and he was the current nude centrefold of *Cleo* magazine. I put two and two together.

'You put on make-up while I'm holding a thief at gunpoint?' I asked in disbelief.

'I couldn't go up looking like I was,' she declared. No wonder it took ten fucking minutes before the bloke bolted.

Being marathon day, every available cop in Queensland was on duty; it took an hour before they arrived.

'Why didn't you pursue the intruder?' asked the female police officer.

'And get arrested for indecent exposure? I was stark bollock naked and holding a shotgun at the time,' I answered, to laughter from all.

But coming ashore, after spending a decade at sea with healthy lungs, plus the added stress of separation from Wendy and Joel, and owing the banks squillions, all took its toll. I was becoming physically ill – on top of the mental stress that had me eventually go down in a screaming heap, an emotional waste-land. It was killing me. I felt worthless, drowning in the suburbs of Brisbane.

One day I rang Wendy to say hi to Joel. She took the opportunity to tell me she had filed for divorce; my maintenance, in my absence, had been determined and I was behind in my payments! Could it get any worse?

I owed a fortune to the banks, I was unemployed and on the dole.

And Ness's visa was running out.

Our only reprieve was on the days Lizzy took us down to the Gold Coast. My car was gone, repossessed, and simply being out of the flat and by the sea was a breath of fresh air.

Then, on one such trip to the Gold Coast, I came up with the break I needed.

Seabrake is born, October 1982

I was at the wheel of Lizzy's Honda, on the highway back to Brisbane with my mind spinning, searching for a way out of this mess. For the first time in my life I had no plan. The night when we'd got caught out at sea in *Papeo* in a Force 12 gale came to mind; perhaps both situations seemed as desperate.

That bucket on a rope had saved our lives, without a doubt. If only I could patent a bucket tied to a rope. Suddenly my mind began to focus on the idea. Boats don't have brakes – and that brake had worked. Someone would buy the idea if it was patentable. What I knew about patents you could fit on the back of a postage stamp, but I knew it provided exclusivity. Something that could be patented could be worth money. A lot of money.

Why had it worked? I was focused on something two-staged, something that could do what the bucket had done. For some crazy reason an umbrella kept coming to mind, the opening and closing of an umbrella, something that didn't give drag – then something that did, the action of an umbrella. To this very day I can remember when it finally hit me.

'That's it – that's definitely it,' I said aloud, planting my foot on the accelerator.

'What?' asked the girls as I drove like a man possessed, in search of a newsagency so I could buy a pencil and pad to sketch it out while it was fresh in my mind.

I drew the first brake for boats in the world 15 minutes later.

What I saw in my mind's eye on the road home, even down to the colour, is what eventually went into production.

In principle, what is required is a device that will tow straight and true, that will have minimal resistance until it's required to create drag – when it will have enough drag to hold back a vessel being forced forward by big waves, just as the 300 feet of hemp rope and bucket had. And no, I didn't draw an umbrella!

At that point I had no idea that what I had engineered was ingenious, certainly unique, and certainly viable. In effect, I had turned around the logical way to create drag (the umbrella) and put a pointed end on a bucket – then, with a 'folding in' action I incorporated four doors into that leading, pointed end. By incorporating a 'spring' to keep the doors in their conical shape and strong enough to resist exposing the 'bucket bum' until required, I had my two-stage device. The nose-cone is where the rope would connect, and a shaft running back from the nose-cone to link the four doors (much the same as the wires in an umbrella do) made it simplistic, idiot-proof – once I had worked out what tension the spring needed to be.

Now full of hope, with a plan, I contacted a patent attorney in Brisbane city and made an appointment with Mr John Callanan. I had $10 to my name, and a pencil sketch. I put $5 down on a dress for Ness and bought a return train ticket to the city, leaving me with $1.12 in my pocket (I still have that $1 note, and the 10 cent and 2 cent coins), and headed to town.

Mr Callanan was the dirtiest smoker I have ever met, ash all over him as well as his desk, but attentive, more interested in me than my invention. I thought it was going nowhere, until he learnt that I was a returned serviceman.

'Does it work?' he asked.

'I wouldn't be here if it didn't.'

'Then you let me worry about the money and this end of it – you go and build a prototype that works.'

That was it. I left his office with a model-makers agreement, a provisional patent (one year's protection) and a heart full of hope.

I sold everything I had of value, including my Franchi shotgun, so I could return to Melbourne with Mandy and Ness as they were flying out of Melbourne to go home to England. I didn't know if I would ever see either of them again.

Ness's ex-fiancé was back in England, and I had nothing – certainly not until I sold *Friendship* or Seabrake got off the ground.

But first we had to deliver *Friendship* to the allocated receiver down in Surfers Paradise to sell. She performed as she was supposed to, with the fuel tanks back further, and the water tank relocated: 22–24 knots all the way from Brisbane to Surfers. So much for the naval architect's 'expert opinion'.

Ness almost bought her at auction chasing a fly away, and I left Queensland with my tail between my legs.

* * * *

Seeing Ness and Mandy off was traumatic. It seemed to be one goodbye after another, but saying goodbye to Ness after a year together was not just sad, it was a great loss. It felt like a very lonely journey ahead.

I started work on the Seabrake prototype, drawing up properly scaled drawings, thanks to Tech Drawing in my school days. I also needed money. The meagre income from the dole wasn't going to help me get a model-maker to build my prototype Seabrake.

So began a stint as a movie extra, and working for a personal security service. Soon I would be crossing paths with liars and con men. Little did I know there would be many.

It started with the sea. The bloke Mandy had taken the suitcase to in Queensland was looking for skippers in a venture he was working on, and gave her his number. I began there.

This guy – let's call him Winton Hayes-Clarke – was a man in his late seventies, with a plan to introduce a fleet of clipper ships for charter along the east coast of Australia. He seemed amicable, even gentlemanly, and was by his own account very wealthy, having purchased four or five of these huge clipper ships still in service around the world. My job would be to bring one from the USA to Australia.

I was interested, but explained I had no ticket to cover that size vessel, nor had I any experience in sailing vessels. Winton was unfazed; he said he had qualified sailing masters, he just needed me as a delivery skipper. Being desperate I agreed, but I wanted to know more before I dropped everything.

It was January 1983, summer in Australia, I had the name of a model-maker and the drawings for Seabrake were well advanced, but I still had no income. Whenever it came to discussing a retainer or meeting the rest of Winton's team, there were delays. Something wasn't right. The name John Benson, from the affluent suburb of Toorak, had been mentioned.

I called him, to learn the whole thing was a scam. Winton was a well-known con man.

The most disturbing thing for me was that a whole host of university kids were paying this bloke real money for their airline tickets to crew on these ships. I phoned the Fraud Squad in Melbourne, and set out with John Benson to expose this prick!

It got worse. Not only was he taking money under false pretences from kids, he was engaged to the daughter, and beneficiary, of the head of one of the country's largest finance groups. I had met her and her mother with Winton at their home.

I had wasted a month with this jerk, but I wasn't walking away until he was behind bars.

The police warned me he had criminal connections and would turn violent if cornered. But he was in his seventies, and even given he was 6 foot 6 I wasn't too fazed about Winton posing any physical threat.

I invited him over. I didn't even give him time to sit before I set him straight on what I knew, what the Fraud Squad knew, and every university in Melbourne now knew.

'And if you think you have tough mates, I'll introduce them to some I know,' is where I ended. 'Now fuck off – I have your fianceé to call next.'

He clenched his fists, thought about it, then turned on his heel. We had already contacted the Melbourne media with the full story, they were staking out his house.

That night 'The Australian Tall Ships' story broke. His game was up and he had the cops to contend with next.

I did phone his fiancée, a lovely lady, beautiful, much younger than Winton, and totally shocked by the news. Her mother had her suspicions all along, however, and it came as no surprise to her; most importantly, my call was timely – they were about to part with a lot of money.

Winton Hayes-Clarke did try to have me stop a bullet in a St Kilda hotel a few weeks later, but instead his shooter got a tap on the shoulder from a couple of burly cops. I'd walked into too many ambushes not to see this one coming.

From the bad came the good. Ness was coming back. She had rung to say she couldn't live without me, and back she came, on a one-way ticket, in the late summer of 1983.

With Ness at my side again, and Joel just a couple of hours away, I was getting my life back. I was still broke, we were living in a dive in Caulfield South, Melbourne, with no furniture – but we did have a Morris 1100 car, although it was stuck in third gear.

Only now can I appreciate what Ness had given up to come back, we were living in virtual squalor.

But John Benson liked the way I went about business; more importantly, he liked my honesty.

'So, what now?' he asked.

'Keep working as an extra, and build my prototype,' I replied.

'Tell me about your invention, I might be interested,' said John Benson.

Under a 'letter of confidentiality' Mr Callanan had drawn up for me, I showed JB my provisional patent on Seabrake. He was a boating enthusiast and a millionaire through his insurance firm.

'Bring me a working prototype, and I'm in. Don't show anyone else – OK?'

'OK!'

I was working as an extra on the TV mini-series *Waterfront*, with Jack Thompson, about the dock workers' strike in Melbourne during the Great Depression. I had also made the list for Group 4 Security. I now had three jobs, while Seabrake took up all my spare time. My mental and physical health was showing cracks, I was smoking like a bark hut, no exercise, poor food. I was a ticking time bomb. My relationship with Ness was under real pressure – I was obsessed with building our future, not taking time out for the present, a mistake that we all often make.

Ness, God bless her, didn't pack up and go straight back home to wealth and security. Instead, she sat out those cold days on Port Phillip Bay as we ran back and forth trialling my prototype behind a friend's boat, or sat alone in our shitty flat. I was able to pay the model-maker and the clock-scales hire – the latter made to weigh vegetables, not measure the drag of a bucket behind a boat! Working with a cone-shaped piece of mild steel, made to my dimensions, then scribing out four doors equally spaced around the cone, which had a bucket-shaped base 24 inches in diameter, we measured the amount of drag and modified the design. As we progressed, the drag went from pounds to tons. But I still had no idea that my radical design was real science, enough to win design awards one day.

* * * *

Group 4 Security was Sir Peter Abeles' company, and it provided Australia with an international level of personal security. Sir Peter owned the huge transport empire TNT, as well as Ansett Airlines at that time.

For G4 he selected only ex-servicemen and ex-police; he was looking for specialists. I had made it into the final group of around 18 from more than 300 applicants. He employed a British guy (whose name I forget), who had left being in charge of all gambling money taken on, and off, Hong Kong's government-controlled horse-racing courses, to head up this new branch of TNT security.

We were essentially high-echelon security, often personal protection to international VIPs, covering anything from book signings to the transportation of tons of legal, restricted drugs, the raw product for medical opium.

This English boss took a liking to me, and we worked together a lot. He had started his security career as an unarmed guard in a Liverpool factory with an Alsatian dog as his only protection. He showed me the scar that ran from his chest to his waist where a guy had gutted him with a square-mouth shovel. The dog had saved his life.

He and I did a job with state and federal cops to transport around 8 tons of pure medical-grade cocaine. All in broad daylight, down a well-known highway, and with no more than a handful of guys. We took it in cardboard boxes from the chemical plant to Melbourne's Tullamarine Airport, where it would go to Scotland for medical use.

Myself and John Benson, the only man in Seabrake who delivered on every promise he made me.

I played a major role – in fact I led the convoy, because I knew the route so well – and that, believe it or not, was from Port Fairy. I knew every road and short-cut, away from towns and cities, so our convoy could keep in sight of each other.

There was a moment my Russian driver misunderstood my directions and ran the lot of us up a dead-end street! He hardly spoke any English, my Russian was non-existent, but we worked through it successfully.

We stacked the cargo in aircraft bins, the kind food is stored in on board, then watched it loaded on and the doors close. The job went without a hitch.

With Seabrake closer to completion, and earning real money once again, Group 4 was just a job. However, through death threats on the boss, Sir Peter, and being stationed as his personal security at Ansett's HQ for several days during a strike, I got the job of a lifetime – providing security when Prince Charles and Lady Diana opened the Bourke Street Mall.

At the security briefing in Myers department store, in the pre-dawn, I stood with a mix of palace security, special UK security, AFP, and state police. The royal couple stood on a dais in front of Myers for the opening. Although I never formally met either one, it was a thrill to see the Princess up close. She was a lot taller than I expected and even more beautiful in real life.

The Pommy boss offered me a management position with the company, relocating to the Dandenongs someplace. I turned him down, much to his astonishment.

'You'll be set for life, mate – this outfit is only getting started, and you'll be a boss from the original foundations.'

How right was he? Group 4 started with only a handful of us – today it employs thousands, and provides security to military bases all over Australia, and more. Had I stayed there, who knows how different my life would have been.

And then there was my acting career.

'Do you have any relatives living in Australia?' I asked Greta Scacchi, in her role as an immigrant coming to Melbourne in the 1920s. I was the immigration officer, picked I'm sure as I was the only one old enough to play the part! However, for $80 cash in hand I'd have said anything. All the die-hards on set, tragics waiting for that one big break, stopped talking to me after that.

But *Waterfront* was coming to a wrap, and standing on Station Pier all day as an extra wasn't my thing either.

For the record, Jack Thompson is a great bloke, a real down-to-earth Aussie icon, who sat with us extras and talked, or played cards, between scenes.

But now I had to make some serious money and pay back all my debts. I declined the offer of more work, and left.

With a working prototype, I needed a good lawyer who could set up a contract between JB and me. I picked a name out of the phonebook.

It was a 'free first consultation' deal. The lawyer was very impressed that I'd come this far on my own, but suggested he call a firm of specialists to do the contract I needed: Davis and Ryan at 1 Little Collins St.

I waited while he called. After explaining what I needed, he gave my name. Then he paused, looking a bit astonished.

'Have you ever drunk fine scotch whisky out of a Vegemite jar?' he asked. Then it struck me.

Mr Ryan.

Des Ryan, to be precise, although I always called him Mr Ryan when he chartered my boat. It was always Des who did the bookings, maybe three times a year, and he always had a group of senior men with him – what they all did was never declared, but I assumed they were lawyers.

It was a tradition at settling-up time that Des and I had a scotch – except one night every glass aboard had been smashed in rough weather, so I washed out a large Vegemite jar and we shared the same glass.

I was put on the phone.

'You had better come up and see me,' he said. 'If it's boating and you say it works, that's good enough for me.'

Off to 1 Little Collins I went, opposite the Hotel Windsor and State Parliament – the real top end of town.

I couldn't believe my luck. This man had spent many hours at sea with me, he knew my capabilities and he knew me – a little rough around the edges – and that this was way out of my depth.

We reminisced over many good and bad charters, and I learnt those senior men he had brought along had been judges, QCs, politicians.

I then had to fill him in on my personal life and the shit I was in financially. 'Tell your Mr Benson you'll have an agreement for him to look at soon, and in the meantime add up all your debts.'

I left feeling quite drunk.

* * * *

'How the fuck did you get Des Ryan? I couldn't afford him!' JB was astounded when I took in Des's agreement.

When I told him, it gave little relief. It was an agreement I never thought John would sign: $100,000 up front, and then it only got worse – for JB.

An annual consulting fee of another $50,000 paid quarterly, in advance. A minimum royalties clause to ensure they didn't just buy it and sit on it, but went into production quickly or it would send them broke.

Mr Ryan did government contracts, he really knew his stuff, and he made my agreement bombproof.

I sweated blood for a week, convinced JB would never sign.

But John Benson signed the agreement, saying it was too big for him to do alone, he didn't want to spend millions on just one project. He needed a 'big brother', and he had someone in mind.

The further irony was that JB's counsel was none other than Frank Smith, the recently retired Australian Commissioner of Patents – an old foe of Des Ryan's for many years, Des being a patent attorney.

Seabrake is born, October 1982

This only made Des more determined to put together an agreement that tied Frank up in knots. With a done deal, *Friendship* finally selling, and myself out of debt, life was good again.

With money, I could buy wheels that had more than one gear! By chance I became friendly with the owner of a South Yarra video store, who was leaving for Sydney to manage the comedian Rodney Rude. All his friends were vying for his amazing house in East Melbourne, and for diplomacy's sake he offered it to me.

Ness and I took it in a flash. It was right behind the Hilton Hotel, its back door was in George Street, and it was a seven-minute walk through the Botanic Gardens to 1 Little Collins Street.

Money was rolling in, I was driving to Port Fairy to have Joel for the weekends and holidays. The pressure was off. Ness and I were rebuilding fences. It was a great time in my life.

Now as I look back, it's a time of many memories, some happy, some sad. I guess, in hindsight, I wish I had spent more time living in the moment, enjoying it all, instead of planning so hard for the future.

Marching with 7 RAR, Anzac Day, Melbourne, 1984 stands out.

'Good onya Corporal Abernethy,' someone shouted from the crowd. There was my dad, face grey from exhaustion, smiling, giving me the thumbs-up. That was the last time I would ever see him.

Just four months later we were at the Sydney Boat Show launching Seabrake to the world. I got back to our hotel that night to news from Wendy, my ex-wife. Dad had died. He died of a ruptured aorta, bleeding to death almost immediately at the age of 69.

It broke more than my heart, it broke me to pieces. I sat on the floor in my room, with my back against the bed, and sobbed. I stayed like that for most of the night.

At least he had lived long enough to see me make something of myself, and provide love and support to Joel, his grandson.

I saw Joel often now I was back in Melbourne, and he and Ness got along just great. We took him to places he loved, skate ramps, tram rides,

The towing tank, AMC, Hobart. That's when we knew Seabrake was a winner.

the zoo – after Port Fairy, being in the big smoke was an adventure. One day I came home with a six-week-old blue heeler puppy for Ness; she called her Schipper, after the writing on the side of the shoebox I brought her home in – Schipp for short. Now Joel had a mate everywhere we went.

With the agreement that I had licensing the 'worldwide rights to manufacture, market and sell' Seabrake came my responsibility to support, and consult with, the licensees to ensure it made it through to production as soon as humanly possible. They were investing millions of dollars. My first job was to produce evidence of Seabrake's capabilities, to take to government departments for endorsement into the fishing industry initially, then commercially worldwide for all ocean-going vessels. The Australian Maritime College (AMC) in Hobart, Tasmania, was my first scientific test.

Dr Martin Renilson was in charge of the hydrodynamics department there, and he and I hit it off straight away. We both loved a scotch, and

I learnt more about science over a jar of quality spirits with Martin after work than I did from years at school.

He was a bushy-bearded Scot with a great sense of humour, but I couldn't get my head around the fact that he had never been on boats! He had a PhD in Ship Stability – 'Broaching-to' – yet he had never been in rough water, much less on a boat in a Force 12 gale.

Ben Lexcen, of America's Cup winged-keel fame, had been the last one in the college's towing tank, developing his invention that had beaten the Yanks at their own game.

The tank was around 10 feet deep, and about 100 yards long. Atop sat a platform like a train trolley, which ran along the tank. Electrically powered, it towed the items attached to it – Seabrake in my case, Bennie's keel before that – the length of the tank, measuring scientifically everything occurring in the water below.

At the end of the tank there were two fail-safe electronic beams to apply an emergency brake should the operator fail to end his trial manually.

This is where my real education began; everything you can think of is pretty much the result of science in some form or another, and Seabrake more so than I ever imagined.

Martin was very sceptical that my device would have 'variable drag'. The prototype was fully functional, and he could understand the mechanics of it, but couldn't understand how a 24-inch diameter device would vary its drag ratio as I was explaining it had.

'Only one way we'll know,' he declared in his broad Scots brogue.

In the earliest stages it was showing signs he'd not expected, drag 'curves' (ratios) that were going up with each run. The maximum speed the trolley was allowed to safely work at was 6 knots.

'We have to go faster Martin,' I kept saying. 'Until we get around 8 knots you're not going to see its true effect.'

I showed him my notes from our very primitive Avery clock-scale results. And now, into our second week of testing, he believed all I had predicted to date.

Against his better judgement, and college rules, he had his operator tweak the trolley speed up.

'Just one run.' He was adamant.

'Just one,' I agreed.

We stood or sat on the trolley for every run, and at 6 knots it felt like you were doing 80km in a 35km zone. On our 'one run' it felt like we had broken the sound barrier.

That is until we hit the back wall – both 'fail-safes' couldn't stop us in time, we ran the extra 10 or so metres into the solid wall with a bang so loud it brought down staff from the offices above.

Everything that wasn't bolted down on the trolley was in the water.

'F O O K!' said Martin, regaining his feet. I thought he was referring to the crash, until I saw he was pointing at the towing bar measuring the drag levels – it was bent in its own axis like a boomerang.

My little invention had suddenly gone from being a patentable bucket on a rope to an international revolution. The drag curves now clearly showed not only a variable drag device but a scientifically-proven device capable of doing all I said it would: that is, prevent a vessel 'broaching-to' and surfing before a wave.

A visiting professor from the Maritime Academy in Southampton, in the UK, where Martin had studied, asked to meet me that afternoon.

'Tell me, John,' he said, 'how did someone with your *lack* of academic background design something as remarkable as this?'

'CDF, sir,' I said, without hesitation.

'CDF – I don't think I've heard of that?'

'Common dog fuck. Seat of the pants stuff, sir.'

I can still see the look on his face.

Martin's report was worth its weight in gold. He was one of two in the world at that time with a PhD in Broaching-to, and coming out of the AMC it carried weight internationally, as the college had worldwide credibility.

JB was very pleased with me, as was the board of Seabrake International.

Now they had a unique commodity, a world first, as big as the Marconi radio to the marine industry, some were saying.

Patented, with a scientific surveyed report, they had a 'one-off' for every boat in the world. It was priceless. Think about that for a second – 'brakes for boats' for the first time ever. It was as big as having the exclusive rights for every boat worldwide. Do you have any idea how many boats there are in the world? What could go wrong?

Now production was the priority.

Since our launch at the 1984 Sydney Boat Show, we had had people queuing to buy a Seabrake. RFD, the British inflatable life-raft and lifejacket manufacturer/distributor, signed-up for it, they wanted to sell it. All the big operators in the marine industry wanted a slice of the action. Seabrake was hot property.

So hot that the inevitable greed that comes along with something like this didn't take long to raise its ugly head. But who would have thought it would come from within, key people in Seabrake International?

Early on, Des Ryan told me what normally happens in all these great invention stories. It's called 'kill the inventor'. Not physically – but find a way to cut them out, as royalties are forever.

But not even Des could believe the ringleader in this case would be the ex-Commissioner of the Australian Patents Office, Frank Smith. He had been appointed to the board of Seabrake International and he, along with others, conspired with the owner of some backyard rotary moulding setup in Sydney to change my design and steal the concept.

Mr Callanan in Brisbane saw their patent application and alerted me. As soon as I brought it to JB, they had an Anton Piller order activated, essentially a search warrant for the guy's factory. They were caught with the lot.

A Supreme Court action ensued – costing a fortune – as they were even spreading to the United States, where court action also had to be taken.

Frank Smith died shortly after the long court cases, from shame, they say. His was a long fall from grace, from head of the Patents Office to common thief, a very public disgrace.

His co-conspirator was also dead – dead in the marine industry, anyway, as the court case costs took everything he owned, including any reputation he may have thought he once had. In fact, Seabrake sank all the crooks.

But the America's Cup was on the horizon, it was coming to Australia, and we were on it.

Seabrake would move to Perth, Western Australia, in 1986, where production was to begin in Fremantle.

Again, I was under enormous pressure – I was the only one who knew Seabrake inside out and back to front. But who could I trust? John Benson certainly, as everything he ever promised me, he delivered on. Everybody became an expert five minutes after seeing Seabrake: how it could be better, cheaper, easier to manufacture. But Seabrake is a lifesaving device. It's done properly.

I had to fly to Perth to the manufacturers and work with draughtsmen, tool-makers, and quality-control people who knew more about Seabrake than I did – which is why no production model had ever worked.

And Ness was still unwell, still struggling with alcohol, despite her promises. Today, I know that she was suffering a disease, something that totally controlled her. Back then, I just knew that I loved her and I was going to cure her. More pressure! Every time I got on a plane I worried constantly that I'd get the call saying she had come to harm while pissed.

I had helped her start her own modelling agency so she had something to keep her occupied; she blamed being bored as to why she drank. She had around eight girls on her books and plenty to do, plus she was modelling too.

Then I arrived home from a trip early to discover she was cheating on me.

We had a huge argument, and she went back to the UK. Although I met a lovely girl who made everything feel right – given my time again I believe she could have been the one – it was not to be. Soon some of Ness's girlfriends began knocking on my door late at night. It was back to the old charter days, and Gabriel's parties. I was single again.

But when you love someone, sex doesn't fill the void. I still loved Ness.

Things got to breaking point. I had been having medical problems since 1982, but my lung condition was back. I was smoking heavily, I was having massive neck and back pain, and I was drinking a lot.

One night, sitting at my desk in East Melbourne, I began crying, and my next memory was waking in a hospital. I got up to discover people in padded rooms in straitjackets. I'd only ever seen straitjackets in movies and it was a shock to learn they actually existed in real life! It was a private psychiatric ward and my GP had brought me there. Was I that crazy?

One of the doctors asked me to write down what was troubling me and left me to it; 24 hours later he was back to collect my 'book' – I had written non-stop for hours.

L–R: Seabrake original prototype, mild steel; Proto1, fibreglass original fully working unit; the first production unit; and the fibreglass model Mk2 Seabrake.

'You're not insane, nor going insane,' was his verdict. 'You need a rest. No work for three weeks!' It was a no-brainer. I arranged a holiday in the Whitsundays, my mate Nifty Nev came with me. We sailed all around the islands and based ourselves at South Molle Island.

My sore back and neck weren't improving, but my mental health certainly was; we had the sailboat for two weeks, then planned on a week in Surfers Paradise on the way home. It was doctor's orders.

In Surfers Paradise I went for a massage, my back was killing me. Afterwards I walked back to our hotel and went to bed. When I woke I was paralysed with pain, I couldn't breathe, it took me ages just to reach the bedside radio and turn it up full bore. The look on my face, and Nifty's when he came to investigate the noise, said it all.

I was rushed to hospital.

'No wonder you're feeling crook, mate, that's your left lung there.' The young radiologist showed me the X-ray. My left lung was the size of a lemon, and my heart, now that my lung cavity was full of air, had been pushed to just under my right collarbone. I later found out I was only minutes from death.

The old 'You'll feel a slight discomfort' trick was warning enough. I saw a long tubular device in a sterile sleeve get passed to the doctor; Nifty was looking on.

I was that sick, death would have been a blessing.

I went from extreme pain to immense relief in a second, as the doctor punched that rod between my ribs into my lung cavity. Green infection sprayed everywhere. Nifty fainted, not me, and they don't come any tougher than Nifty.

Apparently my lung had been infected for some time, and when it collapsed (a pneumothorax) is when my problems began. That rod releasing all the infection and air was the best feeling I'd had in a month.

I stayed in Allamanda Private Hospital for three weeks with the rod in my chest, it was bloody horrific. In the meantime Ness had returned from England, but we hadn't reconciled.

Seabrake is born, October 1982

Alone in Allamanda I discovered the real legacy of Vietnam.

My left lung was like a serious burn scar, thick and thin; a simple cough is all it would take to tear the thin layers.

They said it wouldn't be my last medical emergency if I kept smoking. What do you do when you're stressed as a smoker? Smoke! It would take two more pneumothoraxes and a lot more besides before I quit.

Then came the call I had dreaded

It was late at night. I was back in Melbourne. Ness was in The Alfred Hospital – she had been in a car wreck and had a ruptured spleen. She had asked that I be called. I went immediately. Yes, she'd been pissed.

The only good news was that it had happened practically in front of The Alfred, and they had wheeled a gurney from the hospital to collect her from the car. She was lucky, a couple of shiners from hitting her head and a ruptured spleen from hitting the wheel. I could tell her parents she would make a full recovery.

I visited the hospital regularly, and we spoke about reconciliation. I was leaving Melbourne for Perth for a year, for the America's Cup, and it could be a new beginning. I proposed to Ness while she was still in hospital, and she accepted. The new beginning started there.

America's Cup, Perth, 1986–1987

I had been travelling back and forth to Western Australia for months, working with the manufacturers of Seabrake, who specialised in underwater equipment, primarily in the oil industry. Being on the ground on a daily basis could only expedite matters, as each component in Seabrake's assembly had to be independently produced, and to my specifications – not those of the manufacturer, who was always looking at cost and short-cuts.

Every production unit I had trialled to that point had failed, and I couldn't understand why. Being there where I could trial again the next day, with modifications, could only speed things up. The company sent Ness, Schipper the blue heeler and me to Western Australia and set us up in a brand-new townhouse, purpose-built for the America's Cup, in the suburb of Churchlands.

The problem we were experiencing with Seabrake was caused by 'internal pressure' preventing the doors from opening, and when I pushed the envelope to higher speeds, much above operational speed, the units simply exploded. My mild fibreglass prototype unit had by now been trialled at speeds of 20 knots, and behind navy vessels, commercial fishing vessels, practically every type of vessel afloat, without a hitch.

Was it the material, the high-impact plastics we were using, or was it a design fault? The injection moulding tools for *each* size unit cost $1 million – changing component tooling was expensive, but I was sure I had found the problem. The venturi ports (or tubes) that ran through

Seabrake from front to rear were one piece on the prototype, but in the manufactured unit they were in two sections, joined.

The clock was ticking, and I was responsible for producing a marketable item, for which I was being handsomely paid. I glued together the joins to prove my theory and it worked straight up. Next morning bright and early I arrived at the manufacturing plant, and on the way to the manager's office I began tearing drawings off draughtsmen's boards in my rage.

'Day one I told you – change any part of this design and it doesn't work. Who authorised the join in the venturis?'

'It's easier to make,' he replied.

'I don't give a fuck. Make a one-piece venturi or I'll be recommending we take our business elsewhere. This fuck-up is on your head!' And on that note I left.

By week's end a new tool was producing one-piece venturis, and the first unit I trialled worked a treat. It also turned out to be a better way to assemble Seabrake: a win-win.

With Seabrake back on track I had time to take in more of Perth and the Louis Vuitton Cup – the lead-up to the main event. The Louis Vuitton Cup saw all those contenders from around the world vying for the opportunity to challenge the America's Cup holder.

The 1987 America's Cup was in the hands of Alan Bond, and Australia.

Challengers race each other for months in the lead-up to the final race, so every day there was a 12-metre race going on out on the water.

Ness scored a job with a promotion company for the duration of the Cup and was busily door-knocking, selling wares to the big end of town while the world focus was on Perth.

The whole town was in party mode, especially Fremantle. The greats of the sport were all there, Dennis Conner and John Bertrand to name but two. It was bright lights, all-night entertainment, and high living – it's a rich man's sport, and you needed to be rich even to be a spectator.

The first shipment of 4000 Mk1 Seabrakes bound for the USA, coming off production at the factory in Fremantle, Western Australia.

Through Seabrake we were in the inner circle.

One morning, JB asked me to join him for a meeting with Frank Matich on Frank's boat. Matich, of racing car fame, was interested in a Seabrake.

We arrived at a spectacular brand-new boat – around 90-feet long – and JB spotted a boat tied up beside us with a For Sale sign on it.

'Now that's the sort of boat for you,' I told him. JB had been on my case for ages to help him find a good boat.

'You like that?' Frank asked. 'I own it, if you're interested – that's my old boat before this.'

It was a 60-foot Grand Banks, a great live-aboard, and in perfect order. By nightfall JB owned it.

Now I had a boat to skipper, in addition to my Seabrake role, but what a windfall – I had a trial boat at my disposal 24/7, and with the Canadian syndicate eliminated from the Cup challenge, Seabrake International took over their berth and allocated area in Fremantle Harbour.

Each day we could get right up close to the action. It was a three-layer boat-viewing priority: syndicate boats closest to the course, followed by commercial boats (being us) and charter companies, followed by the outer circle of the general public. We were so close we could hear the racing crews talking.

Seabrake had appointed a new general manager, and it was his job to host potential outlets for Seabrake by bringing aboard the boat any, and all, who could advance our cause. I met some amazing people from all walks in life. But the crooks were still circling Seabrake.

It had me beat why, at the end of each day, the new manager unloaded all the left-over food and booze from the boat. He would arrive every day with new stock. I smelt a rat, and I was right. Not only was this guy hosting gambling parties at home, on the company's food and booze, his house was furnished with paintings and property belonging to Seabrake. JB sacked his arse, and he was lucky not to do time; apparently it wasn't his first offence.

* * * *

There was a lot of great racing in the lead-up to the actual America's Cup of January–February 1987. The Kiwis are always great contenders, and the new boy on the block, also a local, was Kevin Parry, with Iain Murray on the wheel of his boat, *Kookaburra III*.

They went on to challenge American Dennis Conner – beating Alan Bond in the Challengers round robin series and outing him in the regatta for the first time in 13 years. Being there for every race was something.

Ironically, Ness and Alan Bond's girlfriend had the same surnames: Bliss. I had met Diana with Alan Bond in their 'love-nest' as the media called it, in Sydney. Diana Bliss was a beautiful, down-to-earth, natural lady who always made me feel good simply being around her.

I remember being at their place for a party and someone saying, 'You do realise that's a $54 million painting you're leaning against?'

It was Van Gogh's *Irises*.

However, during the Cup, Alan had made noises that he could be interested in investing in Seabrake, and had asked Ness and me to join him at Observation City, a hotel he built for the America's Cup overlooking the course. Of course we went, although Seabrake's rights were already licensed, which I had told him. But you don't say no to the guy who was hosting the whole show in his home town.

That Christmas, 1986, two things of note happened – Schipp the dog got pregnant, and we stayed bogged for a week on the beach at Denmark, west of Albany, after I took the Land Cruiser just that extra bit too far out onto a beautiful beach. I didn't want to spend the break digging out the vehicle, so we pitched our tent and laid back, catching enough fish every day to live on without touching our stores. I even gave surfing a try, with a board I had bought Joel for Christmas. He was the only thing missing.

Local boy Jon Sanders, who was carrying two Seabrakes, timed his second lap of his triple world circumnavigation to a tee, arriving back in Perth waters for the Cup. My whiz marketing mate, Rik Dovey, had arranged for a plane to tow a Seabrake banner overhead, as we were also sponsors, and I broadcast the whole event live on radio from out on the water. In the end, Dennis Conner won back the Cup in a 4–0 victory.

With the Cup run and won by February, JB wanted me in the USA, where our first shipment of Seabrakes was headed. As things turned out, the boat going back across the Great Australian Bight with the best Bass Strait skipper I knew, veteran commercial fisherman Brian Newman, wouldn't have made it without a Seabrake. Brian told me they copped a four-day hiding that would have sent them to the bottom without Seabrake. Forget every other endorsement that followed – that was the greatest compliment from a man I respected more than any other; he had seen more bad weather in Bass Strait than any man I know. What's more, he went on the record and put that in writing.

America's Cup, Perth, 1986–1987

When JB's boat arrived back in Melbourne it went into St Kilda Marina, where Ness and I, and three dogs (Schipp had had puppies), took up residence. It was great seeing Joel after being away for so long, but being young I don't think it affected him as much as it did me; in any event he was thrilled with his pup Buddy, his surfboard, and his own cabin aboard when he stayed with us each weekend and all the holidays.

Ness also took advantage of our location to spread the Seabrake gospel, starting with the boss of the Water Police when they came into the marina late one night. The chief inspector, I believe that was his rank, came aboard and invited me to do a trial behind their boat. Not only did we get to include that footage in our promo video, by year's end most of the Water Police boats carried Seabrakes.

With two container-loads of Seabrakes on their way to the USA, the company's chief negotiator and I flew out to California via Hawaii. In a purpose-built box, like camera equipment, I had one Seabrake to conduct trials. Even back then in the '80s it caused some panic for customs, as to all intents and purposes it looked like a bomb on the X-ray.

Puppies: 'production' by Schipper!

Arriving in San Francisco for my first trial we discovered the box wouldn't fit into a cab trunk.

'We'll need a limo,' announced my companion.

It was my first ride in a stretch limo, and arriving at the Westin St. Francis Hotel in Union Square I felt like royalty – it's in fact where the Queen had stayed when she visited the USA.

During the America's Cup, contacts had been established in the States for potential investors, distributors, even manufacturers. It was my job to demonstrate Seabrake, and my companion's to negotiate contracts for Seabrake International. Day one saw me trialling it behind a very expensive yacht out of San Francisco's main marina, past Alcatraz prison and on under the Golden Gate Bridge for lunch.

I was living the dream – more importantly, I was proving to the world that Australian innovation is world-class.

Lee Marvin was at home in Nevada when I called, and he was adamant that I come out and stay with him: 'Pam's in New York with the kids – we'll have the place to ourselves.'

I simply couldn't, I had day-to-day commitments. It would be to my lasting regret.

I went on with my negotiator companion to Los Angeles, Marina del Rey, the world's largest man-made harbour. We were meeting a cartel, some of the richest businessmen in LA, I was told. Exclusive clubs lined the water's edge, with gorgeous young blondes serving drinks to club members under palm trees. It was impressive.

The boat we were using on this occasion was a large motor yacht. On our way out to sea the skipper pointed out John Wayne's home, Michael Jackson's new house, etc. Then I did my thing and showed them how we could lay beam-on to the swell and not spill a drink, with Seabrake reducing 90% of the roll.

It was a very successful trip, and while we had been away an Australian government department had finished its extensive report into Seabrake's export value. On a fraction of the available US market, they had concluded Seabrake's initial market entry was worth $100 million.

That document was a licence to print money. Keeping in mind this was the USA alone, not the world market, and again, that this estimate was based on the bare minimum, as governments tend to do – it was a product with potential to bring hundreds of millions of dollars into Australia. What could go wrong?

But the trip ended very sadly. Back home, I walked into our apartment and had just put down my bags when a TV news flash reported Lee Marvin had died! I phoned Pam.

'Once they opened him up, John, to see what was there, the exposure to air only sped up the cancer,' she said. 'He was riddled with it.'

I was devastated, and angry at myself for not going to see him – and pissed off with Lee for not saying a word.

Ness and I returned to Fremantle, as guests of Seabrake International, for an Australian Design Award presentation for Seabrake, with legendary Aussie yachtsman John Bertrand as a guest speaker. It was a huge honour, with the WA Governor making the presentation, and John Bertrand endorsing Seabrake. The company also donated a 40-foot boat to the WA Sea Scouts, duly fitted with two Seabrakes.

I was also honoured to be contacted by the publisher of the book *Made in Australia*, which lists me, with photos of Seabrake, on the opposite page to Ben Lexcen's winged keel.

* * * *

Now for the first time in my life I had a tax problem – I know, nice problem. With Seabrake International meeting all my expenses, and the money I was earning, I had exorbitant provisional tax to pay each quarter.

'You need something to pay tax on, outgoings,' my tax accountant said. He went through a list of proposals, eventually saying, 'A run-down farm, for example – fences, dams, land improvement.'

Bingo, he said the magic word. Farm. I knew what the doctors had said back in 1971, but if it was more a hobby farm, in the right location, it would be the perfect solution; both Ness and I loved horses.

We went farm shopping. Every weekend for months we were off to look at a new place. Each week a property at Bendoc, Haydens Bog, 400 acres for a ridiculously low price, was always there.

'Where the fuck is Haydens Bog exactly, Ness?' I finally asked. It was 1988, so we used good old paper maps to eventually find it, tucked away in the alpine region of Victoria's north-east, a mile from the New South Wales border. We arranged to inspect it.

The Bonang Highway is 90km of hairpin bends from Orbost to Bendoc, on a narrow gravel road with logging trucks coming at you continually. That's the good news. When we finally arrived, a bushfire had been raging for weeks, and the only accommodation available was filled with firefighters. The Delegate Hotel on the NSW side of the border is where we arrived, and next morning we headed out to look at 'Fairview'. It was aptly named – you could see for bloody miles! The house and land were on the western side of Mt Delegate, with views out over the Cottonwood Ranges, and onto the nearby Snowy Mountains. Ness and I looked at each other as we stepped from the car. This was it. We both knew it immediately.

It was perfect, it was a goat stud, all electric fencing (no barbwire), 200 acres of cleared land and 200 acres of bush running up Mt Delegate. It needed re-fencing for horses, more dams; it had only an old shearing shed and haystack as structures, apart from the odd shelter here and there. The house was small but liveable, room for improvement, and an asking price about half of what we had seen, for twice the value.

We bought it.

Woodville Lodge, from 1988

They say be careful what you wish for. I'm not sure I ever wished for it, and I know I'd never dreamed I would find myself where I was – a young inventor with many millions seemingly within reach, an astonishingly beautiful wife, an idyllic horse property high in Australia's Snowy Mountains. But it was to prove the best and worst of times.

My time as a consultant with the company ended in May 1988, and since returning from Western Australia I had been working on new designs and models.

Fixing the 'doors' made the unit effectively a drogue, and there was a market in this field also, as only antiquated canvas-style drogues were available. A monocock, or hard-bodied device, didn't exist.

I produced two more totally new concepts – the HSD (High Speed Drogue), and the Mk2 Seabrake (a pop-base version), which did away with the four doors altogether. The beauty of the Mk2 was that it required only two manufactured components as opposed to nine components with the Mk1, making it a much cheaper unit to produce.

These new designs were renegotiated into our existing agreement, all being patented and protected, with the IP remaining in my name. The company would be left in great shape with follow-up product I had prototyped and successfully trialled. Seabrake International had also signed up the large Japanese multinational company Marubeni (Komatsu) as a worldwide distributor, and RFD New Zealand, who had been with us since the 1984 Sydney launch.

The future looked great, and it was now simply a matter of manufacturing to a global market. Or so I thought.

Now renamed 'Woodville', our farm was our piece of paradise, a breath of fresh air, literally, at 1800 feet above sea level. I had not lived in the mountains before, and certainly not in an alpine region.

We moved at the beginning of winter, in June 1988.

Steeped in history, the little township of Bendoc was part of the Victorian Gold Rush in the 1850s, with alluvial gold discovered in the Bendoc River in 1855, and the Morning Star mine starting in the region in 1857. By 1911, the lucrative Victoria Star Goldmine operated at Bendoc. When we moved to Woodville, an old Chinese cemetery had been uncovered at the rubbish tip nearby, testimony to the Chinese communities who had, like so many, hoped for riches during those pioneering times.

Our place had an old goldmine on it as well, although after my Vietnam tunnel experience only Joel and Ness went in.

Where in centuries past they laboured for gold, we set about building our dream horse property, just Ness and me and the dogs at first, with Joel coming for school holidays.

It was a golden time. Living high on a mountain-top in mid-winter with a panoramic view of our alpine surrounds was not only peaceful after the city, it was romantic. If it was bitterly cold, or snowing, we had a huge supply of cut firewood – we could just roll back into bed for the day and watch the falling snow as we made love.

Although the house was too small at first, a builder mate – with the help of my new Farm Boss chainsaw – took out the back wall and propped up the ceiling on jacks, and by nightfall we had a new lounge-room twice its original size. Two open fireplaces and a slow combustion stove provided all our cooking and heating needs, and we had 200 acres of timber for an endless supply of fuel.

It became apparent very early that Ness had a magic touch with animals, all animals. I need only look for the three dogs to know where she was – they never left her side. And as our farm became established,

Ness was the Pied Piper. Horses would whicker at her mere presence, and all the broodmares got their evening meals *heated*, bran and special mixes to warm their tummies for the night.

Geese, chooks, ducks and all living critters on the property were her babies – even feral cats in the haystack.

Where men I know would tread warily around stallions, she had a way that would melt them to her touch, they never played up.

For a girl who had grown up in a very privileged life, Ness was just as much at home covered in horse shit as she was modelling on a catwalk. It surprised many, none more than me.

We also got to know people, like John and Carol Ingram at Craigie Station, who sold us a great ex-racehorse, a 14-year-old gelding called Flag. He was followed by a beautiful chestnut mare called Brigalow, for Ness. We rode the extremities of our land and beyond into the surrounding national parks and state forests.

There wasn't much financial worry. I was on minimum royalties, paid quarterly, in advance. Into the fourth year of our agreement, indexed, it was still a tidy sum.

Building our future. Joel and me, Woodville, 1988.

It was a 16-hour round trip to fetch Joel in Port Fairy for the holidays, but I loved every minute of it. We had some great times on the road. Like the night he fell asleep, and it was so cold the wiper rubbers stuck to the windshield in mid-swipe. I climbed out and started peeing on the windscreen to free them up, only to jump a foot off the bumper-bar when they started up again. Joel woke up to this sight. He laughed his head off.

Actually, snow was a new thing for me. It was a big learning curve to drive in it for the first time. I could leave Melbourne in bright sunlight and need chains on the tyres before I reached home.

The previous owners had been under contract to a chip-milling company, who wanted us to extend the deal. I refused. But, while I was sourcing timber for the house extension from the local mill, I asked the owner about selective logging – taking out a tree here and there, with us taking posts and rails for our fences in lieu of royalties.

It was a perfect arrangement. Our property was almost opposite his mill, and during winter they couldn't log in the state forests, which effectively shut them down. Now they could take timber from our place, just a short distance away, and remain open all winter. This handshake agreement supplied enough posts and rails to fence 80 acres, and was the best win/win deal of both our lives. It stayed in place for eight years without a single hitch.

We needed the post-and-rail fencing. Horses and wire are a deadly combination – young horses, especially, don't see wire, and so we rid the place of all wire where we intended to hold horses.

On his stays, Joel helped Ness and me put up fencing and he also learnt to ride on old Flag, who was the ideal age and temperament for a learner.

I had set two rules before buying the place: there would be no Shetland ponies, and no stallions – stallions are a handful and Shetland ponies can be little bastards.

We intended to breed horses as it was a horse area and nobody else was doing it, it was mainly sheep and cattle territory. As the farm took shape, four horses quickly developed into a dozen before Christmas of our first year. Rather than just focusing on thoroughbreds, we intended to breed stockhorses and kids' ponies – there is always a good market for them – but, again, temperament is paramount. This is how the first rule came to be broken.

We went half-shares in a Dartmoor stallion. Dartmoors are a small, strong pony with an excellent temperament, and only a handful existed in Australia then – I believe Zorro, our little jet-black steed, was one of only five in the country. We landed up with five stallions.

As the horse stud grew, I got my Australian Horse Trainer's Licence – to train racehorses – and we continually had a racehorse, or two, in-work, and racing. This was in addition to breeding 30–40 foals every year.

We soon became a focal point for anyone with an interest in horses.

Our immediate neighbour had a three-year-old colt still running with his mother that needed to be broken in.

Even though I was riding daily, I hadn't sat a young green horse since I was 20; I was now 40 years old.

Having mouthed, saddled and ridden this young colt, he hadn't put a foot wrong – that is until I rode him out of the breaking yard for the first time, dismounted to open a gate and was halfway back in the saddle when his head disappeared between his front legs and he pitched me high in the air. That earned me a broken elbow, but you must get straight back on, or the horse has won the day.

On that same day we purchased a beautiful Palomino Anglo-Arab mare as a breeder – she had apparently been badly broken in and not ridden for years. Di was her name.

Soon after Di arrived I bought some cattle at the local cattle sales. Cattle and horses complement each other when you rotate them around paddocks. But we didn't know the cattle had only had calves weaned off them that morning before the sale.

In bed that night, Ness and I heard cattle bellowing close to the house – too close, their paddock was half a mile away. I got up to find cattle everywhere, searching for their calves in the dark.

We had no stockhorses, only Di, who hadn't been ridden in years. In the black of night I caught her, saddled her, and fitted a bridle with a Pelham bit and chain. Then I held my breath and climbed aboard.

Far from trying to buck me off, she took off after the cattle as if she'd been doing it the day before. I really held my breath as I unfurled my stockwhip and gave it a crack. She never even flinched.

Di and I worked through the night rounding up those cattle; she was as good as any stockhorse I'd ever ridden. Being part-Arab, she had endurance, and part-thoroughbred she had speed; the perfect combination.

But here I was, an upstart from the city, who arrives in iconic Man from Snowy River country and starts a horse business. The local horsemen had been wondering who I was.

One night, coming onto dark, two riders came up our drive. Brother and sister as it turned out; Clive and Ivy Jamison, our neighbours from Haydens Bog. They were in their late seventies.

'Ever seen a brumby?' asked old Clive, as our conversation got onto horses.

'No – can't say I have,' I answered.

He slid to the ground and offered me the reins.

'You're looking at two – caught and broke both of them,' he said. 'Take a ride – see what you think.'

I knew what he was thinking: 'What's this city slicker doing up here?'

I climbed aboard and turned the horse towards our roadway. It was a mile to the mailbox and a mile back. I galloped the horse there and back.

'You did a good job breaking him, he goes well,' I said, handing back the reins. Actions speak louder than words.

Old Clive soon paid another visit. He and a few of his hand-picked family and friends had permits to 'run brumbies': catch them in the Kosciuszko National Park. He invited me along.

Di was the only horse I had capable, the rest being thoroughbred broodmares, racehorses or ponies. The horse may be OK, but I had never ridden at full gallop down mountains in heavily-timbered country with wombat holes everywhere to break a horse's leg, and my neck.

But I accepted Clive's offer and began training myself and Di on Mt Delegate, feeding her well, rugging her, and having her shod. We were ready by the time Clive and the crew were set to go. Alan Mathews, Clive's daughter Debbie and son-in-law Peter made up five riders in all.

Getting into Kosciuszko National Park was a day's work: trucking our horses to the outskirts of the park, unloading them, then riding to a log cabin named Ventry's Hut, which had a rough, log-fenced yard to hold our mounts.

Debbie and Peter would follow us later in a 4 x 4 with our stores. After seeing the film *The Man from Snowy River*, and in particular that scene where he rides straight down the side of a steep mountain, I thought it was pure bullshit. That is, until we reached Ventry's Hut.

It was up and down mountains just like that all the way. You need a breast-plate (a leather strap across the horse's chest to stop the saddle sliding back) and a cropper (a leather strap around the butt of horse's tail to stop the saddle going forward).

Dogs also play an important part in brumby running. First they pick up the trail, then they round up the herd, heading them to stop their escape. Dogs that go for the heels are of no value, as they only drive the herd away. Once they come across a herd, their barking can be heard for miles, and that was our signal, to follow the sound.

Day one we climbed and climbed – at one point I could see Mt Kosciuszko covered in snow, so close that it appeared we were above it. The dogs had picked up a trail and were in pursuit. They were only a mile away, but a bottomless gully lay between us.

By late afternoon we decided to split into two groups: Alan, Deb and Peter down onto the Snowy River, and Clive and I taking the ridge above. The river looked like a small creek snaking its way through the vast wilderness. There was no way I was galloping Di straight down that steep drop. In fact, when Clive suggested we go down to where we could hear the dogs barking, our horses couldn't use their hind legs for anything other than skids – sliding under their bodies with their front legs acting as props to edge their way a foot at a time, straight down. But the brumbies were near, even though mountain goats would have had trouble keeping their feet in this terrain.

After descending 1000 feet straight down, the barking was now much louder and closer. Clive stopped and pointed. On a knoll 500 feet below us, a magnificent black stallion, covered in sweat, reared and pawed at the pack of dogs around him. We edged down. As soon as we reached the ridgeline where the stallion had been, brumbies could be heard rushing through the bush.

'Catch the foal,' the other group shouted, as a bay filly flashed by.

Without a single thought, I hit Di with both heels. Clive was at my side.

'Grab the tail,' Clive yelled. Di was right on the filly's heels. I leaned out of the saddle and reached for the filly's tail, just reaching it with my finger-tips. The brumby filly found another gear and shot ahead. That happened many times, until Di's front legs pushed the filly off-balance, just enough for me to get a good hold of the tail. I grabbed and hung on for dear life, pulling up Di, and the captured filly.

'You beauty!' cheered Clive, tossing his lasso over the filly's head, but she was spent, and happy just to stand at Di's side, blown out. I slipped from the saddle to take Clive's end and tie it off around the nearest tree – with her wind back, she'd be gone again if I didn't.

'Watch those hind legs – she'll kick your head off,' warned Clive, later telling me how one of his mates had been kicked in similar circumstances and lost an eye.

Nobody could believe I had caught a brumby on my first day – some had been trying for 20 years. It was only to get better.

Next day I caught a chestnut filly, after all five of us took off after her. We got there first on Di's uncanny endurance and speed.

It was unprecedented – two brumbies on my first run. But not all our brumby running ended happily.

Sometime later, when we went back in to the park, both Debbie and I were riding young horses we were breaking in. Our role on young horses was to follow, not chase.

On this trip, an ABC crew were in there filming, and on our first morning Clive spotted brumbies close to the hut.

The film crew took off on foot as we hurriedly saddled up. Debbie's horse began playing up even as she tried to saddle her.

Sensing us, the brumby mob bolted, with Clive and Pete in pursuit. Deb and I followed, and her horse began to buck. The further they went, the worse it looked. Eventually the horse, with its head between its front legs, tossed Deb over its head and into a snow gum. I went to her.

She was unconscious. On closer examination I saw she wasn't breathing. She didn't have a pulse. She was dead.

Her horse, without a rider, quickly caught up to Peter, who fortunately came back; only weeks before he had completed his first aid course with the SES. By the time I had removed the branches from where Deb lay and gently rolled her over, Pete was there.

'Mate – she's not breathing, and no pulse,' I told him, as he stared in shock. 'Pete – for fuck sake, it's been too long – she needs CPR!'

Still he was paralysed in his saddle, looking down.

'PETE – FOR FUCK'S SAKE!'

Then it hit him. He went into action, mouth to mouth. As he crossed his palms on her chest to begin heart massage she gasped, long and loud, through her purple lips, and she began to breathe, rough and erratic at first, like an engine missing, then more settled.

'Mate, she hit that tree hard, real hard, with her back,' I told Pete.

We inspected her back and to our horror we saw a haematoma the size of a football between her shoulder blades. She had to have a broken back, at best.

Then Clive arrived. She was his only child.

'She's gone?' he asked from his saddle, more a statement than a question as he looked me square in the eye.

'No, mate, unconscious, she's going to be fine. But we need to get her to hospital.' I tried to sound calm.

The ABC film crew had a Land Cruiser station wagon; we sent the cameraman to bring it up. Between all of us we gently got Deb in across the back seat, and I knelt over her from the floor to stop her rolling.

With Pete at the wheel we began the slow journey out of the wilderness towards Delegate. En route we came in contact with a CFA firetruck that radioed ahead for an ambulance to meet us – which took place near Delegate River Tavern. Pete had to drive the ambulance while the driver attended Deb in the back. I went on to the tavern and had my fair share of scotch before returning to Ventry's Hut.

Deb had five shattered vertebrae. Had she not started breathing when she did, if Pete had pushed down on her chest we may well have put her in a wheelchair for life.

She made a full recovery and was back riding again a year or so later, much to her doctor's annoyance.

The High Country is no place for the faint-hearted – but is some of the most beautiful country I have ever seen, and the only way to fully appreciate it is on horseback.

I have to add, brumby running and horse riding in national parks has since been banned. The two I caught we bred from, and cared for, which is a hell of a lot better than their mob got later on, when National Parks and Wildlife hired shooters to cull them from helicopters. The wounded bled to death, or lay with shot spines till they died of starvation or thirst. And they say they are conservationists. I call them fucking hypocrites.

But in many ways our life was idyllic – although we worked bloody hard. Farm work is endless, no matter what sort of farm it may be.

Our days started early, 5.30am if I had racehorses in-work. I'd float them to Bombala racecourse 20km away then, back at the farm, feed all the stabled horses, clean out the stables and lay fresh straw every day.

During winter our broodmares were doubled-rugged at night, then one rug taken off during the day. Remember, we had 50-plus broodmares.

If I had young horses to break in I would start that after breakfast, while Ness fed out around the paddocks, checking each horse as she did.

There was also other maintenance and infrastructure to take care of. As a developing horse stud, we were constantly extending our post-and-rail fencing, building new dams, building new stables, working with vets and farriers – always there is a horse needing medical attention, or a racehorse needing new shoes. And there was always firewood that needed to be cut and carted.

But as honest as our long, rural days were, storm clouds were gathering over our paradise in the mountains.

Seabrake, and the business world, was never far away.

It was both a blessing and a curse. Technology was starting to make a difference. With fax machines and mobile phones coming onto the market, even living in the bush meant you could do business with the city.

Every night there were dozens of faxes for me to go through, after working the farm from dawn till dark, and sometimes travelling for work. It was in my best interests to help out. The company paid my expenses to attend boat shows around the world, as investors always like to meet the inventor, and I was training salespeople at the same time.

After the business successes at the America's Cup, the company set up representatives in each state in Australia. Never doing things by halves, they took up offices in prime waterfront locations, with staff driving expensive cars; to them, it was all about the perception.

Austrade were also very active in assisting with Seabrake's overseas expansion; we were now well established in the USA, Japan and New Zealand, attracting interest from across the globe.

Then I began hearing rumblings about various companies associated with Seabrake International having trouble getting paid; my IP payments were also late.

JB confirmed that Lorraine Investments, the Nicholas company, were having cash-flow problems – not Seabrake International. The Nicholas brothers had spread themselves thin in multiple venture-capital businesses and the October 1987 'recession we had to have' had caught up to them.

They owned multiple desalination companies, which were all still in development stage. Mike Nicholas had also purchased Erakor Resort in Vanuatu – which a cyclone had blown away – and the historic cattle station, Tom Groggin Station, in the Victorian High Country. In short, they had a really serious cash-flow problem. It would be a gross understatement to say they had over-extended themselves.

It was around this time two very significant things happened.

The good news was Ness was pregnant. The bad, that Lorraine Investments had an administrator appointed and JB was forced out of Seabrake International.

John Benson had been there since day one; if it were not for him there would be no Seabrake International. He put up the money to develop Seabrake, he backed it with millions of dollars of his own money, he brought in Lorraine Investments, he fixed every problem. John Benson was the only person in the history of Seabrake who delivered on every promise he ever made me. Now he was out, and I was dealing with an administrator.

Under the terms of the licence agreement, should the licensee default it all reverted to me.

Having an administrator appointed was one of the clauses I could give notice to terminate, and if this was not rectified within 90 days the agreement was at an end. I was owed a considerable amount of outstanding royalties, and manufacturers and other creditors were owed large amounts of money.

Seabrake could survive. It was not the cause of Lorraine's demise and it had international distributors in place. I had never expected Lorraine to default. They'd spent in the vicinity of $13 million, and were poised to recoup that and hundreds of millions more.

Months and months of negotiations, false promises, and unsuccessful resolutions to save Seabrake International went down to the wire; thousands of units in the USA and around the world, as well as tooling and company assets, were to be sold off.

As the licensor I should have been kept in the loop, as most of these assets were to revert to me; tooling especially, as nobody could produce from them without a licence from me. Mysteriously, it all disappeared – the liquidator bought the time to cash in on everything he could until there was nothing left.

I never saw a dollar of the tens of thousands I was owed, and I'm sure there were many more just like me. But the real damage was that Marubeni withdrew; they were the key to Seabrake's future.

As a multinational – with tentacles reaching into the marine industry globally – and as the distributor, that was a greater blow than the closure of Seabrake International.

Meanwhile, Joel had come to live with Ness and me. He was around ten years old and had finished primary school. Joel loved being up on the farm. He had grown up at his mother's, and he took it upon himself to ask if he could start secondary school at Bombala, with us; he had made new friends here on his school holiday visits. The Port Fairy-Warrnambool area had a huge drug issue among the youngsters then – I thought getting him to the bush would protect him from all that.

Wendy and I were amicable; she had remarried and was still teaching in Port Fairy, and she and Ness got along. I was all for it and Wendy agreed.

So Joel started his secondary school education at Bombala High School.

His half-brother was born shortly thereafter. On 7 March 1990, Samuel Desmond Abernethy arrived fit and well at Cooma Hospital.

Ness's parents were out from the UK for the occasion. Her waters broke around midnight during the worst storm we had ever had up there.

The two-hour drive in those conditions, with the contractions down to a minute apart, was a night we will never forget. But now we were a family of four.

Having grown up on a farm myself I knew how lucky I had been, but also the downside – the isolation, and the lack of those facilities that city kids have. Joel had to make that transition. Like myself at the same age, he wanted to learn to play guitar. So we purchased a black left-hand electric guitar and amplifier, and it never left his hands.

With 400 acres of our own, and miles of surrounding bush, he also loved to shoot, trying his hand at foxes and feral animals.

I taught him the basics of firearm safety, as my father had taught me, too. Joel listened, and understood.

I had sown down 30 acres of oats, which had attracted every kangaroo for miles around – if I wanted to save the crop, I had to do a cull.

Joel was as keen as mustard, and with his semi-automatic Ruger .22 with 20-round magazine he was out to impress his dad. I took my 30-30 lever-action Winchester.

We left the house to Ness's parting words: 'Please don't shoot any mothers with joeys.'

Joel and I lay in wait on the path we knew the roos would take, and sure enough, just before dark they came – a hundred or more.

'Just the big bucks mate – head shots, OK?' I whispered.

His rifle had a telescopic sight and, as it was the smaller calibre, I told him to shoot first. A big buck stopped about 40 metres from us and Joel took careful aim, squeezing off a single shot. He missed.

With the entire mob now spooked, I fired on a large roo, finding the heart. It dropped stone dead.

We walked towards the body: 'I gave you first shot – and you've got telescopic sights,' I jibed.

'Yeah, but you've had lots more practice, Dad … being old and that!' he replied.

As we reached the carcass, in the fading light, I saw movement.

'Please don't let that be a joey,' I said aloud.

Joel pulled the uninjured joey from the dead mother's pouch.

'Ness is going to kill you when we get home,' he said, with relish.

I carried the joey home under my jumper, where it felt warm and secure – more than I could expect when I walked through the door with Joel eagerly shooting his mouth off.

'Dad shot a doe – with a baby joey in its pouch!'

But Ness's heart melted as I produced a little head with flicking ears.

I tried to explain.

'I don't want to know!' she said, and that was it.

The joey had his own pouch an hour later – my jumper sewn across the waist and the sleeves tied around the firescreen, in prime location near the open fire. From then on, Ness and Sam fed him formula bottled milk from the vet's. That was the most expensive roo I've ever shot.

As Sam grew, Joel became both big brother and protector – so long as Sam didn't try and touch his guitar. We had some great family times up in the mountains.

But the clouds on the horizon grew darker.

After Seabrake International reverted to me, I now had a horse stud as well as an international company to run. Put simply, there weren't enough hours in the day to do either properly, and to re-license Seabrake meant being away from the farm a lot.

Leaving Ness with two kids and all the horses created additional problems. We both had our hands full.

Friends and neighbours could fill my shoes back on the farm, but nobody could fill my shoes with Seabrake. The horse stud was costing money, not making it – so Seabrake, and only Seabrake, was our sole chance of survival.

Des Ryan set up meetings with numerous prospects to take over the licence, but nothing acceptable came forward.

At one point I was made an eight-figure offer to buy me out. I've never made the amount public, and I won't do that now. I could have accepted, but it would have cost a lot of Australian jobs, not to mention export dollars. I had been through too much to simply sell out. I had always sworn Seabrake would remain Australian-made.

The story of my refusal made the cover of Australia's leading business magazine of the time, resulting in an invitation to go on the *Today Show* on Channel 9 Sydney.

I was contacted by Steve Liebmann and interviewed by Liz Hayes. The story angle was that more great Australian innovation was being sold to overseas interests instead of remaining Australian-owned and operated. I stated on air that I wanted Seabrake to always be Australian-made and owned, and if not by me, then by an Australian company – as indeed it is today.

When I came off air, Steve informed me that Malcolm Turnbull was sending a car for me to be taken to his office.

'Who's Malcolm Turnbull?' I asked.

At that time, Malcolm Turnbull and Neville Wran, the former Premier of New South Wales, were in partnership as merchant bankers. I spent an hour with Turnbull, then an hour with Wran, who spent much of the time explaining how he regretted not retiring earlier as Premier, rather than expressing any interest in Seabrake.

I wasted weeks with the Wran-Turnbull solution. I recall Wran referencing Corn Flakes constantly as his yardstick for brand name and value. Why Corn Flakes I shall never know. But when their offer of 1% of what the Americans had offered came in writing, I took great delight in referencing Corn Flakes in my reply. Their offer was an insult, and what they were really offering was their brand (names) and 'promises'. They probably thought I would be impressed with their involvement and financial backing. Nothing could have been further from the truth, which I also mentioned in my reply.

A company affiliated with the impresario Michael Edgley, called MEH (Michael Edgley Holdings), eventually took up the worldwide rights to Seabrake.

The new company was called Seabrake Technologies, based out of Melbourne and again licensed through Des Ryan's agreement. With $13 million already spent on development and promotion, international

Woodville Lodge, from 1988

Sam and joey, on the bottle, Woodville, 1992.

distributors in place, and a marketable, in-the-box, completed product, it was a goldmine ready to begin production again.

But by now I was back in debt, owed almost $150,000 by Seabrake International, with solicitor fees, ongoing IP costs, and the cost of running a horse stud that was intended to eat up my tax burden. My dream had become my nightmare.

On advice, given the uncertainty that I would ever see a dollar out of Lorraine Investments, my best option was enter into a Part 10 'Deed of Agreement' – the same as JB had been forced into. We were both victims of the same incompetence. However, should MEH Seabrake Technologies get Seabrake back on track, I could trade myself out of trouble. The farm would be safe – Ness and her father had that in their control, at arm's length from Seabrake – but I still needed income to keep it afloat.

Under enormous pressure yet again, I had three black-outs over a short space of time. I'd had a few before this, too. I just collapsed unconscious; I didn't know what was causing them, and I didn't have the time, or the money, to properly find out. This in turn caused huge worry for Ness, and she started drinking again. Stress piled upon stress, as it does.

My best friend up there at this point was Dr Brian Carroll, our local GP, who sent me to Canberra for tests. Nothing showed up, stress was the obvious cause.

Making it worse, with racehorses in-work I had to be up at 5am, and by the time I was done with Seabrake at night I was getting three to four hours' sleep. I was exhausted beyond sanity.

By year's end, MEH Seabrake Technologies' managing director did a runner to South Africa with what money they had, leaving the company insolvent, and me high and dry yet again.

It was the same old pattern. Seabrake was seen by everyone as a cash-cow; simply being a part of it was a licence to beg, borrow or steal money.

Those who took on licence agreements expected people to come out of the woodwork with open cheque books and make them rich, without having to do a thing.

The horse stud had grown dramatically, from a couple of saddle horses to five stallions, 50-plus broodmares, and a crop of new foals every year.

I had to lease an additional paddock just to provide enough feed for them. We now had a registered Australian stockhorse stallion in addition to being a registered Australian thoroughbred horse stud, Woodville Lodge, with our own brand and racing colours. The kids' ponies were practically sold a week after birth, although none left the property until they were well-handled and going to hand-picked families.

Despite these successes, the horse business was still costing money, not making any.

But Sam was growing up, and Ness and I had been together for over a decade. We decided to get married, and the farm would be the ideal venue. We hired a large marquee and invited around a hundred people, friends and family from far and wide.

But, highlights aside, in my world back then, stress and trauma seemed to invade both my personal and business life. It was one long, hard fight, and the going was heavy. Seabrake led me along paths I couldn't have imagined. After Michael Edgley Holdings failed, I was introduced to a

Sydney-based company, a publicly-listed venture capital group. It again produced urgently needed income, but it meant being away from the farm a lot more.

I had also patented a collapsible version of Seabrake, which I had put on the back-burner while licences were in limbo. The collapsible version I named GP, for 'General Purpose'. It had many advantages over the solid-bodied Seabrakes. It didn't require expensive tooling to produce, it took up less space than hard-bodied units, had many more applications, and it was a fraction of the cost right across the board. It also appealed to the yachting fraternity much more than the earlier units, and there was a huge yacht-market worldwide.

With the Mk1 Seabrake I had proven to the world that it genuinely did all I claimed it would do. The highest level of maritime approval at that time, and probably still, was the US Coast Guard. I personally went to West Palm Beach, in Florida, to demonstrate Seabrake to the US Coast Guard in the worst weather conditions possible, leaving them with a unit they were so impressed by that, in a first, we were allowed to publish their approval in advertising material.

I sought to achieve the same for the GP model, as it was a highly effective emergency steering device in addition to its many other uses. The Australian Maritime Safety Authority (AMSA) are Australia's equivalent of the US Coast Guard, and again I successfully demonstrated the GP Seabrake for their approval.

It has since accompanied many Sydney to Hobart contenders as an emergency or secondary means of steering.

How a product with so much going for it continually fell into the wrong hands is beyond comprehension – but it did yet again. The company that now held shares in Seabrake was at the big end of town, run by high flyers; and with a Harvard hot-shot running their venture capital business, they thought this bunny from Bendoc would come to heel so long as they held the purse strings. Wrong! I had been jumping through hoops for too long.

The upshot of it all was that a contact of an old army mate of mine arranged a meeting for me with Mr Bernard Ahern. 'Don't be late,' the contact said.

I'd not heard of Bernard Ahern, yet he was a giant in the trucking world – introducing the first petrol tankers into Australia – and an equal to the billionaire Lindsay Fox.

When Bernie sold his trucking empire, he bought the famous Melbourne law firm of Frank Galbally, a prominent Australian criminal defence lawyer. Bernie, to my knowledge, wasn't a lawyer himself, but he had the sharpest mind of any man I have known. Suffering chronically from emphysema, he always had a cigar burning in the ashtray. He was not a man whose time you could waste.

After an hour of discussion, finding out all he could about me, Bernie read through the material I had brought, not lifting his head once to look at me – just thoughtfully drawing on his cigar.

'So, where are your share certificates?' he asked.

Having never been involved in limited companies or owned shares before, I didn't have a clue where he was coming from. Bernie faxed asking for a copy of the share register, and two hours later learnt that no shares existed.

Bernie had me head straight to the Melbourne office of share registrations, insisting I bring back a formal copy of what he wanted – it was now beginning to make sense. If no shares were issued to me under the 'investment agreement', my deal with the venture capital company was null and void.

The next day was my birthday; Bernie insisted that I be at his place by 8am. By now the Australian Securities Commission (ASC) investigation department had been advised that the share register was not available. It was at this point we discovered the company had been suspended from trading on the Australian Stock Exchange the day before.

With all this going on, the Seabrake HSD model was still being manufactured and sold through RFD Melbourne, who were also licensed by the company. Realising the consequences of what was at stake, and the seriousness of their position with ASC, I was invited to a meeting in Sydney.

To cut a long story short, the company made way for another investor.

RFD Australia had now produced a marketable GP model, which gave the NSW-based majority shareholder in Seabrake two variations of the original model and an opportunity to hit the ground running.

He had enough investment capital to buy into a licence with me, now amended to accommodate the collapsible model. He had taken his time in committing, even to the extent of meeting with John Benson, who had shown an interest in becoming involved in Seabrake again. Although JB ultimately decided otherwise, he did advise on the whereabouts of the original Mk1 tooling and where thousands of Mk1 Seabrakes still were in the USA.

A new company was formed: Seabrake Australia Pty Ltd.

Meanwhile, in Florida, someone had registered Seabrake America Inc.

I travelled to the USA to check out the situation, and returned to Australia fairly confident a deal could be struck once those involved were licensed with the patents that I had in place.

For licensing reasons, I had to remain at arm's length to any agreement, but I would remain a consultant to the company, and would retain all the IP in my name, as had always been the case. Seabrake Australia Pty Ltd's majority shareholder had to pay the IP costs, as well as royalties. In the deal, Seabrake Australia would provide me with a company car and meet my expenses.

Despite progress on the business front, there wasn't much to be cheerful about. Things on the home front were not good. I was now paying three people to help Ness on the farm in my absence, but she resented that I was 'getting away from the place'.

She considered my trips abroad holidays, although nothing could have been further from the truth. I was fighting tooth and nail just to keep Seabrake alive. For all of us.

I guess the end began the night I arrived home from my first US meeting. I walked in to a note from her saying I should come down to the coastal town of Merimbula.

After 20 hours' flying and the six-hour drive back to the farm, what was another hour?

I arrived to find Ness the worse for wear.

I packed Joel and Sam's bags, picked up a lit cigarette burning in the ashtray and left with the boys. It was my first cigarette in years. It started me smoking again.

Against this backdrop, Seabrake America Inc was duly licensed. Now, more than ever, it was imperative that I supported the Americans. This was Seabrake's last big opportunity.

Ness and I had another huge fight the day I was flying out for the USA, again over the fact that I was going 'on holiday', leaving her with the two boys and the horses, despite the help and support I had arranged. She couldn't, or wouldn't, understand that every dollar coming in was from my work with Seabrake – if I was to stay home, we would soon lose everything.

In the United States there is a boat show somewhere every day. My American colleagues listed those we should attend – keeping in mind Seabrake had not yet been publicly displayed in the USA at that point.

I started at the Seattle Boat Show, then travelled on to Miami, Boston, St Petersburg (Florida), New Jersey and many more. The biggest show, however, was Annapolis, America's sailing capital, and home of the US Naval Academy.

I left for the Annapolis Boat Show feeling lousy. Our booth was the smallest, most insignificant stand that I had ever presented Seabrake at – an 8 foot x 10 foot T-shirt stand outside the main pavilion. There was only enough room for two HSD units, a sizeable TV to run our promotional video continuously, boxes of brochures and, hanging from each side at the entrance like Chinese lanterns, a GP24 and a GP36 collapsible Seabrake.

My colleagues and I looked at each other as they opened the gates the first morning, wondering how in the hell we would make any impression. By midday we had no such concern. The video, which had always been a show stopper, had hundreds of people watching it. It ran for 13 minutes, and most people stayed to watch it at least twice.

Back in West Palm Beach, 400 of the collapsible units had arrived from RFD in Melbourne; by day's end on day one we had sold all 400, and had orders for another 200.

It had blown us both out of the water, neither of us expected anything like this. I reported the good news back to Australia – preparing them for a second order. We still had a week of the show to go.

And then we heard from RFD that unless certain business issues were resolved, no further units would be coming our way.

RFD eventually went ahead and wound up Seabrake Australia Pty Ltd.

I was between a rock and a hard place. On one hand I had a family and a farm to support, first and foremost. On the other I had a product exploding onto the world market through the USA.

Once again, I was left holding the baby – and owed money.

As a rule, one disaster is soon followed by another. I came home to find Ness sitting in the dark in front of an open fire. I can still see her silhouette, and the drink and cigarette in her hand. She just came straight out with it, and told me she'd been unfaithful.

Suddenly everything I had been doing on the farm for eight years meant nothing.

Miraculously, I found a buyer for the farm in less than a week.

I took off with Ness and the two boys, destination England via West Palm Beach, Florida. Ness and I were through. She could go back and live with her parents.

Farm life to bright lights and back, 1995-2000

It had been one hell of a turnaround, from 400 acres in paradise and a secure future, to God knows where, and God knows what.

All I knew was I had to get my private life sorted before doing anything more with Seabrake.

I was Sam's legal guardian, having been granted sole custody by the Canberra Family Court when he was just two years old. It remained in place until he turned 18.

I was at the end of the road.

So, I put all our belongings into storage and used my frequent flyer points for air tickets for all of us to Los Angeles. Joel was thrilled at literally bumping into Jerry Seinfeld at LAX, Los Angeles International Airport – he spoke to Joel to apologise to him.

Sam was now old enough to take it all in. We intended to stop over in Florida to take him to Disney World, hire a car to visit the Florida Keys, and check in on Seabrake America in West Palm Beach.

Ness and I were barely on speaking terms, but remained amicable for the two kids. After covering the Keys and West Palm Beach, we drove to Orlando and booked into a hotel right at Disney World. There followed another argument between Ness and me.

I'd already had the final straw, I didn't need any more. Soon afterwards she left for England, and the two boys stayed with me.

It was a nightmare. We were in a whole new ballgame. I had two young boys to care for, no home, and my entire life and income dependent upon Seabrake America Inc.

I stayed on for a week and all seemed well; they wanted to manufacture out of the USA, which we were still negotiating, but sales were good, and everyone seemed happy. I had a night in the hospital at West Palm Beach, which was later put down to stress. I was so hurt, it was probably a combination of stress, grief and a lot of uncertainty.

When we arrived in the UK I knew it was going to be tough. Ness made arrangements to come and visit, and seemed to accept the situation as it was. I was looking at schools for Joel, Ness had a school lined up for Sam. Business arrangements were looking like I could base myself in the UK. A fresh start seemed likely.

Just as Joel was about to start school, I got an urgent phone call out of the States about some personal tensions that were affecting the business. I had to get out there. I loaded Joel, much to his delight, and returned to the USA, leaving Sam in school and staying with Ness and his grandparents.

I bitterly regretted doing this. Sam needed me more than Seabrake, as did Joel, but Seabrake was still our meal ticket. I had no choice.

Joel and I were living at the same hotel I always stayed at in West Palm Beach. I was on a first-name basis with all the managers and staff. Weeks turned into months, and still no resolution – which in turn affected supply of the product. My concern now was finding a good US manufacturer.

Switlik Parachute Company, out of New Jersey, were the ideal people. They had been in business since World War II, supplying parachutes to the US forces then, and ever since. Richard Switlik Jnr and I met up at his factory, and he invited me to stay at his home. Everything went according to plan.

Back at the hotel in Florida, however, all wasn't going to plan. The manager met me in the lobby. 'Mr Abernethy, when you have a minute we need to talk about Joel. We have had the police here looking for runaway children – and complaints over noise from other guests!'

Joel, who was the staff darling, had been scoring all the left-over booze when they cleaned the rooms. Joel had his own drinks trolley!

On a more sinister note, he had been hiding a runaway kid in our room and had refused the police access. With his 'cute Australian accent' he had a close following of some 20 local kids (mostly female) who idolised the ground he walked on. Practising his electric guitar on the fire-escape for better acoustics was the final straw.

I marched him down to the front desk, where he gave an undertaking none of the above would ever be repeated. I had only been gone 48 hours!

Switlik wanted in, and their product quality would equal RFD's out of Melbourne – but things still weren't straightforward with the American business. And that affected my royalty stream.

Joel and I had been in the USA for almost six months by now. I was living off my overdraft and I needed to get home.

My mate Cubby, Kevin Cuthbertson, got the fright of his life at the sight of me at Sydney Airport. I was that ill.

But Cubby excels at making things happen, and within an hour I found myself sitting before a Veterans' Affairs advocate. My health had been neglected far too long, I was too busy to make specialist appointments.

'If you won't do it for yourself – do it for your sons,' both the advocate and Cubby said, every time they mentioned *'pension'*!

I was 47 years old, not a bloody invalid. However, I lost the argument to Bluey, the advocate, and Cubby, my mate. Together they saved my life.

Joel went back to Bombala High School, and we moved back onto the farm, as the new owners had left it untouched since we moved out – we'd sold the horses when we sold the farm. The new owners welcomed us back, given we had been extremely generous in our hand-over.

I dragged the fax machine out of storage, reconnected the power and phone, and boxed on, calling for all the support I could get.

Austrade and the Australian government had contributed enormous support both financially and through representation, and I asked them now to help protect their investment. ASIC and the Ombudsman were

Kevin 'Cubby' Cuthbertson CSC. Mentor and mate through it all!
(That's Cubby on the right.)

brought up to speed too. However, not one single organisation – nor individual – did any more than 'note' my complaints and need of assistance. No help was forthcoming. I was on my own.

So I did what I should have done years earlier. I went it alone, licensed RFD to manufacture the GP model, by agreement had RFD distribute the HSD – which was also my product, manufactured out of Melbourne – and semi-retired.

Joel and I moved to the coastal town of Merimbula, in New South Wales, in late 1996. I rented a three-bedroom apartment and supported Seabrake outlets across the globe. I still owned all the patents and trademarks. Where there was life, there was hope.

Then my fledgling sense of security came crashing down. One night I called the UK to speak with Sam. A stranger answered. Sam was in hospital and undergoing a second lot of surgery. I froze.

'What happened?'

'Struck by a car,' was as much as I was told.

I was frantic. Hit by a car and they were still operating on him days after the accident? You think of the worst possible scenarios. It took two full days before Ness returned my calls.

His foot had been completely severed at the ankle. If he were to walk again he would have a permanent limp. I gave Ness till Christmas to bring him home, or I would be over to collect him. He couldn't travel until then.

My place on Monaro Street was big, three huge bedrooms. When Joel and I first moved in there was space galore, although it didn't take long for all that to change. He had many friends, he had finished his Year 10 and was working at Magic Mountain, a local tourist park.

Then Ness came back with Sam.

It gutted me, as he tried to run to me at the airport. It broke my heart to see him hobble.

I decided to get him swimming, using flippers to extend his damaged tendon, one flipper on his bad leg, nothing on his good one.

Again fate intervened. When I was in the local sports store buying his flippers, the owner recognised me – he was originally from Geelong and, being in the fishing business, he knew who I was. He told me his brother-in-law had just bought a new boat but didn't have the right ticket. Would I skipper it?

No way.

I had two kids to look after, and my ticket would have expired years ago, I thought. They didn't give up; next the brother in-law arrived at my door.

The boat, a 48-foot Randell, required a minimum Master Class V to skipper it. Nobody in town had that ticket then, but he bullshitted me that he had a skipper arriving in six weeks' time – he just needed me until Christmas.

Thoroughly convinced my ticket was no longer valid as I hadn't skippered a boat in around ten years, I agreed to go with him to Waterways, the NSW equivalent of the Marine Board of Victoria. For some reason the boss there took an immediate dislike to me, to the extent of calling me a liar! Immediately I demanded he call Thieg Enevoldson, boss of the Vic Marine Board, and chair of the EMMA Committee, head of all states and territories.

The look on his face said it all, the fact that I even knew who this bloke was. He made the call.

'I personally examined him, one of our best,' Enevoldson said, over the speaker phone. 'If he's there, please put him on.'

Mr Smartarse Waterways fell over himself to be nice to me from that day onwards. It was a shock to learn my ticket was still valid: a 'Grandfathers Ticket' as they are known. When Dip and I did our Master's Certificate, we had to do the lot: a radar course with air force techs, 'Celestial Navigation – Sextant and Dead Reckoning', in Bass Strait, no GPS in those days, and a six-week course to pass. It had taken Dip and me two years.

So now I was back driving charter boats. I'd completed the full circle. There were around a dozen charter boats operating at the time out of Merimbula, but *Sea Wolf* was the largest, and a very good sea boat.

I had the two boys at home, and Ness, since I'd agreed to let her stay while Sam settled. She stayed longer than that, but when she moved out she continued to live in Merimbula.

There were good things to come of this time.

On my first morning driving charter boats, I met Daryl 'Snowy' Turner.

He had recently lost his son and was doing it tough – he couldn't sleep, which is how he met me at 5.30am down at the marina. He told me he was an ex-boxer and had fought on the under card to Allan Aldenhoven, Welterweight Champion of Australia.

Allan and I were mates, had been to Vietnam together, and had both boxed in the army. Snowy and I became mates for life.

In Merimbula at that time, street gangs, packs of runaway teenage boys, were throwing their weight around in the main street at night. More to the point, every night a shop was being broken into. I had seen what was happening and warned my kids away.

What we needed was a venue; kids need somewhere to hang out together. I asked Snowy if he still had any of his old boxing gear around, which he did, and I still had my heavyweight bag and training mitts.

I approached the RSL, which had its old unused building right on the main street. Since I was an ex-digger, with a plan to get these thugs off the street, the president accepted my offer. If we maintained the building, paid the electricity and cleaned up the streets, then we could have the building rent-free. We shook hands on the deal. Now to attract the kids.

Three simple rules applied: no alcohol, no drugs and everybody off the street by 9pm.

The first night was a disaster, two kids turned up – stoned and unimpressed when we turned them away. Night two was better – five kids, two had been sniffing aerosols.

By week's end the word had spread, and only kids who were straight were turning up, in groups of three, four and five – strength in numbers.

It wasn't a gym to teach boxing – it was a place to hang out and hit a bag, off the street.

My father had a great saying: 'There is no such thing as a *bad* kid.' Circumstances, and bad parenting, is what turns good kids bad, and most of these kids were runaways from good families. Since Merimbula was a place where they had fun on family holidays, it was an easy destination to choose when they left home.

The thing that struck me early was the generosity from the community, and notably one sports store on Victoria Road, Sydney.

When Snowy and I explained what we were doing, and why, equipment came out of the woodwork – 'samples' the guy kept saying. It was thousands of dollars' worth of gym equipment, gloves, headgear, bags, pads and weights.

Suddenly we had enough equipment for every kid who came through the door – and Snowy was sparring 50 rounds a night, teaching these kids how to protect themselves. Boys, girls, they all queued up to go two to three rounds with the old pro. It was a real winner, and most importantly we had the kids' trust.

What was in it for us? Nothing, except showing them that our time, and all this, was for them – that we cared about them, and our town.

One night a young girl arrived alone and began belting hell out of a heavyweight bag, not just punching it, kicking it – hating it. Some of our leaders moved to step in, but I stopped them, letting her go until she collapsed in tears. Norma, our secretary, treasurer, everyone's mum, took her in her arms and let her cry it out.

This kid was being molested by her step-father, abused. What pissed me off even more was that it had been brought to the attention of the cops, and the Department of Community Services (DOCS). But the end game for me was when I learnt one of the cops was strip-searching this 14-year-old girl in the public toilets – and this had also been reported, to no avail.

The cops told me I'd made a big mistake when I went over their heads and straight to Queanbeyan Police HQ, but it perturbed me little. I did the right thing.

With equipment, kids, rules, and free school bands once a month, at $5 per head to pay the power bill, we were rolling. Within a month, break and enter in the main street had stopped. Local businesses approached me with donations – a hotel proprietor donated soft drinks for our dances, the supermarket donated chips, the bakery put on a sausage sizzle, with all proceeds to Snowy's Gym. I invited the cops to drop in anytime (but leave your hats in the car). Only one ever took me up on the offer – Jacko. He did his job, but he had a ticker and the kids respected him. More Jackos I say – he could relate to the kids and have fun with them. He wasn't the enemy.

I had also got a 1976 VW Superbug convertible. I couldn't help myself. It was red, cheap, and I couldn't buy it quick enough. Another box ticked. But she was a tired little VW Bug, she needed urgent restoration. I started from the floor up – new floor, seats, motor, eight coats of two-pack aviation paint (the Westpac Chopper was in for a repaint); my new bug was now Westpac red, with a new canvas roof.

I loved my new car, loved her. I even drove her in winter, for the first year anyway, with the roof down.

It was also around this time Ness and I got divorced. It was a horrible time for us all, but there's little point in bringing that up now. It's long ago, and in the past where it belongs. Our divorce was approved in 1998.

But my health was still giving me a workover. Another pneumothorax saw me back in hospital. My life had been turned upside down. I no longer knew who I really was, my relationship with my boys was sometimes strained, nothing was working well. Looking back now, I guess it's because my self-esteem was so low, I was so stressed, hollowed out by the events of the last few years. I no longer cared about my past, present or future. I was on autopilot. The reason I kept going is because I am a survivor. I reasoned I'd weathered the storms before.

Adding to my woes, I couldn't say no when mates called on me.

I went into partnership on a yacht, I was back skippering – why not do something really different?

Whale watching was all the rage – but nobody was doing it from a yacht. A guy I had known since Vietnam came up with a proposition of an equal share. I had the tickets, experience and know-how, and he was a certified chartered accountant, so could take care of the financial side of things. I was to hire and fire crew and run the boat day to day, while he would promote, pay, and manage accounts from Sydney.

He set up an account for our new venture, and my TPI – Totally and Permanently Incapacitated, a Veteran's pension status – back-pay went into it.

In all I put in five to six years running the lot. Apart from the very occasional visit from Sydney, my partner did nothing.

I did however pull off a coup with my marketing slogan 'See a Whale Under Sail – the Traditional Way'. The advert in the *Canberra Times* attracted the high end of the market, which is where we specialised –

embassies and consulates were booking charters. Having silver service gourmet meals and BYO drinks all served up by a hostess, with limited numbers of guests, made it a very special, personal experience.

Sam had made a full recovery. The one-flipper trick *did* the trick. He had gone from almost crippled to being an effective striker with the Merimbula 'Grass Hoppers' (under 8s soccer team), running with no limp. I had no background in medical recovery for such an abhorrent injury, but I figured if the surgeons had gone to so much trouble, twice re-joining his foot to his leg, the tendons were the key to mobility. He loved to swim, and if I could extend the tendons by putting a flipper on his bad foot, it would not only extend the tendon, but it would strengthen the ankle. It took a year, but I was right.

This was also the time of a journey into the past, right back to Vietnam. It is a trip I will never forget.

In 2000, when the East Timorese conflict began, my old battalion, 7 RAR, now 5/7 RAR, were deployed. This upset a reunion we had been planning for over a year, in Darwin. With that off the agenda, my mate suggested we go to Vietnam instead. I thought he was joking at first, but he was deadly serious. Graham 'Eddy' Edwards, MP for Cowan, Western Australia (now retired) and I were both 7 RAR and mates. He lost both legs just below his scrotum in a mine incident, one of three times he was wounded in Vietnam – that, however, being his last time.

Every day the phone would ring, and it would be Eddy: 'Come on mate – you were already going to Darwin for a holiday, make it Vietnam.'

A 'holiday', I thought. My memories of Vietnam were all bad – who the fuck in their right mind goes back to the scene of their worst nightmares? I kept refusing, until one day Eddy caught me at a weak moment and I agreed. Before day's end, his personal assistant had faxed our itinerary, including accommodation, stop-over in Bangkok, and return fares. I was going! Anzac 2000 in Vietnam.

As crazy as it may sound, returning in peacetime was more concerning than arriving in time of war.

Eddy, myself and Phil 'Macca' McLean out of Brisbane, all mates from 7 RAR, made the trip. Soon after our arrival and on the road to Vung Tau, the first landmark of note was a Foster's beer factory, and the foundations of the road had been laid by Australian engineers back in our time.

Modern, clean, and staffed by friendly Vietnamese, our hotel was in downtown 'Vungers', as we had known it during our R&C days. Back then it was wall-to-wall brothels and bars and Allied troops; now it was fewer brothels and bars, and Russian oil crews had moved in.

Travelling with a disabled person is a real eye-opener. You realise how much you take for granted. You worry whether the wheelchair will fit through the front door of a building, whether the doorway into the toilets is wide enough – and is there a lift to our room? It goes on, and on. How do you board an aircraft where no boarding bridges exist? On a forklift of course.

Eddy had done this trip before, and alone. Any time you think you're having a bad day, think for a minute how much worse off you'd be coping in a wheelchair for a week, much less for life. Obstacles, always obstacles, and people always looking down at you. I found it more polite, if not more comfortable, to sit or squat to talk to him.

We visited a lot of old sites where we had served 30 years earlier: Dat Do, the 'Horseshoe', Nui Dat, Lang Phuoc Hai, the Long Hai Mountains and the paddy fields where we had set ambushes night after night.

The fire support bases we had built were now thriving suburbs with streets and lighting, and the old route road from Dat Do to the coast was now a freeway equal to the best anywhere in Australia.

From a dirt track on the back of an armed personnel carrier to sitting back in an air-conditioned Toyota Tarago was a bit much at first, and casting an eye over the paddy fields where we had lost mates was sobering.

The 'Badcoe Club', an R&C centre on the beach in Vungers, was now almost gone; all that remained was the swimming pool and some of the old barracks, now converted to family homes. By now, I'm sure, very little from the past would be recognisable.

Anzac Day started with the International Red Cross collecting us at 5am for the drive to Long Tan, site of the legendary battle between D Company, 6 RAR and a Viet Cong regiment in monsoonal rain on 18 August 1966.

We stopped at the Long Tan police station to collect the plaque that's affixed to the memorial cross for special occasions.

I shall never forget the hundreds of flickering candle lights emerging through the rubber plantation, all headed towards the cross. The Vietnamese lost hundreds, to Australia's 18 fatalities, in the bloodiest battle we fought during the war.

From Ba Ria we went on to Ho Chi Minh City (Saigon) for an Anzac Day service with the Australian and New Zealand embassy staff and officials. It had been quite a day, and even more surprisingly there were some 400 ex-pat Australians living in Vietnam at that point. I think I had a drink with each one of them.

Then came another eye-opening visit. Eddy had been delivering wheelchairs that WA Rotary had been making for kids in Vietnam, and he asked me to accompany him and take some photos.

I was shocked at what I saw.

There were four and five kids to a bed, no windows in the hospital, and it was as dingy as a prison, not a place of healing.

We waited and waited to see one of the wheelchairs; Eddy figured out it was being assembled as we waited. When it did arrive, it took my breath away. They had dragged some terrified kid, with both legs missing, out of his bed and pushed him towards us. Since the war, kids had been continually standing on landmines, as after heavy rain the mines moved in the sandy soil. What was safe yesterday was today's minefield. It was gut-wrenching to see this poor child displayed the way he was.

We left the hospital very pissed off; somewhere sat a lot of unassembled wheelchairs from WA Rotary, which Graham respectfully requested be in use for his next visit.

On our way back to the hotel we spotted a Huey helicopter in front of a museum, a chopper left behind, so we decided to take our photos with it. As I was doing just that, two guys approached.

'Say man – which unit were you guys?' This in an American accent.

I realised they were journalists. 'The mighty 7th – 7 RAR,' I replied.

'Huh – you're Australian. Australians weren't in the war!'

'Tell him that,' I said, pointing in Eddy's direction. 'He lost both his legs here supporting America.'

They looked at each other in disbelief.

It took little to convince these two we were for real. It truly is amazing how many Americans don't know Australia was involved.

Next morning at breakfast, Eddy tossed a newspaper in front of me. There was a picture of him beside the chopper, and a very long article in *The New York Times*. More Americans knew about Australia's involvement in Vietnam after that edition.

Eddy had one formal duty to perform on our trip, and that was opening a new wing at the Ba Ria orphanage. This was started by Australian

Eddy and me in Vietnam, 2000.

troops during the conflict. After the war, the land was purchased by Australians and the orphanage was built by Australians.

It truly is a sight to behold, equal or better to any similar facilities in Australia, with all the mod cons. Even in 2000 the kids had computers.

During our tour, our Padre forbade us to throw parts of our ration packs to kids going through Ba Ria, or anywhere.

'Give it to me and I'll take it to the orphanage,' he used to say.

This was because when Aussie armed personnel carriers or trucks were passing through, the kids would come running – we would give them our barley sugar (emergency ration packs) and cans of fruit, cheese, whatever. It was only a matter of time before one of these kids went under a wheel, or track. It's good to know that from humble beginnings now stands a tribute all Australians can be proud of.

Our last night in Vietnam, coincidently, happened to be the twenty-fifth anniversary of the fall of Saigon, and a big night had been arranged at the Rex Hotel for both sides to attend, North Vietnamese generals as well as Australian MPs. The Rex had been an HQ for the Americans throughout the conflict.

As we entered the foyer a swarm of camera flashes came our way.

'What's happening?' Eddy asked, submerged in the throng of people surrounding us.

'Some guy being interviewed on TV,' I said.

'John McCain probably,' he replied.

He was right – presidential candidate Senator John McCain soon sought out Eddy at the end of his US *60 Minutes* interview and, with his wife and son, joined us in the foyer.

John McCain had returned to where he had spent many years as a POW; as a navy fighter pilot he was shot down over the North.

'I'm a loser,' he said, when I asked him how he was doing. He was referring to his defeat in the US electoral lead-up. I assured him he wasn't.

'You must be very proud of him,' said McCain, nodding in Eddy's direction.

'His arse is a lot closer to the ground now, but he'll always stand 10-foot tall in my eyes,' I answered.

Tears filled John McCain's eyes. He shook my hand, unable to reply, before making a bolt for his motorcade. He was one American serviceman the world should acknowledge in a big way. He was a true legend.

* * * *

I can still recall clearly the day Sam announced: 'Mum has stopped drinking.' It was the year 2000.

After waiting for almost two decades, I was sceptical to say the least. However, it turned out to be true.

Ness had joined Alcoholics Anonymous. I guess we all take our own time to right our wrongs, get well, give up things that are bad for us. Ness's turning point came when she was in a car wreck that could have killed her. As I write, she has not had a drink for nearly 20 years, and I am so proud of her.

I now had a place in a cluster of apartments, with a pool – which thrilled Sam, as he practically lived in it. I had a girlfriend, Barb, I was taking whale watching charters – life seemed to be turning in the right direction again. Seabrake under RFD was ticking along nicely.

Another of my diggers from Vietnam had taken up the lease on a pub in Victoria's Alps, a goldmine of sorts as it was the last pit stop before the high-priced ski fields. It flourished during the season, with crowds stocking up on booze before hitting the slopes for the weekend.

My Vietnam mate called me with a crisis on his hands; his mother-in-law had passed away in the UK and his wife had gone back to England. With the ski season only weeks away, could I help him out for two weeks?

Why he chose me was apparent; he was short on friends and big on acquaintances.

But I needed a break from my surroundings and agreed to go, although you could write on the back of a postage stamp what I knew about running a pub.

The days were long, starting at 7am and rolling into bed late every night, only to do the same thing next day. It was also bitterly cold – I hate the cold, remember!

Ski season was gearing up and the crowds were building every weekend, and on Friday and Saturday nights we had live bands, which also attracted the locals.

One night, as we got home late, the phone rang – and I could tell by the expression on my mate's face something was terribly wrong. When he hung up he looked at me in shock.

'What's up?' I asked.

'He's having a heart attack – and the ambulance hasn't arrived!'

'WHO?' I demanded to know.

His father-in-law was having a heart attack at home on his own in the UK.

'He called an ambulance 15 minutes ago, but it hasn't arrived,' he added.

'What's the address?' I asked.

With the address I called my mate Cubby, who was still with the Australian Federal Police.

'Leave it with me,' he said.

After Cubby's call, INTERPOL produced an ambulance in the UK, which got there first and saved the man's life.

But my mate had to go to the UK. I drove him to the airport, and contacted an old 7 RAR digger who had just sold his pub. 'Bear' had been Squirrel's number two on the machine gun after I left 8 Platoon.

In less than 48 hours, Bear drove from the Queensland border overnight to take up the role as publican. He knew the game – how to hook-up barrels, what to order, how a pub should be run. My role was manager, do the banking, pay staff, the general dogsbody.

We soon had the pub running well.

As is the case with all new publicans (apparently), the dregs of society came in during the first few weeks to 'try out' the new boss, test their limits so to speak. In this pub we had only one, a known groper of women, a common thief who would buy his drinks from anyone's money lying on the bar, a reputed tough cowboy with a rodeo reputation that he loved to spruik about.

Husbands had stood back, afraid of this animal as he grabbed at their wives, yet he was still tolerated within the community. He had created a scene, groping a customer, on my very first night, so I put up on the blackboard that he was barred for a week.

The day after I posted the ban, his mate asked me if I really meant it.

'Let me put it this way,' I said matter-of-factly. 'You tell your mate from me that should he try and break my ban I'll give him the toughest eight seconds of his life.' Eight seconds being the time required for a rider to stay on a bucking animal in a rodeo qualification. His mate laughed at that.

Then I got back to the hotel late on a Friday evening after running errands, and spotted this jerk sitting at the front bar as large as life. I made a beeline for him.

'Abo, mate, how you doing?' he said.

'Can't you read?' I pointed at the ban on the blackboard.

'Nah ... it's all good mate, let me buy you a drink,' he retorted.

I caught Bear's eye behind the bar.

'Don't serve him another drink and let all the staff know.'

Bear reached and took his glass.

'You're nothing but a c..t,' the jerk said to me, loud enough for most in the bar to hear.

'OUT!' I said.

Now, as for old mate's reputation as a fighter, from what I'd heard, he was a 'king hitter' – all his victories had come from his opponents not seeing his punch coming. Given that he was ten years younger than me, had two eyes and two lungs, he figured I'd be easy meat.

I opened the front door and indicated he go first, I wasn't turning my back on him. As he stepped onto the outside deck I saw him clench his fist, and anticipating his haymaker gave him the perfect four-knuckle grounder as he began his swing – he went down as if he'd been shot. It took well under eight seconds.

Where I got the strength, I will never know, but I took hold of his belt and the scruff of his neck and hurled him face-first off the landing onto the dirt in the carpark. The wind that came out of him when he landed sounded like a truck applying air brakes.

I went back for his hat, throwing it after him.

What I had overlooked in my rage was that at least a hundred people had just witnessed what had happened, the full glass front of the hotel gave a clear view.

Even his brothers who were in the bar at the time didn't bother to intervene. It had been a long time coming, was the general consensus, and from that night onwards we never had any trouble, from anybody.

In total I was there three months. Bear stayed six weeks and did a mighty job, all at his own expense. Neither Bear nor I received as much as a thank you from our old digger mate.

My stay came to an abrupt end when I passed blood, and an X-ray revealed I had an aneurism of the aorta, exactly what had killed my father.

'Get home immediately and get to a specialist,' the doctor said.

I was offered a 'house-sitting' low-rent arrangement, which enticed me into a two-storey home on Fishpen, an up-market waterfront area in Merimbula.

From here I could walk out the front door, hop in the tender, and motor right to the yacht. Joel, meanwhile, had gone to Canberra and was landscaping for a living.

It was also a time when Seabrake moved from one home to another. RFD had been involved in Seabrake since the 1984 Sydney Boat Show launch. As the exclusive manufacturer, with distribution rights, Seabrake wasn't getting the potential distribution outlets that were available to us.

Joel was now a director of Seabrake Australia Pty Ltd, as was my long-time friend and 'Power of Attorney' Cubby Cuthbertson.

We discussed the possibility of relicensing distribution – and ultimately found that Burke Marine in Sydney were the biggest and best in Australia/New Zealand. As they manufactured all their own products, Seabrake was a simple process for them, and it opened up some 500 outlets to us. It was agreed I sit down with Burke and negotiate a deal.

Martin Burke, the founder and owner of Burke Marine, was a very successful sailmaker, and had moved into the Sydney suburbs and expanded his business to include a wide range of marine products.

Seabrake is unique, and Martin had a good knowledge of it from our successes at boat shows where he also exhibited. He was immediately interested in an exclusive manufacturing/marketing and distribution agreement. We struck a deal and moved everything from Melbourne to Sydney. The stage was set for expansion – Martin had a new product and we had much broader distribution.

My aches and pains and blackouts were still a hindrance. Plus, after a day's sailing, my left arm and shoulder were so sore I couldn't sleep with the pain. I was referred to a chronic long-term pain specialist, who diagnosed: 'Something is badly wrong, but what I don't know!'

More ultrasounds and X-rays were scheduled.

While I was having the ultrasound on my left shoulder, a door behind me hit my chair; the technician asked me to pull my chair forward, leaving the scanner in place on my shoulder.

When I lowered both arms to move the chair, the technician gasped, 'My God – don't move!' She summoned her colleagues to look at the monitor.

The action of opening up my shoulder in order to move the chair had revealed a bone spur inside the joint socket, which had previously been hidden from the scanner.

The spur, the size of my little finger to the first joint, was growing off the ball end of my upper arm bone, catching and sawing the main tendon every time I moved my left arm – 95% of the tendon was sawn through.

'My God, you must be in agony,' said the technician.

'You think! Could this be the cause of what I have been bitching about for the past 18 years?' I was really angry when they turned the screen for me to see.

I was referred to a top shoulder specialist at Sydney's North Shore Private Hospital, the man who performed most of the National Rugby League players' shoulder reconstructions, I was told.

Easy-peasy, he assured me – keyhole surgery to saw off the spur and you'll be home in 48 hours.

An hour after surgery they had me doing physio, stretching rubber bands that were coded in various colours to show increased or decreased resistance. The tendon would grow back, I was assured. The biopsy report revealed a small fragment of metal – shrapnel. Like the formation of a pearl in an oyster, the bone structure had evolved from the tendon irritation, forming around the metal.

Another legacy of Vietnam, and I found the photo to prove it years later. There it was – the trickle of blood right where it had gone in on the night of 30 April 1970. I had been photographed with Squirrel the next morning, with my shirt off.

You didn't think of it at the time, we all suffered bleeds during contacts, often simply gravel rash or flying debris drawing blood. With the adrenaline pumping, and others seriously injured to worry about, you would never feel a thing.

But this started my heavy opiate intake, for the pain. Small doses of Endone at first, then much larger doses of Oxycodone were to follow.

The pain I was experiencing had originated from the tendon, becoming a referred pain through my left side and centring in my spine – at its worst the pain would then create a spasm in my chest.

A year earlier I had been struck by a car one night, crossing the road in torrential rain. I was piggybacking Sam when it happened, and the driver put his lights on just before impact – enough time for me to shield Sam and launch us onto the bonnet. I took the full impact on my back, against the windscreen, resulting in a broken shoulder blade. Months after, I went back to my GP complaining of intense pain in my spine between my shoulder blades. Nothing was determined, but the pain persisted.

Further investigation in Canberra with lots of different specialists, including a vascular surgeon looking into my aortic aneurism, all produced nothing. On one occasion I spent a month in hospital being monitored by four independent specialists; nobody could find any reason for the pain.

However, after 18 years of doctors telling me my blackouts and pain in my left shoulder/back was 'all in my mind', I knew what real pain was like – and that doctors aren't always right. All that resulted, however, was an increase in pain-relief medication.

* * * *

In the winter of 2003, Joel and I, and my partner in the yacht, decided to take the boat to Queensland for three months. Joel and I would take the boat to Brisbane, and my partner would fly up and join us.

We left Sydney Harbour, stopping at the Hawkesbury River and Port Stephens before heading onto Coffs Harbour. Late at night, staying well offshore, I heard Port Macquarie Radio forecasting 'light winds of 10–15 knots and calm seas'.

We were directly abeam of Port Macquarie and in rough seas with 30–40 knot winds. I radioed-in our position and conditions, which were immediately updated on air, and was thanked for the advice.

Two hours later, as we ploughed on into even worse conditions, a 'Mayday' call blared through our radio, a frantic skipper in a vessel sinking beneath him. He was so close to us we could see his lights and called him up; it transpired he was making for Port Macquarie in an 80-foot commercial fishing vessel and shipping more water than his pumps could disperse.

He wanted me to take him and his crew off, impossible in those conditions – our fibreglass hull would have been smashed to smithereens coming alongside his vessel. I reluctantly had to tell him this, and reassured him should he sink and take to his life-raft we would come back and assist.

We monitored his progress and radio calls to Port Macquarie, where he was advised that the entrance was now closed due to the conditions.

Somehow he made it as far as Port Macquarie and, against all advice, decided to run the bar, the entrance, for the safety within. He never made it. We listened to the drama unfold – the vessel went down in the entrance, fortunately without any loss of life.

The wind was peaking at times in the realms of 60 knots out of the north-east, off our bow essentially. Going into a head sea, the danger is nowhere near as bad as a following sea. The east coast compared to Bass Strait is as different as chalk and cheese; the ground swell on the east coast is much, much smaller – but in these winds it was a very high and uncomfortable chop. In a yacht it was far more doable than in a power boat, and with only a storm jib sail up, and motoring, I was in no fear of losing our ship.

We battled on all night, at times making only 1–2 knots into the head-on conditions. The forecast was now 'correct' – gale force! The state of the sea in the early light was sobering; I have never in my life been in such a confused sea. The waves were coming from *all directions*, there was no pattern, just huge lumpy waves crashing into us from all points of the compass. We decided to make for Trial Bay, a small township with an entrance I hoped would be deep and wide enough for us to seek shelter. We had now been in these conditions for over 24 hours, and both Joel and I needed sleep, if nothing else.

It took us the whole day to reach Trial Bay, and when we got close enough to establish radio contact I asked whether the entrance was safe to attempt. 'No – not in a fit,' came the reply I wasn't expecting – but I could soon see why!

The entire coastline was a mass of foaming surf. I came in close enough to see cars banking up on the cliff-tops to look out at us in the furious sea.

At that point, Coffs Harbour Water Police called me, offering to take Joel and me off the yacht, and to leave her to sink.

After all we had been through in the past 36 hours, the look on Joel's face showed he was all for it, but the same applied as with the fishing boat – for two vessels to come alongside in those conditions would be suicide. I gave them my opinion, thanked them and said, 'I'm standing off to sea!' The deeper the better.

We were only several hundred yards from the beach, we could see people clearly – but most clear to me was the look of horror on Joel's face. 'Do everything I tell you to and we'll be OK,' I assured him.

Spinning the wheel to starboard, away from land, we took off at a great rate of knots, covering in two hours the same distance that had previously taken us 12 hours.

Coming onto nightfall we were 20 miles offshore; here I set up a Seabrake, and a back-up Seabrake should we lose the first for whatever reason. Joel worked up on deck, furling away sails in extremely dangerous conditions, at my side in the darkness; it was a baptism of fire for him, and I can't say enough how proud I am of him and the courage he displayed all through those hours of hell.

'Put your head down mate,' I told him, as we drifted downwind in the gale. I stayed on deck and, to my sheer horror, as I looked south, the sky lit up with lightning like I have never seen before or since. It lit up half over land, and for miles out to sea – and it was heading straight for us.

I think this was my most fearful moment in all my years at sea, even more so than the night we used the 'bucket brake' to save us.

On this night I had my son on board with me. My fear wasn't for me – it was that I may have brought about both our deaths. The feeling of guilt and despair was overwhelming as I watched this massive storm rapidly approaching, growing bigger and darker by the minute.

With the flashes of lightning I could see Joel cuddled up below, asleep by the time his head hit the pillow. Then came the sound of heavy rain

Like father, like son — a girl in every port.

drops striking into the sea, coming closer and louder. All around was pitch black.

As I stood in the cockpit at the helm awaiting the onslaught, checking and re-checking that the Seabrake was out and positioned correctly, the first heavy drops started hitting our decks, each sounding like a rifle shot in the quiet that came with the rain – so loud it woke Joel from his deep sleep.

Between us and the land I could make out the sheets of rain pouring down and rippling the sea surface. Then, as quickly as the rain started, it stopped. It dawned on me that the wind had also stopped. The eye of the storm was my immediate thought, I had heard of such things but never experienced it.

It was as if somebody had switched off a fan, and the edge of the falling rain – like a waterfall only 200 yards away, kept going north around and past us towards the land.

I stayed on deck smoking for an hour afterwards, waiting for the other end of the storm to engulf us. But the sky cleared, I could see the glow of townships along the coast, the sea had settled like a lake, and the barometer confirmed that it wasn't wishful thinking. Knowing that I was in, or close to, the shipping lane, I burnt every conceivable light possible, set the alarm at 6 miles on the radar, and rolled into my bunk.

As I closed my eyes I made a promise to myself, a promise I have kept to this day. Get Joel safely home to Sydney after this trip and I will never go to sea again. The old hands had always told me: 'When it's time to quit, you'll know it.'

The following day we made Coffs Harbour. I had promised Joel the biggest steak in town once we tied up, and little did I know the restaurant above the marina centre was owned by one of Dip's best mates, a guy I had taken out many times on my boats at Port Fairy.

The harbour master was also an old mate of mine from Melbourne, who gave us a great berth. Sitting up to a huge steak and numerous schooners over dinner, I saw two police officers enter and speak to Dip's mate, who pointed out Joel and me.

'Well, I must admit I never thought I'd ever see you two again,' said the senior officer, offering his hand. The Water Police.

We learnt that the sea had been the worst on record, even boats inside the marina had been badly damaged, with waves coming over the sea wall.

'When you said you were going off to sea – we all thought you were mad,' said the copper.

'Had it been anyone but Dad skippering I would have taken my chances heading for shore in my lifejacket,' Joel confessed.

What happened that night is still a mystery to me. An act of God? Good luck? Who will ever know, but it was significant enough to end my career at sea. I have not set foot on a boat since. It is, however, fair to say that my decision to go out deep that night probably saved our lives, as in close the storm did most of the damage along the coast.

Deeper is always safer in my book, always has been. The closer to shore you are, the more the seas stand up over shallow ground; but, equally as important, it broadens your options with more seaway. Lose an engine or mast close to shore in those conditions and you can kiss your arse goodbye.

* * * *

With Burke Marine now manufacturing and distributing Seabrake, Martin asked if I'd go to METS (the Marine Exhibition Trade Show) with him.

Held in Amsterdam in November of each year for the marine industry as a whole, it's where you find new products as a distributor, or go in search of new distributors. Burke Marine at this point were Australia/New Zealand, and Martin sought to expand his network overseas – piggybacking off Seabrake, as it was unique, and already had international acceptance.

METS is conducted under a country-by-country status, whereby all exhibitors from the same country are grouped together. Austrade was our principle co-ordinator. Martin and I set off together for the ten-day show not really knowing what to expect.

Our first appearance was with a relatively small group of Australian businesses, at a guess I'd say no more than eight or ten – all well-known international brands for the most part.

On advice, we would be extremely lucky to sign up one international distributor in our first year. Those successful in the industry know that consistency is your greater strength, more so than the product itself. Come back again next year and we can see you have substance, as well as a good product. From memory, we signed up two or three on our first visit.

By the second year METS there were more Australian companies, and those who had expressed interest last year were now ready to sign.

I had been to most of the big international boat shows over two decades. However, this was my first trade show, where it's all about distribution through a very well-informed industry. The area under cover was enormous – apart from Seattle's Kingdome stadium, I think it's the next-biggest by far.

Back home, with the overseas expansion going well via METS, I had the brainwave to do some expansion work of my own.

I knew practically everybody in the industry from Perth to Cairns, so I invested in a motorhome and hit the road. I bought a six-berth Mercedes Benz, as I planned to spend a lot of time in it.

The model I chose had three double beds, a shower, toilet, galley, the works! I had a custom-made aluminium storage locker fitted on the back for my generator, tools and Seabrakes, which gave me self-sufficiency should I go bush for a week or so. No pulling down tables or settees to sleep on at night – simply pull up, step back out of the cab into the cabin and pour a Jack Daniel's at day's end. Nice.

At the same time as my change of lifestyle came the horrible news that my lifelong friend and best mate Squirrel was gravely ill. Leukaemia! He was in hospital in Melbourne under treatment, but the prognosis wasn't good. It simply broke my heart, as he had been to visit me in Merimbula the previous Christmas, where we had sat in the sun overlooking Merimbula Lake, reminiscing and, as always, with Squirrel filling me in on his beloved kids.

Tragically, he lapsed into a coma soon after his chemotherapy began and passed away without regaining consciousness.

I am proud to say that all his mates from 8 Platoon were at his funeral, giving him an honour guard as he left the church, including his Platoon Commander Lieutenant Greg Lindsay MC, who had only weeks before been diagnosed with a brain tumour and advised not to fly. It is the only time we have had 100% attendance of all the boys, which is testament to how much Frank 'Squirrel' Squillacioti was revered by all. RIP mate.

* * * *

Prior to our third METS, my doctor had reviewed my aneurism and decided, given my father's history and subsequent death, that he would operate when it had reached 5cm – it was only a whisker under this, and therefore probably meant my last METS. I had told Martin that, in view of the upcoming operation, which was a very big deal, I had considered selling my interests (IP), as neither Joel nor Sam were really interested in taking it over.

Then, at our third year, in 2007, no American exhibitors were there.

'Where are the Yanks?' I asked a Canadian guy.

'You haven't heard? The industry is on its knees – people are walking off $3 million boats in Fort Lauderdale and leaving the keys in the ignition. Recession – big time,' he concluded.

The old adage 'When America catches a cold – the rest of the world catches pneumonia', struck like Big Ben. If I was considering selling Seabrake beforehand, it was definitely up for sale now.

I have learnt that in tough financial times the first thing people stop buying is luxury items. The leisure industry, boating, gets hit hard. How big or how long it was going to last this time was anyone's guess, but I'm no gambler when it comes to my livelihood.

On our last night in Amsterdam, all the Australian exhibitors went out for dinner, and that's where I dropped my bombshell. I said it was my last METS and Seabrake was for sale. When asked who the buyer was, I candidly replied, 'Maybe Martin.'

As soon as I got home I went straight into sell mode – the company was valued, a broker was appointed to sell it by tender, and I planned just one more trip before hospital – Darwin.

My specialist had told me that an AAA (abdominal aortic aneurism) operation is bigger than open-heart surgery, insomuch as I'm gutted like a rabbit, before my aorta – which is the largest artery in the body – is clamped off and the damaged area replaced by a piece of artificial tubing. I had around 8–10 inches to be replaced.

It was also my MP mate Graham 'Eddy' Edwards' last year in politics, and he was joining me on the trip from Cairns.

I was still in a lot of pain, and stressed – with the sale taking three months to run its course via the selling process we had chosen; so I was monitoring my health as we went. Fortunately, wheelchair-bound Eddy had good access into the motorhome via the side entrance, and we hit the road out of Cairns as the tender process went into phase one.

Ironically, we were helped out by the army, all those years after being diggers together ourselves.

On the road from Normanton to Cloncurry, in outback Queensland, we blew a rear inside tyre in gale-force winds. As I hesitantly climbed under the motorhome to look for a secure point to place the jack, the wind was so strong I was afraid it would rock us *off* the jack. I thought I could hear Eddy talking to me above the noise of the wind, then suddenly a face appeared, looking under the rear of the vehicle.

'How's it going'? asked a friendly young bloke, clad in army fatigues.

'Not so good,' I confessed. 'Where the hell did you come from?' Keeping in mind we were in the middle of nowhere and hadn't seen another car all morning; due to the wind I hadn't heard his vehicle pull up. Eddy was happily chatting to his two companions.

They saved the day, literally. I really don't know if my jack would have been safe enough to lift her in those conditions. As Eddy and I looked on, the wheels were removed using a trolley-jack – the spare was fitted and we were back in business in minutes.

This crew were out of Townsville RAEME (Royal Australian Electrical and Mechanical Engineers), in two vehicles, heading for an army base at Mount Isa to service and repair army vehicles out there. If ever there was a made-to-order crew, it was them. Not just content to help out a couple of old diggers, every routine stop they made they would wait till Eddy and I went past, then follow on for a while to make sure we were all good.

That night we caught up with them at the Irish Club in Mount Isa and returned the favour.

The tender progressed through to the final stage the same day I returned to Cairns, three months later. And yes, if you haven't already guessed, Martin Burke won the tender. The broker had emailed every prospective buyer worldwide in one hit, some 50,000 businesses, and letters of interest proceeded to the final three contenders. I had final say, and as Martin was the last Australian standing it was an easy choice. I was thrilled.

In addition to the existing product, I had patented a new design – a Power-Anchor, a very large drift anchor, which Burke Marine had prototyped under my direction. This was included in the deal. With a recession coming I knew Martin would weather the storm; he was big, with many options to survive where others would fail – which became the case.

The payment process was in three instalments, February 2008 being the final and largest of them all.

I was sweating blood by New Year, and until that final payment was made, watching and listening intently for news of the recession hitting Australia was nerve-wracking to say the least. Martin could have pulled out at the last minute, conceding only the two smaller amounts already paid – but the gods were still smiling upon me and the final payment came through before the 2008 recession reached our shores.

I bought Joel and Sam cars, became debt-free for life, and forgot about Seabrake almost as quickly as I had conceived it.

Retired, I could now concentrate on my health and start writing my first novel, which I began while I was in hospital.

Knowing that I would be laid up for the best part of a year after having the AAA operation, I decided to take Joel and Sam away with me in the motorhome for a road-trip. Collecting Joel from Canberra, we then headed north, spending time at The Entrance and Port Stephens for extended stays.

Having the two boys on board was a real treat, they were enjoying it as much as I was – and it's a time I will always cherish. Joel and Sam were much more than brothers, they were best mates. The older they got, the closer they became.

The time came to go for my operation in John James Hospital, Canberra. I had no idea what to expect. The boys took me there. I'm not sure if they feared the worst, but my sister Judy and brother-in-law Ray also came to Canberra from Victoria. My memory of waking up in post-op is vivid, even though I was doped to the eyeballs. Ray and my sons were there, Judy had a cold and kept away. The pain was immense, and being trussed up like a Christmas turkey only added to my ordeal. I had tubes out of me everywhere, I was uncomfortable, but I was alive. The operation had been a success.

Hospitals are a great place when you're really sick, but for the first time in my life I was panic-stricken every waking hour. I could not settle, nor was I my usual jovial self. I had to sleep on my back, as my gut, from brisket to balls, was held together by wire staples –the zipper club, some call it!

With only one good lung, I always had difficulty lying flat on my back – combined with pain and a feeling of suffocation, I was in a constant state of paranoia and simply wanted to get up, which wasn't going to happen! Eventually the nightmare ended, and after two weeks Joel came to drive me home to Merimbula. As I was forbidden to lift *anything*, Sam became my appointed carer, so my motorhome went to Ness's property at Millingandi, 4km out of town, where Sam now lived with his mum.

The recovery was slow and painful, and now I was on higher levels of pain killers in order to function at all, I had become a prescription junkie – as I was to later discover! Seven months after the operation, I thought I was well enough to travel, and with Sam as co-pilot we headed for Cairns.

As you do when you're feeling better, you tend to over-do it – but like a bloody idiot I went surf fishing for blue salmon! That night back in the motorhome I had severe gut pain, but never thought the day's fishing had anything to do with it.

Back in Merimbula a month or so later, my GP immediately saw the problem – I had given myself a hernia. The entire line of my scar from the AAA was bulging, I had torn open the gut lining and all that was holding my guts in was the outer layer of skin! You have to go back in for it to be repaired, my GP advised.

If I thought the AAA operation was an ordeal, it was a walk in the park compared to what followed. The scar tissue from the previous operation had to be cut away to provide a clean new join to heal, and having been torn apart once before, a reinforced strip of material was sewn over the join to provide additional strength.

This second operation was done in Canberra, by a different surgeon. Once out of post-op the same horror show began all over again: being restricted to lying on my back, immense pain, and a constant state of asphyxiation and panic! Only this time I had a real sense of doom. I could feel my mental and physical state slipping each and every hour of the day.

On a Sunday afternoon about five days after the procedure, I knew I was dying, and should I not get outside help before nightfall I would not make it through the night.

Marshall O'Brien had done a psychologist appraisal on me for Veterans' Affairs some years earlier. He had remained in touch, both professionally and as a friend. I called him. 'Should you not get here soon I feel I will not survive the night,' I told him. He was there within the hour. The look on his face as he entered my room said it all – pure shock!

He abruptly left the room, returning soon after with the intern doctor on duty. 'I know this man, he needs his respiratory physician urgently,' Marshall demanded.

An hour later, an elderly gentleman (not my normal respiratory specialist) came through the door – he also took one look and then stepped into action: 'Get that drip out of him – reduce oxygen!'

Nurses and doctors came from all directions for the next hour, and slowly but surely my feeling of complete demise began to reverse. I was sat upright at Marshall's request and again I felt better.

To the day I die I will never forget that elderly doctor returning to my room in the early hours. 'Good thing you called your friend when you did – you nearly didn't make it. Had I not got here when I did, you *wouldn't* have made it,' he said, squeezing my knee before disappearing into the night.

Marshall O'Brien stayed with me all night, falling asleep in the chair by my bed.

It took years to eventually find out what exactly had happened. Marshall said I looked like the Michelin Man when he arrived. 'Your head and body were twice their normal size,' he said.

Officially I was drowning in my own fluids: instead of nose tongs to supply the oxygen, I had a full-face mask, which apparently meant I was poisoning myself with the excess nitrogen that was being recycled. That's why you see so few full-face oxygen masks these days – as I understand.

In any event, I had now been gutted and re-zipped twice in as many years, and the nerves that had begun to grow back after the initial operation were again severed and also doing a repeat. I couldn't feel any part of my gut.

Again, I was on light duties, with Sam as my carer. My motorhome was still out at Ness's, only this time I didn't go surf fishing – I finished my first novel instead.

Christmas was coming and Joel was going to spend it with us – it would be the first Christmas we'd shared as a family since Ness and I split in 1995. I was really looking forward to it.

On Christmas Day, Ness put on a huge meal for about ten of us; it was an amazing day.

I said goodnight to Joel and Sam, who were sat side-by-side behind Ness's bar, and then went to bed, around 11-ish – I couldn't party like I used to.

Then the true nightmare began. Around 5.30am I woke to Ness hammering on the door of my motorhome.

'It's Joel. The ambulance is here, it's not good, so prepare yourself,' she said, as I struggled to take it in.

Ness took me inside to the bathroom.

The scene that greeted me was the worst moment in my life. Joel was on the floor, with Sam over him, totally distraught.

One of the ambos gently eased Sam away, and pronounced Joel as deceased. Sam and I held each other and wept uncontrollably on the floor beside Joel's body. I could not, nor did I, bring myself to look at Joel's face before I took Sam outside.

We sat there for an hour in each other's embrace, in tears that will never end.

In a state of shock, I realised I had to call Wendy.

I knew I must do it as soon as possible, as the longer I left it the harder it would be. Our son, our child – her only child – was gone.

Words can never express how hard that call was to make. I was inconsolable, and I had to break the news to Wendy, on Boxing Day, that her baby was gone.

We had no idea of the cause of death; the coroner was there, as were ambos and police, but until the autopsy was complete we had to wait.

I knew Joel had consumed a lot of alcohol during the day, a lot. Sam found him sitting on the loo – asleep, Sam thought. Then when it became clear he was unconscious, Sam gave him CPR for an hour.

The ambos said to me later they don't know how he physically did it. 'We certainly couldn't – on our own.'

Now I truly knew what it was like to be a parent who has lost a child, like my mate Snowy – who was the very first person to arrive when the news spread.

Snowy cried as much as we did, it bought back the horror of his loss. Words are inadequate to even attempt to describe that depth of loss, grief and sadness. No parent should ever bury their children – the hole it leaves in your heart, and life, is there for eternity.

While we waited for the coroner's report, Sam, Ness and I went to Joel's apartment in Civic, Canberra. I guess with my own medical woes, the X-rays up against the lounge-room wall were the first thing that caught my eye. He hadn't mentioned being sick, or getting X-rays done, but I did recall his concern at having a broken nose through sparring; he had taken up boxing in a big way a year before.

When I read the report I was immediately concerned, and more so when I found his doctor's letters. He had been experiencing light-headedness, and the X-rays and scans were of his heart. My obvious conclusion was that it was an issue with his aorta, which is hereditary. He had an appointment to go to the heart specialist after Christmas.

I find it terribly difficult to write about Joel's passing, and funeral, but I must, for all those who loved him and came from far and wide to say goodbye.

In his last years he had been working with children through the Ted Noffs Foundation, where he became such a popular mentor that the head in Canberra insisted Joel complete the certification necessary to really advance his potential. He went back to school, completing his second year of qualification with high marks, and he was ready for a career helping young people from disadvantaged backgrounds.

The coroner's report confirmed what I had suspected, but not in my wildest dreams could I have anticipated what Joel would have learnt had he attended the heart specialist after Christmas.

Of his two major coronary arteries, one was 90% blocked, the other 80% blocked. He was a walking time bomb, a massive potential heart attack, which ultimately happened on 26 December 2010, five days short of his thirty-first birthday.

There are no blessings in this tragedy. But if there should be, it would be that Joel had spent the best Christmas Day ever with family and friends, and passed away at home with us, and not somewhere else alone. Christmas has never been the same since, and Boxing Day is a day Sam and I will always spend together while I'm still alive.

A home at Millingandi

Sam had always wanted to join the army, and after Joel's passing he was even more determined, but I was adamant – NOT INFANTRY, there is not a big demand for 'hit-men' when you get out! Get a trade. So engineers was his choice, but first he had to get in.

Not until my first phone call to Sam during recruit training did it hit me just how hard he would be doing it. For the first time in his life he had neither parent to turn to when he was up against it.

He sounded terrible, almost broken – which is the reason no calls are allowed for the first six weeks. The Defence Forces are not for the faint-hearted, and during initial introduction into the army it's all about bonding – building mateship and teamwork. Recruit instructors (RIs) don't want their subjects calling home every night for moral support; that comes from within, within yourself and within the ranks.

I was in my motorhome on the way to Melbourne when Sam called. From the tone of his voice I knew all wasn't going to plan – he had just been bawled out for forgetting to wear his hat when heading outside to make his call.

Quickly it took me back to my first weeks of rookies – back in the bad old days when bastardisation was the rule of law and RIs could get away with anything their heartless little hearts could devise to humiliate or punish you. I had the benefit of leaving home at an early age and working in shearing sheds for an introduction to tough love. The army, by equivalent, was boarding school, as they couldn't drag you outside and beat the shit out of you, which was par for the course back when I was shearing in the '60s.

Sam knew I'd been through the same and survived.

'Cop it sweet mate. Remember your mistakes and soldier on, get your back up – or start bitching and trust me you'll play right into their hands.'

The benefit of having been in the army and an NCO meant I could reassure him that much of what he had already seen was par for the course, and knowing he was better than many who continually fucked up is what he needed to hear.

'Let them be little tin gods – just get through rookies and your day will come,' I promised.

Sam had always been popular and a leader at school and sports – once he got to his unit I felt he would excel. His strong point being he was always generous, with his time for others as much as with his possessions.

After his first 12 weeks, Ness and I, and my sister Judy and brother in-law Ray, drove to Kapooka, New South Wales, for his March Out.

That feeling never goes away, the stirring of the heart when a band strikes up and seeing a company of men perfectly in step march out onto the parade ground.

Sam, being tall, was at the front of his platoon and we spotted him easily. I was so proud of him, and delighted that he marched exactly as I had, head steady, arms straight and mechanical; he was a soldier from head to foot and it showed.

After the parade we embraced, and he whispered in my ear: 'Joel has been with me every day here.' It broke my heart that Joel wasn't there to see his brother.

There is no greater endorsement or accolade than that of your peers, and every soldier, male and female, in Sam's platoon rated him their best recruit – which he would have been awarded had he not told a lie to cover for a mate's mistake during a weapons drill. That cost him the award – but gained him much, much more in my eyes, and those of his peers.

After his corps training at Puckapunyal, where I had done my rookies, he was posted to 2 CAV (2nd Cavalry Regiment) in Darwin. Transport was the only opening for him at that point. He rang me, gutted.

'Darwin! There's just a tin shed out there in the desert!'

'Really,' I replied. 'Wait till you get there mate. I wish I'd been posted there.'

Sam arrived in Darwin a couple of days before Christmas, and as it was the first anniversary of Joel's passing I wanted to be with him. I flew up and stayed a week, hired a car and showed him around. His eyes got wider the further we went – there were female backpackers everywhere!

'Dad, this is Paradise,' he said, smiling from ear to ear. Now I knew he would be OK.

I wasn't OK though.

After Joel's funeral I went to a place deep within myself, where nobody else could see. I couldn't listen to music, I couldn't look at his photos, I avoided anything remotely connected to him. I packed all his belongings, from clothes to letters, and then I drove with Sam to Port Fairy with Joel's ashes, leaving everything with Wendy.

As I handed over a box full of letters I told her he had superannuation, as the related letters had always come to my address. Subsequently, Wendy discovered that due to accidental death there was an insurance policy, two in fact, that totalled around $90,000.

That was exactly what we needed to do something to honour Joel's legacy, his love of kids and music. Together, Wendy and I explored many options, until Wendy found the perfect solution.

The Australian Children's Music Foundation (ACMF) came to her attention. It is a not-for-profit organisation that inspires creativity and helps talented children through weekly music lessons Under the directorship of Don Spencer – a much-loved Australian children's television presenter, songwriter and musician – it helps musically talented children without financial support to achieve their dreams. It was perfect. Wendy contacted Don and we devised a plan that would

Joel and Sam, brothers in arms and best mates.

be eternal, not simply a one-off payment. It was Wendy's idea to call the legacy the Joel Abernethy Advantage.

Each year the ACMF provide Wendy and me with the names of various children and their circumstances. It could be a young girl who needs singing lessons, or kids who can't afford their own instruments – they range from Indigenous children in the Northern Territory to suburban kids in Sydney. But the two essentials are there: music and helping children. The principal amount was placed in a trust, where the accumulated interest each year goes to a child, or children, keeping it an ongoing annual award, and one to which anyone can now donate to raise the amount of principal. It's been a great success and getting better each and every year.

While that was a bright, good thing, I was in a dark and desolate place.

I cut myself off from the world I had once known, my world view changed, my outlook changed, I was a shell. I had no hope, no optimism, no dreams.

Except where it concerned Sam. Besides him, I had no interest in pursuing relationships, certainly not romantic ones. I became a recluse. I went from outgoing entrepreneur to sad hermit. The motorhome played right into my choice of lifestyle, I was a gypsy, a nomad drifting on an open road.

My health was again in decline, as I drank too much, smoked, and never ate proper meals. Each year at the beginning of winter I would head north to warmer climates and remain there for three to four months at a time. I could go weeks without any contact with other human beings – I could even spend a whole week without leaving the security of my home on wheels.

In 2012 my blood pressure was always high, I was constantly in pain, and my GP had exhausted ways to improve my circumstances other than by increasing pain-relief medication, namely Oxycodone and Endone in higher and higher doses.

With winter approaching, I decided to head north again, this time to Darwin, via Adelaide and up through Australia's Red Centre.

When I left Merimbula, my GP gave me a script for my medication that would last three or four months. My blood pressure on that day was 160 over 98.

The next day I arrived in Mansfield, country Victoria, and went into a chemist to have my script filled. I didn't feel well, so while I waited I had a free blood-pressure test. It was 190 over 120. The pharmacy wanted to call an ambulance but instead booked me in to see a local doctor.

Their concern was real, especially as I was driving alone to Darwin. They insisted I see a vascular specialist as a matter of urgency.

I called my GP, who made an appointment for me to see the same pain management specialist (not heart specialist) in Canberra. That night I drove 500km back to the ACT, to see the pain specialist first thing the next morning.

To my astonishment, he gave me a quick examination then told me my problem wasn't a heart condition – it was grief!

'You're grieving the loss of your son. I'm going to prescribe you something I want you to sip from the bottle whenever you feel down.'

He scribbled out the prescription and handed it to me.

'Just look out the window at the birds and trees, stay relaxed, go and see your other son in Darwin,' he said.

With that advice, and armed with a new prescription, I turned around and drove back south, headed for Adelaide.

When I had the script filled out, I asked the chemist what it was. Liquid Oxycodone was the answer.

At this point I was taking around 160mg of Oxycodone in tablet form daily, and around 15–20mg of Endone on top of that. To 'sip' unmeasured doses of Oxycodone at will, on top of what I was on, in the very simplest of terms was the equivalent to handing a drunk a bottle of scotch while he was behind the wheel.

I must emphasise that both my GP and my pain specialist knew I was driving on my own from Merimbula to Darwin. I should also like to add that, like a dummy, I simply took whatever medication I was prescribed without question. I learnt later that I was on 'Hillbilly Heroin' – I was becoming a prescription junkie!

I blew an inside rear tyre just before Mildura, and while I was changing that tyre I nearly fainted several times. At this point I had not taken any of the liquid dose.

It was a long, long journey – but eventually I arrived; however, I was exhausted, and the heat only drained my physical resources even more.

After a time, I went to see a local doctor, who was aghast at the amount of pain killers I was on, but even more so that I had driven this far with such elevated blood pressure, and on the advice of my doctors. He suggested that I get home as soon as I could and see a doctor, or a heart specialist.

I caught up with Sam, but mostly lay on my bed in the air conditioning for weeks on end, building up strength for the return journey. It was a half-life.

The shortest way home was across the top of Australia, through Mount Isa in Far North Queensland.

However, instead of heading for the coast as I normally would, I took the A2 through Longreach, then the Mitchell Highway from Charleville to Dubbo before Canberra and home. On occasion, mainly at night due to the pain of driving all day, I took a short swig of my liquid Oxycodone to get to sleep. Normally one Valium would do as a sleeping tablet, but due to the amount of shit I was on I was afraid I wouldn't wake up. When I got home I drove straight to Ness's and collapsed in a heap. I just wanted to lie still, be calm and sleep.

Sam arrived home for leave and again took me under his wing, doing my shopping so I didn't need to drive. He also joined the gym, as he had become a gym junkie since entering the army.

He had gone to the gym one morning and I was struggling with a splitting headache I couldn't relieve. I rang my sister Elizabeth, the medical guru in the family, and filled her in on what had taken place recently.

She insisted I go to hospital straight away, given the headache and the symptoms of the past months. As we were talking, Sam returned – he had forgotten his towel. 'God – Dad, are you alright? You're grey!' He hustled me into his car.

I was on a first-name basis with many of the staff at Pambula Hospital, I'd been there so many times. Casualty was full of tourists with fish-hooks in their hands, and sick kids.

The nurse behind the counter knew me, took one look and led me straight through.

There was a locum on duty who I didn't know; he was young, and preoccupied with a laptop in front of him.

'Any pain in your left arm?' he asked.

'No.'

'Any feeling of weight on your chest?'

'No.'

'Any hot or cold flushes?'

'No'
'Any chest pain?'
'No.'
He went back to his laptop and I lay there feeling lousy. Sam watched on, worried.

'Mate, go to the gym,' I said. 'I'm OK and you can pick me up on your way home.'

Then I was hit with an overwhelming rush of hot and cold flushes, and an elephant sitting on my chest, followed by an agonising pain all down my left arm. I loudly reported each event to stunned looks from the nurses and the doctor.

Suddenly, out of nowhere, came a tall young male nurse, who swept everyone aside, unlocked the wheels of the bed and pushed me flat-out through Emergency to the end of the ward.

'Stay with me, John – you're having a heart attack, I've got it,' he assured me, as he slapped on the electrode pads for a defibrillator.

As I struggled for my life all I could see was Sam's face beyond the huddle. He had not long ago lost a brother, and now he was watching his father die. In went a needle, and within minutes I could feel the effect, life being restored to my body.

It was 20 minutes from when Sam and I had arrived at the hospital until I had the heart attack. Ness was out for the day and Sam would have been at the gym for at least two hours had he not forgotten his towel. I would most certainly have died on my own in Ness's lounge-room, all but for that towel.

'You've just had a minor heart attack,' said the young male nurse, Dan, who had saved my life.

If that was a minor heart attack, a mid-range or fatal couldn't be any worse in my book. It was like nothing I've ever experienced, nor ever want to again. That night I was taken to hospital in Canberra, where an angiogram showed up the blockage. I was conscious and chatting to the doctor while he inserted a stent into my heart.

'No more smoking – next time you will not be so lucky,' he warned.

I was discharged on New Year's Day, 2013. After a heart attack it plays on your mind, how in an instant life can be taken from you and you are powerless to do anything to save yourself. My confidence had never been lower.

Again, on the advice of my 'practising professionals' – my GP, and my heart and pain specialists – I tried new medication.

My initial woes – spinal pain between the shoulder blades, muscle spasm of the diaphragm, shortness of breath – continued. The pain specialist came up with a tablet that had a calming effect but weakened me considerably more.

One day I had to go into town. Parking close to the main street, I began walking the short distance to my destination. My head started spinning, my legs gave out, I knew I was going to faint, so I collapsed onto a chair in front of the bakery in the main street and called 000, fearing another heart attack.

How embarrassing, to be wheeled off the main street on a gurney, straight into the back of the ambulance.

'Mate – I don't know what's happening here,' said the ambulance guy, 'but your heart rate is ranging from 21 beats per minute to nearly 200 beats per minute!'

I was taken to hospital and stabilised. Now, both my GP and pain specialist knew that I was born with a very slow-beating heart; resting, it was at 48 beats per minute – asleep, it dropped to 33 beats per minute. The medication the pain specialist had put me on was to slow down my heart. In fact, he had slowed my heart down so much that it almost stopped. This was the last straw. I sacked them both. Many said I should have sued both their arses.

I guess if you neglect to service your car for years on end, drive the guts out of it day and night, it's finally going to blow, or will certainly need major works. This is what I had done to my body; even when it was screaming out for a check-up, I was always too busy.

One of my favourite sayings is: 'God builds a great car – shut it down and give it rest, and it heals itself.' I had never learnt to shut down, or rest – and now, aged over 50, I was paying the price.

My biggest mistake, however, was not getting a second opinion. I just stuck with those same two medics for years. And to endorse this, the Department of Veterans' Affairs (DVA) have in triplicate every dollar of taxpayer's money this pair wasted 'practising' on me.

As it stood, I had numerous specialists in Canberra who I was seeing on a regular basis for heart, lungs, spinal, gastro, physio, orthopaedic, chronic pain, skin cancer ... the list goes on.

But the debilitating pain that was turning me into a cripple was still no closer to being resolved. Short of enough Oxycodone and Endone to tranquillise a horse, it continued to escalate.

One morning, as my mate Nifty and I were preparing to drive to Canberra, Nifty needed to relieve his Chinese bladder (as he liked to call it), and I decided to do the same.

To my utmost shock and confusion, I was peeing black.

At first I thought somebody had pulled a stunt on me, laced my coffee or the like, but it concerned me enough to call my doctor.

'Probably a small vein is weakened, the blood will come out as black – no big concern but come and see me when you get back from Canberra.'

As the day went on, the need to take a leak increased; however, each time I tried I couldn't pass any urine.

By late afternoon I was in pain, bloated, bursting to empty my bladder. Taking to a Fyshwick restaurant toilet I refused to quit. After 20 minutes I finally succeeded. To my horror it wasn't urine, not even black urine, it was minced meat followed by a gush of black lumps of congealed blood before bright-red blood in a steady flow. I knew I was in trouble – big trouble. Nifty took me straight to Pambula Hospital, where arrangements were made to send me back to Canberra, to National Capital Private Hospital. A urologist (add this to the list) met me upon arrival.

He gave a clear, concise, professional, assessment, which set me at ease, along with his calm and thorough demeanour.

A couple of hours later in post-op he was there to greet me from my return from the anaesthetic.

'Small tumour,' he reported, in the same calm manner. 'It is a new growth, I have got it all – and got it early'

'Cancer?' I asked, suddenly aware of the implications.

'Yes – malignant. But you're lucky – had it not bled you wouldn't be here this Christmas.' Christmas was three months away.

'Bladder cancer won't kill you when we get it early, as we have,' he went on. 'We'll check you regularly for the next ten years for any regrowth – and you'll be fine.'

I had lived in fear for years that I had some form of cancer, when my pain could not be diagnosed – but now being told I had cancer strangely didn't bother me at all. I had total trust in my urologist; we would be seeing lots more of each other, but I was going to live.

Well and truly over the local hacks posing as doctors, I demanded to have my undiagnosed pain seen to by a Sydney specialist, a gastroenterologist/general surgeon.

I was referred to a professor who thought that he was the original Hollywood George. His opening line was how lucky I was to have him, 'The best in Sydney'; this was topped off by Skype interviews to reinforce how good he was, and (again) how lucky I was to have him. All of this was at DVA expense.

It became a comedy of errors: first his nurse neglecting to tell me not to shower for 24 hours, as the monitor she had attached wasn't waterproof, followed by the professor setting the surgery date and neglecting to convey to my GP – ten days out from surgery – the need to stop any blood thinners.

Strutting in late on the day of the procedure in his 1950s sports jacket, the specialist halted the surgical staff taking me into theatre, saying that the operation was off – I hadn't stopped my blood thinners.

Apart from the fact that he had no intention of operating – he had arrived in his civilian clothes – he then blamed me for not doing as his nurse had instructed. I'd not spoken to the nurse! But I was in with my GP when the professor neglected to tell him to stop blood-thinning meds ten days prior. I'm now glad he never laid a hand on me.

But, after an eight-hour drive to Sydney and the same to go back home, I gave the arrogant old fool a dressing-down the whole ward heard. This was followed by an apology from the heads of the hospital, who assured me he would be reprimanded for his bad behaviour – and they would seek an alternative surgeon for me. If I would come back.

Now there is only so much a koala can bear. And after the string of dickheads I'd had queued up to rake in DVA money for jam, it was time to bring it to DVA's attention. If every time I turned up for a five-minute consultation for a script, DVA were being billed for a double consultation, how many other Veterans were experiencing the same?

I made direct contact with DVA's head and provided him with details. He recommended I make a formal complaint against the doctors to the Health Care Commission, which I did. God only knows if they are still 'practising' but one thing's for certain, they will never 'practise' on me again.

Again, out of the bad comes good. I was recommended a brilliant surgeon, humble, great bedside manner, and all things a good doctor should be.

For years Canberra specialists had been telling me I had a 'small' hiatus hernia.

'Until I get in there, John [or 'Colonel' as he had nicknamed me], I won't know how big or small it is.' I could be scheduled for the hernia repair prior to Christmas.

At the same time I had found my new home, a relocatable cabin.

Ness offered me land at her place to set up the cabin. Our friendship had survived and grown over the decades, and she had inherited from her father, which had allowed her to purchase a large property inland from Merimbula at Millingandi. It is a beautiful spot, and a perfect place for me to live too.

After all, when we go to happier hunting grounds, Sam inherits the lot – it was a win/win situation. So, in between waiting for the operation, I was working with sub-contractors to have my little house wired, watered and septic-tanked, all in anticipation of coming home from Sydney a new man.

It was supposed to all be fairly straightforward keyhole surgery, not the full-blown rabbit-gutting as before.

I was scheduled for 11am surgery and to be back in the ward by around 2pm. I went into theatre full of cheek and highly confident.

What took place during that procedure changed my life forever. I remember it vividly, and I recorded it on my phone as soon as I could.

In an ultraviolet fluorescent glow, I stood beside a man at the top of a luggage conveyor, watching as my Kathmandu backpack rolled towards us. On the other side of the luggage belt stood my father and Joel, smiling and pleased to see me. I just wanted to leave my bag and go to them.

'Is that your bag?' asked the man at my side – being my blind side I couldn't see him.

'Yes,' I answered, and reached for it. All went black.

I went into theatre on a Thursday morning, and the next thing I knew I was in a ward. A clock on a wall read 2pm.

I could hear a woman's voice saying that the doctor was busy right now. In a panic I thought that I had woken up on the operating table and at any minute I would see the doctor and feel his knife. My heart thumped in my chest, but strangely my breathing felt perfect – the best ever.

However, I was paralysed – I couldn't blink, I couldn't make a sound, I couldn't move a muscle, reinforcing my fear that I had woken during the operation.

From 2pm until 4.45pm I lay there helpless, awaiting a terrible fate, and not being able to call out. At 4.45pm two men approached my bed.

'Sorry, but what I'm about to do is going to be horrible,' said one.

I had been in total dread of giving myself another heart attack all the time I had lain there. Now I was certain that's how I would die. A dreadful nausea filled my whole being. Here comes the heart attack, I thought.

Then as abruptly as it began, it stopped. I could move, cry, talk.

'I just saw Dad and Joel,' I wept.

'Boy – did you give us a fright,' said one of the men. 'You stopped breathing – you died!'

I told them all that had happened, how I had seen Dad and Joel – how I had lain there since 2pm paralysed. I had been ventilated, and sedated – withdrawing the ventilator had been the horrible experience and the cause of my nausea.

To my utter amazement, all three in the EU that day told me they had heard the same description of dying from hundreds of patients before me. What I had seen vividly, departed family members – in my case, Dad and Joel (and Old Nick) – is how others who had clinically died and been resuscitated had described the event.

The instant I had my mobile back in hand I recorded every detail in case I should forget it. And it was now Sunday, four days since I went into surgery. In my life I have experienced some odd, if not inexplicable events, I've seen ghosts, and spirits leaving bodies. What I experienced this time, when I clinically died, was as vivid as the words I now type. Never will I be afraid of death, for if that's what awaits me on the other side there is nothing to fear – only cause to rejoice.

The outcome of my hiatus hernia repair was far from 'small'; as opposed to what all the so-called experts had been telling me for years. When my doctor went in to perform keyhole surgery he got the shock of his life. Instead of three incisions he had to make seven – rather than open me up fully again, which is the last thing either of us wanted.

What he found was that 60% of my intestines had been drawn up into the vacuum of my chest/lung cavity, sharing the space with my one-and-a-half lungs.

After discharge, which saw me home for Christmas, I was to report to my GP. Having sacked two GPs in the space of 12 months, I was referred to a female doctor – young, and obviously still learning her trade … 'practising!' Sam drove me in, and on the short walk from the carpark into the surgery I developed a serious nose bleed – blood pouring out of me due to my blood thinners. I was met by the clinic's nurse, who took me straight into her room and began treating me, keeping me in a sitting position.

In came the young female doctor, who ordered me to lie down on my back. An argument between doctor and nurse began.

'If he lies on his back he will choke on his blood,' argued the nurse.

'Do it,' insisted the doctor.

I began choking on the blood running down my throat, and I couldn't breathe. I sat up. The nurse recommenced pinching off the bleed and applying a cold compress, which immediately fixed the problem. The doctor spun on her heels and left, saying to come through when I was cleaned up.

The situation went from bad to worse.

'I'm NOT going to provide a script for that amount of Oxycodone,' the young doctor said adamantly, when I produced my discharge certificate and specialist's instructions.

'I won't even give a script for half that amount,' she said firmly.

I had had enough. My Irish blood (what was left of it) erupted, sending me to my feet. I gave her a dressing-down in front of Sam that neither he, nor she, will ever forget. I rang the Sydney clinic, who told me to report to the nearest hospital emergency unit, which I did, and my post-op instructions were followed.

It goes without saying that there are good doctors, and bad doctors – and boy have I had my fair share of bad ones. I will even go as far as saying there are honest doctors and bloody crooks with MD after their names.

When you are really sick, the last thing on your mind is partying. And when the sickness gives some short-term reprieve, it's constantly on your mind how long will it be before it's back with a vengeance. Living with yourself under these circumstances is trying enough, there's no joy in one's life.

There is nothing like dying to knock your confidence around.

Coming home from Sydney and moving into a 'building' (my cabin in the woods), not the motorhome, was probably the only uplifting experience I'd had in quite a while. The plumber was still hooking up the water as the DVA limo brought me up the driveway.

'Tomorrow,' he promised, but I didn't really care, I just needed a bed. Looking back now I see the real trauma I had been through, but at the time my focus was simply to walk again unaided. Living with pain was something I'd become accustomed to – the real challenge was to go for as long as I could without spacing myself out again on 'Hillbilly Heroin'.

During my 2008 visit to Darwin, I had decided to go cold turkey – offloading three months' supply of Endone and Oxycodone into a city dumpster. I subsequently learnt that the street value, in total, was around $200,000!

That withdrawal process over eight days locked away in a motorhome in 33 degree heat wasn't an experience I'd like to repeat. In this case the comfort was worse than the cause – being a zombie 24/7 is no life, not for someone like me who has always had self-discipline and self-confidence. To be relegated to no more than a prescription junkie left me with a feeling of self-disrespect and loathing, not a healthy outlook for recovery.

More than ever before I wanted to be pain-free; even more importantly, drug-free. For all of 2014 I had been in agony, and in and out of hospital, perhaps now with my guts back where they should be that would be possible.

Having Sam home on Christmas leave again was total joy. But it wasn't to last. Into my second month of convalescence and getting my head back on straight again, in a settled environment – my cabin in a rainforest with abundant wildlife all around – Ness arrived with news that she had just spoken with Sam, who was now transferred to Townsville, and she feared he was in hospital.

This was followed almost immediately by a call from Townsville Hospital reminding me that Sam had his brain scan scheduled for the morning.

None of this made sense; Sam had just gone back after his Christmas leave and had made no mention of any upcoming medicals. Upon finally discovering that he *was* in fact in Townsville Hospital, I asked to speak to his doctor.

I was totally unprepared for what the doctor had to say.

Sam had been admitted in the early hours of Sunday morning – unconscious from an unprovoked 'king hit', a random and unexpected punch thrown by a stranger. Sam was very lucky to be alive. It was now Wednesday, and not a word from anyone, police or army. (We later found out Sam had insisted that we not be contacted – he knew the stress it would cause us.) His current state was that he was conscious, his swollen brain had stopped bleeding, and he was stable and responding to treatment.

With only two children, one already deceased, this kind of news is any parent's worst nightmare. Even more distressing was the fact he had been on his own for four days, during which time he could have died from his injuries. Eventually I spoke to Sam, who had no memory whatsoever of what had taken place. Assured by his doctor he was now out of the woods and on the road to recovery, I phoned Townsville Police. No answer. I then rang Brisbane Police HQ and reported what had happened to my son. I wanted to speak to the officers who had arranged the ambulance and, according to Sam's doctor, interviewed Sam in the EU upon his arrival.

Sam had a fractured skull, he was unconscious, and the cop put in charge interviewed him shortly after he regained consciousness; apart from having a critical head injury, Sam had been doped to stabilise him and control his pain. Adding insult to injury, this same cop dropped the assault charge against the guy who had punched Sam from behind.

I saw red. I called relentlessly until I finally got to speak to the cop who had attended on the night. In short, he said when he interviewed Sam it was Sam who said he didn't want to lay charges. He even went on to say he knew the individual who had king hit Sam and spoke to him at the scene.

I assured him that Sam did want to press charges!

So began a shitfight that lasted well over a year, and went all the way to the top of the chain of command. A shitfight between Townsville CIB and me – which, however, saw the individual responsible for hitting Sam charged a day or so after my first call.

I set about my own investigation. Knowing the incident had occurred outside the Bank Night Club, that's where I started, and to my dismay found out the club's own CCTV showed the incident. The police hadn't even taken the CCTV. Again, a call to Brisbane HQ quickly rectified that situation. An officer was sent around to collect it a week after the incident.

It took all this time to let the criminal get away with near murder, because the police prosecutor said it couldn't be determined who actually threw the punch that caused Sam's injury – even though the bloke had confessed to hitting him. The club's video didn't show clearly enough who had struck the critical blow; there was more than one attacker, they said.

When I checked out the Bank Night Club, directly in front and to each side of the building I found no less than five city council CCTV cameras; this footage, combined with the club's own video, would have provided 3D coverage of what had happened. But nobody got off their arse to gather the council's CCTV evidence.

Bottom line. While Sam was standing outside the club minding his own business and rolling a smoke, he was set upon and almost killed. Townsville Police didn't do their job – confirmed in a letter to me dated 15 August 2016, which said that as a result of my complaint the Ethical Standards Command had identified areas for 'professional improvement' on behalf of the police in question. It added that managerial action had been taken to 'educate and prevent' a reccurrence of the police handling of Sam's case.

Sam was on his first night out in town, with a married couple. He had only been in Townsville two weeks when all this went down. His attackers were locals and known to police.

And again, without fear of repeating myself, good often follows bad.

Christmas that same year Sam announced to Ness and me that he was bringing a girl home on leave with him.

Now, *that* coming from Sam was the revelation of a lifetime. From the day Sam realised girls were different to boys, in a nice way, he had surrounded himself with them. It was never one, he would arrive home from school with as many as five at a time, and the older he got the better he got at it.

For Sam to bring one girl home for Christmas was a big deal. Toni, a blue-eyed, blonde, Gold Coast model, was beautiful, yet down to earth. They had met on Magnetic Island at a Full Moon party – where Sam had taken it upon himself to handcuff himself to her (they were plastic handcuffs, he assured me!). Unfortunately, Toni could only stay a week with us and had to return to work.

On New Year's Eve at around 2am my mobile rang. I freaked. Christmases were always bad now, and to get a call from Sam at 2am stopped my heart – literally.

'Congratulations – you're going to be a grandfather,' he proudly announced.

'WTF – do you know the time?'

'Toni – she's pregnant,' he laughed.

I didn't know what to say. I always expected Joel to give me a grandchild – not Sam. I was thinking he may settle down to have a family in his forties, not his twenties.

I was tickled pink. New life, a baby, but that lingering question ... they had only known each other a short time – months! As parents do, we asked the questions, are you guys in love, are you getting married? Marriage these days is apparently not an applicable word but yes, he said, we are in love and we want this baby. They had been living together ever since they met, so I guess they both knew each other's bad habits, as the old saying goes. In any event, they were both over 21, adults, and it was their call, nobody else's.

Joel Abernethy II was born on 13 August 2016 to proud and happy parents and grandparents – a gorgeous little man with his mum and dad's blue eyes and good looks. Sam, being military, was entitled to a house, so Ness and I flew up and helped with the move into their beautiful four-bedroom home. What a difference a year makes, from Sam nursing a fractured skull and living on base restricted to light duties, to full-time dad living off-base with his new family.

I was still recovering from my hiatus hernia repair and unscheduled death as a consequence, but the greatest medicine I could have received was a grandson. Sam had declared from the moment Toni knew she was pregnant that if it was a boy he wanted to name him after his brother, as it was to be.

It becomes a bit ironic when your grandson's first words to you are 'Grumpy' – not getting his tongue around 'Grandpa'.

'Grumpy alright,' agreed Ness. It has stuck. You tend to be grumpy when you're constantly out of breath and in pain; when every breath is like breathing through a wet towel it is not only scary – it is daunting and tiring, and will make anyone 'Grumpy' after four to five years! 2017 was a year when the flu started dropping people like flies, many elderly people, and those like me with respiratory issues – when you can't breathe you tend to die.

On 31 August 2017, the last official day of winter, I was in Canberra with Nifty. I hadn't felt well all day and said if I didn't improve by the time we reached Bemboka, the village at the foot of Brown Mountain, I may get him to drop me off at Bega Hospital. I made it home, but stepping out of the warm car into the cold is the last thing I remember before waking up on my deck. Fortunately, I had my mobile, and rang 000. The ambos were there inside 15 minutes, and with my form, decided to take me to Bega – thank God.

I spent a hell of a night in EU; even on pure hospital oxygen I still couldn't breathe, and the oxygen concentrate in my bloodstream was hovering around 85%. I remained in hospital for ten days ... ten horrifying days!

Now, it is this simple. If you have a chronic lung issue and breathing is a battle at the best of times, add a chronic cough, and nose and lungs full of crap, and it is impossible to breathe in. That in effect is why I hit the deck (literally) when I got home from Canberra – while coughing, I couldn't take in air, and being very restricted when I did, I blacked out due to lack of oxygen. Physically I felt like shit, mentally I felt like shit, nothing could be done other than what was being done, and nothing could make me feel like anything but shit.

Plus I was put into solitary confinement, with four walls closing in on me and one window that gave a view of the ward wall just beyond. I was suffocating mentally as well as physically. One night I rang the buzzer in a serious state of panic. I'd never experienced a panic attack before, but I knew I was having a full-blown one.

I begged the nurse to get me out of that room – I would have even taken a VC tunnel system to escape I was that desperate. As it was around 2am, she said she could take me down to the main TV room because there was nobody there. I jumped at it. By the time I was in a wheelchair, moving away from that 'prison', I could feel myself coming good. I didn't turn on the TV or read a magazine – I simply rid myself of the torment of that enclosed space. I sat there all night and watched the sun come up through the huge floor-to-ceiling windows. I felt alive for the first time in ten days. I was never going back into that room!

I insisted upon being discharged, as I had oxygen at home. Ness could shop for my food and keep an eye on me. I was going HOME!

Again, through luck, or the good grace of our Lord, I met one Christine Sullivan, nurse practitioner for Bega Hospital, on the day of my escape. A condition of my bail, so to speak, was that I come back and see her the following week. Little did I know it would be a life-changing event.

Christine is a cross between Florence Nightingale and Mother Teresa, with a strong will to get things done. On my first visit, when I began outlining my medical woes of the past four years, having not even got to the two decades prior, she picked up the phone and called my then-GP, requesting certain things that needed urgent attention. One of those urgent things was an X-ray of my vertebrae in the region where I had experienced such great pain for almost ten years. She wanted me back the next week with that X-ray result.

Now, you may not believe the following, but it's true. After the X-ray, my GP asked to see me. Looking like a mouse coming out of a cheese factory when I entered his room, he handed me the report without making eye contact.

'Crush fracture of the T8 vertebra!'

'Are you telling me I walked around with a broken back and NOBODY thought to investigate the vertebra?' I asked.

'That's what's happened,' said my GP.

When I took the X-ray and report to Christine the following week, she looked at me in dismay. The bone of the vertebra had knitted back together, it was healed – but while I was wandering around with a shattered vertebra, for years, without any form of treatment, I was lucky it never pinched my spinal cord.

This was the beginning of my recovery, the beginning of having a life back again that felt remotely like it had 20 years ago.

From there, Christine came up with the name of a top Canberra neurosurgeon.

Now I was in the hands of professionals and gentlemen.

A full bone-density scan from my neck to my butt revealed no spinal cord damage; the T8 disc was healed and there was no obvious nerve damage. I was finally referred to a real, professional, long-term chronic-pain specialist.

'We'll start with nerve blocks,' the specialist announced.

Having been through that process twice before, I wasn't thrilled at the prospect of having needles inserted into my spine again. But, onwards and upwards.

'When do we start?' I asked.

For the uneducated, a nerve block is the same treatment that a vet applies to a lame horse. He injects a local anaesthetic into the area (nerve) where the animal is lame – and repeats this until the horse can walk, trot and gallop without pain. It's trial and error.

In my case, the nerve endings at the 'wings' of each vertebra are injected – and it hurts like all bejesus.

As in the case of the lame horse, when I can walk out pain-free it means the doctor has found the nerve causing my pain.

It was on the second vertebra injection on my second visit when he struck gold, although it felt nothing remotely like good.

I literally rose 6 foot above the operating table, levitating there momentarily before yelling blue murder and crashing back to earth. Whatever that needle struck, it went through me like a bolt of lightning.

But that was the one that hit the spot. It was an instant fix.

From the moment I walked out to my car I was a new man. I could breathe. It was the first time in over a decade that I had taken a FULL breath; suddenly my ribs and chest had another 2–3 inches of expansion – that needle felt like it had cut a cord around my diaphragm.

From that moment to this, I haven't felt a twinge of pain, from that vertebra in any event.

It's not a permanent thing, I need maintenance work, but after all this time and agony I'm free of pain, I'm active again. I have a life.

And when you think it can't get any better out comes a new drug, an inhaler, for people with COPD (Chronic Obstructive Pulmonary Disease) or breathing issues. It works, and it's on the PBS.

It's also wonderful to see the world again through clear vision – not blurred by A-grade drugs. I could seriously write a book on my medical history and the imbeciles who did me more harm than good for so long.

Nobody knows your body better than you do, always remember that. And always get a second or third opinion if the doctor you're seeing isn't producing the desired result. There are good people out there, who are out to help you – but you have to look.

Epilogue

With age comes wisdom, along with the aches and pains, but in writing my story at the behest of my son Sam, it has been an insight into a life I had taken for granted, I'd been so busy living it. Now upon reflection I see how an innocent country boy changed dramatically due to life's knocks and bumps.

One of my favourite sayings is, 'We create our own luck – good and bad.' And now I know the truth in that.

How different would my life have been had I not volunteered for National Service – would I be a retired farmer in the Western District of Victoria, probably still married to Wendy? Something tells me that was never my destiny. We'll never know.

Do I have regrets? Yes – many! In hindsight I can see the error of my ways. I'm astounded to count the number of times I've resorted to violence, as I've always thought of myself as a lover, not a fighter.

Since my school days I have always sought to avoid violence, and brought up both my sons to be the same. 'Always walk away. Never start a fight – but protect yourself, only when you can't walk away.'

Did the army and Vietnam make that change in me, where I have felt it my duty to take whatever measures necessary to support my beliefs? Was violence sometimes the only way out? I truly believe when you resort to violence you have lost the argument. Then again, never turn your back on principle, or king hitters!

It may appear that my army experience was all bad – on the contrary, it was an experience I firmly believe teaches young people life skills and creates lifelong friends. It teaches team work, respect for others and self-discipline that will see you through life, where others will fail. However, I'm still in two minds about my promotion and being transferred out of 8 Platoon and into 7 Platoon. All my mates were in 8, my boss was the best – being awarded a Military Cross in Vietnam – and 8 Platoon were the only platoon in C Company who had no casualties for the entire tour. But that's the hand that fate dealt me, and you can't argue.

I look back today more than 40 years since being a 20-year-old kid, with less than a year's training, being sent off to war, and responsible for the lives of other young men. I feel vindicated that our medic, Ian 'Flappers' Reid, who I recommended for a citation (three times over 47 years), was finally recognised in 2018 with the Medal for Gallantry for his actions that night in the Vietnamese dry rice paddy. And Pop Cooper, the critically injured soldier whose life he saved, went on to spend more than 30 years in the army. I phoned Pop on the eve of the contact, 48 years later to the hour, at 8pm. I wished him a happy anniversary.

I can't use Vietnam as an excuse for my infidelity – I know the difference between love and lust. I have already said it, I married both the women I truly loved, and the lovers I've had, wonderful as they were, can never replace true love. I will always regret being unfaithful to Wendy and causing her the hurt I did. Now in my senior years I truly know the value of having someone you love, to grow old with. It warms my heart when I see an elderly couple walking hand in hand after a lifetime of sharing the good and bad times together.

All my life I have had a female partner of some sort, but for 23 years now, all through the worst medical woes since my AAA operation, I have avoided a romantic relationship.

When I wandered around Australia for eight years in my motorhome, I had nobody to share those wonderful sights and places with. It was just me and my terrible grief. But I'm still an optimist. Now that my health has, perhaps, finally been restored, I haven't given up hope of settling down with a wonderful lady again. I know she exists. But for now it's me, and me alone.

What else have I learnt? I have been rich and poor, down to $1.12 (which I still have in a plastic laminate), and then a millionaire during the heady days of Seabrake's better years in the 1980s. It's all relative: the more you have, the more you need to maintain that level of lifestyle; alternatively, if you're broke, you've got nothing to lose.

I'm comfortable now, rich isn't any better – but broke is a real pain in the arse. All we really need is life's essentials: food, clothing and shelter – for ourselves and our family – to be able to take the people we love on holidays, and have enough to keep everyone healthy and safe. I have friends who are multimillionaires and are bloody miserable, and I have friends who are battlers and are the salt of the earth and a joy to be around – money doesn't maketh the man, and that's a fact.

For me, after the birth of Joel and later Sam, it was no longer all about me; everything I did was for the long term, for their future.

That was a mistake in one sense, and I regret I didn't spend more time with both my kids in the *now* rather than putting in time for the future. Kids need the love and attention of both parents, they don't understand anything about work, or money – they just want Mum and Dad to give them hugs, praise and encouragement, to be there to read them a story and kiss them good night, go to their school days and sport, see them grow up. Today, even more so than when my kids were little, economic reality means so often both parents are flat out just trying to make a living and maintain a lifestyle. Having a child is life's greatest accomplishment, so make every day count, for yourself as much as for them – don't live to regret that you missed the most wonderful time of your life in pursuit of a future.

There are many things I would have done differently, with the wisdom of hindsight. It's ironic that before I invented Seabrake I was broke, deeply in debt and on the dole. From there I went on to a lifestyle that we all dream about, with success and more money than I ever needed.

I was offered a multimillion-dollar deal to buy me out of Seabrake – an eight-figure sum, a fortune, enough to see me and my kids out for life. I wanted to keep the company Australian-owned and, swayed by advice from my attorneys, I turned the deal down. 'If it's worth that much to them now, imagine what it's going to be worth to you later on,' they said. Greed!

Had I taken that deal at just 35 years of age, how would it have changed my life? I wouldn't have had the stress and workload, I would have had health treatment earlier, I would have had more time with my kids.

But truly, in hindsight, I'm glad that I didn't take that deal. I've seen what that sort of wealth does to people, and in all honesty I feel myself and my children have been better served by working for a living than by being a fat cat where you lose sight of value, and values.

I have so much to be grateful for, things you can't put a price on. I was blessed with wonderful parents, both different in many ways, but both kind and considerate people who taught me manners and principles, life's essentials that have stood me in good stead always, in good times and bad. Not everyone has that start in life, and I have passed my parents' values on to my children. Never take for granted what you have, as you can suddenly lose it.

Do unto others as you would have done unto you. It's good advice. When you have travelled the world as extensively as I have, you appreciate how lucky we all are to live in this wonderful country, Australia. And even then, there are so many who are born into poverty who, through no fault of their own, will never have the same opportunities as others. We are the lucky country, and Australians are the most generous people on the planet in my book. But charity also begins at home. There should be no child living in poverty in Australia. Full stop.

The best days in my life were the days my sons were born. And the worst day in my life was the day Joel died, on 26 December 2010. For every father the birth of a son is a very special event, and Joel was a very special person for all of his short life.

Fathers are supposed to teach their children, but it was Joel who taught me. From a very young age, Joel was never too shy to correct me – if I said there were a dozen ducks on our dam, he would quickly set me straight: 'No, Dad, there are only seven!'

He was never afraid to speak his mind, politely, even if it was to disagree. To this day I consider what Joel would have done when I am in two minds about something. I wish I could have been as good a person as he was – I learnt a lot from him, and there isn't a day that I don't think of him, grieve for him.

He was unique, and I'm thrilled that he will be remembered eternally through his legacy with the Australian Children's Music Foundation.

I am on very good terms with both my ex-wives, who in turn get along with each other very well.

After weathering so many storms, Ness and I enjoy a close platonic friendship. I share a block of land with her on the outskirts of Merimbula, where we have separate dwellings surrounded by rainforest, 600 fruit trees, a huge dam and no neighbours. I think today we are better friends than we ever were when we were married.

Life goes on. Sam, Toni and little Joel live in Darwin, where Sam is a fully-fledged army PTI (physical training instructor), and for the first time in many, many years I am well and happy.

I'm grateful for my good fortune, for my health, for my family and my friends. There's still life to be lived. I'm looking forward to it.

I'm ready to create my own luck again.

THE END

ACKNOWLEDGEMENTS

This story would never have been told if not for two people. My son Sam Abernethy, and my friend and the most amazing editor Gillian Lord.

Firstly, Sam wanted his son to know about his grandpa's amazing life and hounded me constantly to write down as much as I could so he could remember it all. It became a book! (This is a memoir, so bear in mind that over the course of a very full life some people's names may have been imperfectly remembered.)

I met Gillian Lord through my first book, *Drug War*, where I was lucky enough to fluke her through the ACT Writers Centre.

Editors turn words into stories, good editors turn stories into gripping works of art, 'can't put down' books. I'm more than just an ordinary Aussie bloke – I'm an ordinary author who has been inspired, driven and coaxed by an incredible wordsmith who has crafted my tales into books. Thank you Gillian Lord.

Be your own person and do it in your words – that's my message to anyone contemplating this writing caper. But none of us are good enough to do it all alone. Editors make books, and I have been blessed with the best.

REFERENCES

'National Service, Vietnam, 1969–1971'
For details about the operation at Phuoc Tuy, related to the decision to award Ian 'Flappers' Reid a Medal for Gallantry, see:
Australian Government Defence Honours and Awards Appeals Tribunal Executive Summary, *Reid and the Department of Defence [2017] DHAAT 22*, online at defence-honours-tribunal.gov.au/wp-content/uploads/2013/06/Reid-Decision.pdf.
My testimony for the final hearing in Canberra in September 2017 commences on page 16 of the Executive Summary. **Footnote 43 on page 19 reinforces the fact I was acting section commander on the night.**

A colour photo of myself and my diggers displaying a captured Viet Cong flag can be found in the official AWM record of the Vietnam War:
Ashley K. Ekins with Ian McNeill, *Fighting to the Finish: The Australian Army and the Vietnam War*. Sydney: Allen & Unwin, 2012, page 410.

'America's Cup, Perth, 1986–1987'
Ben Lexcen and I appear on opposite pages of the following book (a proud moment!):
Alexandra Towle, ed., *Made in Australia: A Sourcebook of All Things Australian*. Sydney: William Heinemann Australia, 1986, page 196.

www.ingramcontent.com/pod-product-compliance
Lightning Source LLC
Chambersburg PA
CBHW030252010526
44107CB00053B/1675